UNDERSTANDING HOMELAND SECURITY

Understanding Homeland Security

Policy, Perspectives, and Paradoxes

John B. Noftsinger, Jr.,
Kenneth F. Newbold, Jr.,
and
Jack K. Wheeler

UNDERSTANDING HOMELAND SECURITY
© John B. Noftsinger, Jr., Kenneth F. Newbold, Jr., and
Jack K. Wheeler, 2007.

First published in 2007 by
PALGRAVE MACMILLAN™
175 Fifth Avenue, New York, N.Y. 10010 and
Houndmills, Basingstoke, Hampshire, England RG21 6XS
Companies and representatives throughout the world.

PALGRAVE MACMILLAN is the global academic imprint of the Palgrave
Macmillan division of St. Martin's Press, LLC and of Palgrave Macmillan Ltd.
Macmillan® is a registered trademark in the United States, United Kingdom
and other countries. Palgrave is a registered trademark in the European
Union and other countries.

ISBN-13: 978–1–4039–7242–2 (hardback)
ISBN-10: 1–4039–7242–7 (hardback)
ISBN-13: 978–1–4039–7243–9 (paperback)
ISBN-10: 1–4039–7243–5 (paperback)

Library of Congress Cataloging-in-Publication Data

Noftsinger, John B.
    Understanding homeland security : policy, perspectives, and
    paradoxes / by John B. Noftsinger, Jr., Kenneth F. Newbold, Jr., and
    Jack K. Wheeler.
        p. cm.
    Includes bibliographical references and index.
    ISBN 1–4039–7242–7 (alk. paper)
    ISBN 1–4039–7243–5 (pbk. : alk. paper)
        1. Terrorism—United States—Prevention. 2. Civil defense—
    United States. 3. National security—United States. 4. United States.
    Dept. of Homeland Security. I. Newbold, Kenneth F. II. Wheeler, Jack K.
    III. Title.

HV6432.N65 2007
363.3250973—dc22   2006050330

A catalogue record for this book is available from the British Library.

Design by Newgen Imaging Systems (P) Ltd., Chennai, India.

First edition: June 2007

10 9 8 7 6 5 4 3 2 1

Printed in the United States of America.

Transferred to digital printing in 2008.

The authors would like to dedicate this book in the loving memory of Mary Jane Kelly Noftsinger and Lynda Jean Newbold, who through their examples were the ultimate educators

Contents

List of Figures   ix

List of Tables and Boxes   xi

Foreword   xiii

Acknowledgments   xv

Reader's Guide   xvii

Acronyms and Abbreviations   xix

About the Authors   xxiii

One   The Nature of the Threat   1

Two   What Is Homeland Security?   27

Three   Public Policy Issues   55

Four   Information Intelligence   79

Five   Critical Infrastructure Protection and
          Information Security   99

Six   Risk Communication, Psychological
          Management, and Disaster Preparedness   119

Seven   Transportation and Border Security Issues   149

Eight   Future Implications: Imagination, Integration,
          and Improvisation   175

Index   197

LIST OF FIGURES

1.1	Timeline of Noted Terrorist Events	12
1.2	The Progression of Terrorism	17
1.3	The Five Phases of Social Psychological Conditioning	19
2.1	Current Organizational Chart of the DHS	35
4.1	Members of the U.S. Intelligence Community	84
4.2	The Intelligence Cycle	88
5.1	Timeline of Key National Policy Initiatives	102
5.2	Critical Infrastructure Interdependencies	105
5.3	Network Security Risk Assessment Modeling Tool	107
5.4	A Decision Support System for Hazardous Material Management	107
5.5	Organization of the Department of Homeland Security	109
6.1	How to Be a Good Witness Fact Sheet	120
7.1	CAPPS II Passenger Prescreening Process	157
7.2	Secure Flight Chart	157
7.3	Flow Chart of ACE Operations	163
8.1	Quantifying Public Trust	177
8.2	Public Policy Trilemma	178

List of Tables and Boxes

Tables

1.1	Previous Classifications of Terrorism	13
2.1	Total Federal Resources Allocated for Homeland Security, 2001–2006	43
2.2	Funding for the Department of Homeland Security	44
6.1	Risk Communication Dos and Do nots	129
7.1	Eight Key Issues Identified by Public Law 108–90 and the Status of Efforts to Address Them, as of January 1, 2004	169

Boxes

1.1	Terrorism Comparison: Sicarri and Zealots	5
1.2	Terrorism Comparison: Assassins	5
1.3	Terrorism Comparison: Herod the Great	6
1.4	Terrorism Comparison: Attila the Hun	7
1.5	Terrorism Comparison: The First Crusade	8
1.6	Terrorism Comparison: Genghis Khan	9
1.7	Terrorism Comparison: Torquemada	10
1.8	Terrorism Comparison: the Reign of Terror	10
1.9	Terrorism Comparison: the Munich Massacre	11
2.1	Mission and Strategic Goals of the Department of Homeland Security	34
2.2	Directorates of the Department of Homeland Security	34
2.3	Programs Funded by the Office for Domestic Preparedness	46
3.1	Prisoners of War as Defined by the Geneva Convention	72
4.1	International Intelligence Agencies	81
4.2	Sample Presidential Daily Briefing, August 6, 2001	94
5.1	Critical Infrastructure Sectors as Defined in the National Infrastructure Protection Plan	100

5.2   Infrastructure and Information Assurance Initiatives
      Within the DHS   113
6.1   The Seven Rules for Effective Communication
      With the Public   122
6.2   Risk Perception Factors   124
6.3   CDC's Principles of Communication   130

FOREWORD

John O. Marsh, Jr.

*Former Secretary of Army, Former Council
to the President with Cabinet Rank,
Former Member of Congress*

This book by Dr. John Noftsinger, Kenneth Newbold, and Jack Wheeler of James Madison University examines the history of terrorism and its impact culturally, politically, and militarily on society. As the authors correctly observe terrorism is not new, but is more deadly due to technology, and especially as a result of the sweeping information technology revolution.

This discussion of terrorism in a historical perspective is essential to the understanding that will be necessary to cope with this menace. Cultural impacts have too long been neglected. Terrorism is a social cancer that has plagued humankind through the ages. It may go into remission only to recur years later, and often in more virulent form, and in a different place with devastating consequences. The suicidal zealot armed with modern explosives, or piloting a commercial airliner to a controlled crash site is a new face of this cancer.

A recurring theme in this book and one that can not be overemphasized is the lack of awareness by those in a society under attack as to the aims, goals, and motives of the terrorist attacker, who in many cases are mature, well educated, socially well placed, idealists, filled with hatred toward the West, and especially the United States. History is the best precedent in planning either a defense, or a response, and *Understanding Homeland Security: Policy, Perspectives, and Paradoxes* walks the reader through various efforts made by our national government, albeit with differing degrees of success, to cope with this phenomena of indiscriminate violence. The vulnerability of the "open society" is a major concern raised in the book. It can be a stumbling block to effective defenses. In cities with crowded road networks it takes only a fender bender on an arterial highway to cause great delay and major inconvenience. Imagine the detonation of a car rigged with a large bomb on the same highway. The damage could be massive and incomprehensible. But the book challenges us to try to comprehend the incomprehensible.

Considerable attention is given to governmental efforts to develop an effective counter terrorism strategy and policy. This is not an easy task because of multiple jurisdictions in a federalist system and conflicting jurisdictions inside the national government. The threat is pervasive. It cuts across political boundaries and the customary boundaries of departments and agencies. This can raise, and has raised, issues of authority and responsibility, it also can cause, and has caused, ineffective responses, and even inertia. These problems are clearly spelled out, and thereby may be a guide to new structures and new strategies.

The reader is asked to give special attention to the discussion of protecting the critical information infrastructure, a neglected area in our national security. Addressing this should be one of our highest priorities. It has not been, but *Understanding Homeland Security: Policy, Perspectives, and Paradoxes* makes a strong case why it needs to be. This warning has been sounded before in the presidential report on infrastructure protection issued in 1997, and again in Presidential Decision Directive (PDD) 63 and more recently in the President's Homeland Security Directive 7. The message is the same: that our information infrastructure is not only vital, but it is vulnerable. Confounding the creation of an effective program of protection is the reality that eighty to ninety percent of the nation's information infrastructure is in the private sector. Reaching the private sector requires new thinking and new approaches, which are highlighted in this book.

Acknowledgments

This book would not have been possible without the assistance of friends and colleagues at James Madison University's Institute for Infrastructure and Information Assurance and the Critical Infrastructure Protection Program at George Mason University. The authors deeply appreciate the efforts of Mr. Benjamin T. Delp and Mr. J. Gregory Surber, who assisted in the development of this text.

The authors would like to express their sincere appreciation and thanks to the following individuals who provided their valuable input to this work:

Dr. Massoud Amin, Dr. George Baker, Matthew Bates, Dr. A. Jerry Benson, Joshua Barnes, Dr. Douglas Brown, George Hawke, Michael Hutton, Keith Mann, John O. Marsh, Jr., Dr. Kent Murphy, Tiffany L. Newbold, Lucinda A. Noftsinger, Rebecca Rohlf, Dr. Linwood Rose, Kyndra Rotunda, Dr. Gregory Saathoff, Dr. Peter Sandman, Eric Stern, John Stoudt, and Anita Westfall.

READER'S GUIDE

Each chapter in this text will follow an organized pattern providing the reader with key words and definitions, case studies, and table top scenarios. The table top scenario will highlight either a current threat or past event, based on the content of the chapter, in an imagined scenario. For example, chapter one, "The Nature of the Threat," examines the threat of terrorism from a historical and psychological perspective. Chapter one's table-top scenario describes a mock series of bombings in Australia, and tasks the reader to identify key pieces of information that an analyst for the Federal Bureau of Investigation (FBI) might find useful.

The opening chapter, "The Nature of the Threat," will trace the roots and evolution of terrorism using historical examples dating as far back as Roman rule before Christianity came into existence. By understanding the religious, cultural, and social influences of terrorists, one can better analyze terrorism's role in this postmodern era. This analysis will be aided by introducing the student to psychological factors that dominate the current motivation of terrorist activity.

Chapter two, "What Is Homeland Security?" examines the role of homeland security in the post-9/11 era. The efforts of all three levels of government (local, state, and federal) will provide the framework to properly view homeland security and homeland defense policies. The creation of the Department of Homeland Security (DHS), the enactment of the USA PATRIOT Act, and the DHS Threat Level Warning System will engage students to participate in a discussion on the Constitutionality of domestic homeland security tactics, as well as legal and ethical issues arising during the War on Terror.

Foreign and domestic policy objectives bring the Civil Rights debate to chapter three, "Public Policy Issues." The incarceration and trial of Jose Padilla serves as the case study, which will present the protection of civil liberties while interpreting the USA PATRIOT Act. In addition, the authors present both sides of the argument as to whether the United States should engage in diplomacy or military action to fight terrorism.

Chapter four, "Information Intelligence," explores the revitalized efforts of the U.S. Intelligence Community in gathering and analyzing information to thwart the terrorist threat. The chapter will consider the intelligence gathering roles of both the private sector and government before and after 9/11. The work performed by the 9/11 Commission critiquing the U.S. Intelligence Community comprises the case study.

Ever since Bill Clinton's President's Commission on Critical Infrastructure Protection (PCCIP) in 1997, securing critical infrastructures has become a top priority for national security institutions. Chapter five, "Critical Infrastructure Protection and Information Security," investigates critical infrastructure systems, specifically those necessary for the daily routine of the civilian sector; for example: financial institutions, health care networks, water distribution systems, transportation networks, and communications. The importance of securing these interrelated entities will be presented using the 2003 North America Blackout as a case study.

Chapter six, "Risk Communication, Psychological Management, and Disaster Preparedness," discusses one of the primary post-9/11 concerns of trustworthy communication between government and citizens. In addition, thousands working for the government (DHS, FBI, CIA, Military Intelligence), in private firms and in higher education, have researched preparedness strategies to protect the United States against another 9/11. As a result of this research, the emerging field of risk communication is defined, which seeks to disseminate emergency guides and information to the public. Local governments, civic organizations, academic institutions, and local businesses will provide the medium linking disaster response plans to communities across the United States. The authors examine the 2001 Anthrax attacks in the case study.

With President George W. Bush's pledge to protect Americans from terrorism came new regulations and policies regarding border security and the transportation community. Memories of 9/11 have placed a great emphasis on airline travel security. Therefore, chapter seven, "Transportation and Border Security Issues," will address protection issues involving aviation, border, port, and rail security.

The eighth and final chapter, "Future Implications: Imagination, Integration, and Improvisation combines all the elements of the text to provide an outlook toward the future of Homeland Security. Emphasis will be placed on how higher education is developing curriculum, research centers, and outreach centers that focus on U.S. security. This textbook is a result of the new focus at the university level to educate the next generation of Intelligence Analysts. Included in chapter eight is an examination of the nation's science and technology community's role in developing new technologies that have direct homeland security implications.

Acronyms and Abbreviations

ACE	Automated Commercial Environment
ACLU	American Civil Liberties Union
AIF	Accelerating Innovation Fund
ALA	American Library Association
ATS	Automated Targeting System
ATSA	Aviation and Transportation Security Act
AUMF	Authorization for Use of Military Force
BTS	Border and Transportation Security
CAPPS II	Computer Assisted Passenger Prescreening System
CBRNE	Chemical, Biological, Radiological, Nuclear, Explosive
CIA	Central Intelligence Agency
CBP	Customs and Border Protection
CIAG	Critical Incident Analysis Group
CIPP	Critical Infrastructure Protection Program
COOP	Continuity of Operations Planning
C-TPAT	Customs-Trade Partnership against Terrorism
DCI	Director of Central Intelligence
DIA	Defense Intelligence Agency
DIRCM	Direct Infrared Countermeasure
DHS	Department of Homeland Security
DHHS	Department of Health and Human Services
DNI	Director of National Intelligence
DoD	Department of Defense
DoT	Department of Transportation
EDPP	Explosive Detection Personnel Portal
EDS	Explostive Detection Systems
EIJ	Egyptian Islamic Jihad
EMPG	Emergency Management Performance Grants
FAA	Federal Aviation Administration
FAMS	Federal Air Marshals Service
FBI	Federal Bureau of Investigation
FEMA	Federal Emergency Management Agency
FISA	Foreign Intelligence Surveillance Act
FFDO	Federal Flight Deck Officer

FFRDC	Federally Funded Research and Development Center
FinCEN	Financial Crimes Information Network
FOIA	Freedom of Information Act
GAO	General Accounting Office
HCRA	Harvard Center for Risk Analysis
HSARPA	Homeland Security Advanced Research Projects Agency
HSAS	Homeland Security Advisory System
HSC	Homeland Security Council
HSGP	Homeland Security Grant Program
HSU	Homeland Security University
HIS	Homeland Security Institute
HSIN	Homeland Security Information Network
HSOC	Homeland Security Operations Center
HSPI	Homeland Security Policy Institute
HUMINT	Human Intelligence
IAIP	Information Analysis and Infrastructure Protection
IC	Intelligence Community
ICE	Immigration and Customs Enforcement
IED	improvised explosive device
IIMG	Interagency Incident Management Group
IMINT	Imagery Intelligence
INS	Immigration and Naturalization Services
ISPS Code	International Ship and Port Facility Security Code
IT	Information Technology
LETPP	Law Enforcement Terrorist Prevention Program
MASINT	Measurement and Signature Intelligence
MANPADS	Man Portable Air Defense Systems
MARAD	Maritime Administration
MMRS	Metropolitan Medical Response System
MTSA	Maritime Transportation Security Act
NATO	North Atlantic Treaty Organization
NCTC	National Counterterrorism Center
NGO	nongovernmental organization
NIC	National Intelligence Council
NIE	National Intelligence Estimate
NIO	National Intelligence Officer
NIPP	National Infrastructure Protection Plan
NORAD	North American Air Defense Command
NRP	National Response Plan
NSA	National Security Agency
NSL	National Security Letters
NTC	National Targeting Center
ODP	Office for Domestic Preparedness
OHS	Office of Homeland Security
OMB	Office of Management and Budget
ORNL	Oak Ridge National Laboratory

OSINT	Open-Source Intelligence
OSLGCP	Office of State and Local Government Coordination and Preparedness
PCII	Protected Critical Infrastructure Information Program
PDB	Presidential Daily Briefing
PDD	Presidential Decision Directive
PCCIP	President's Commission on Critical Infrastructure Protection
PNR	Passenger Name Record
RANSAC	Russian American Nuclear Security Advisory Council
SBI	special background investigation
SCADA	Supervisory Control and Data Acquisition
SHSGP	State Homeland Security Grant Program
SIGINT	Signals Intelligence
TRADOC	U.S. Army Training and Doctrine Command
TRIP	Transit and Rail Inspection Pilot
TSC	Terrorist Screening Center
TSA	Transportation Security Administration
TSDB	Terrorist Screening Database
TTIC	Terrorist Threat Integration Center
UASI	Urban Area Security Initiative
UAV	Unmanned Aerial Vehicles
USAMRIID	United States Army Medical Research Institute of Infectious Diseases
USA PATRIOT Act	Uniting and Strengthening America by Providing Adequate Tools Required to Intercept and Obstruct Terrorism
UNCAT	United Nations Convention against Torture and Other Cruel, Inhuman or Degrading Treatment or Punishment
US-CERT	United States Computer Emergency Response Team
WMD	Weapons of Mass Destruction

ABOUT THE AUTHORS

Dr. John B. Noftsinger, Jr. serves as Associate Vice President of Academic Affairs for Research and Public Service, Executive Director of the Institute for Infrastructure and Information Assurance, and Associate Professor of Integrated Science and Technology and Education at James Madison University. He has primary responsibility for facilitating external grant and contract funding, homeland security research programs, economic development, technology transfer, and academic public relations and service programs for JMU. He has led the development of an innovative bachelors program in Information Analysis at JMU and is actively engaged in developing economic acceleration policy and programs within the mid-Atlantic region through the Accelerating Innovation Foundation; Virginia Technology Alliance; and Shenandoah Valley Technology Council, which he cofounded. He is a founding member of the Executive Committee of the Virginia Institute for Defense and Homeland Security and Deputy Chairman of the University of Virginia's Critical Incident Analysis Group (CIAG) Steering Committee. Dr. Noftsinger is also a member of the Critical Infrastructure Roundtable at the National Academy of Sciences. He serves as a Senior Fellow at the George Washington University Homeland Security Policy Institute (HSPI). In 2002, Dr. Noftsinger's state-wide leadership was recognized when he was appointed cochair of the Virginia Research and Technology Advisory Commission (VRTAC), which advises the governor and General Assembly of Virginia on appropriate research and technology strategies. He was also appointed by the Governor of Virginia as Deputy Secretary of Education for the Commonwealth. He holds a bachelor of science in Political Science and Public Administration from James Madison University, a Master of Arts in Higher Education Administration and Student Affairs from The Ohio State University, and a Doctorate in Higher Education Administration from the University of Virginia.

Kenneth F. Newbold, Jr. serves as the Associate Director for the Institute for Infrastructure and Information Assurance with a focus on administration and finance for James Madison University's effort within the broad area of homeland security. He is responsible for the day to day operations of the Institute for Infrastructure and Information Assurance including budgeting, external relationships, research and personnel. In his role, Mr. Newbold has helped lead the development of JMU's Information Analysis degree program and teaches a public policy course in the department of Integrated Science and Technology. His research interests include critical infrastructure protection with a focus on the human component of infrastructure systems, intelligence analysis, innovation and economic competitiveness as well as government oversight within the emerging area of homeland security. He is a graduate of Bridgewater College and holds a masters degree in Public Administration from James Madison University.

Jack K. Wheeler serves as a Security Consultant for the Security, Privacy, Wireless, and IT Governance division of IBM Global Business Services, Jack K. Wheeler is a 2006 graduate of James Madison University with a masters degree in Public Administration. While at JMU, Jack served as Graduate Fellow of The Institute for Infrastructure and Information Assurance where he played an important role in assisting the management and research activities for this homeland security-focused organization. His particular areas of experience include the development of innovative security solutions for the hazardous materials transportation sector, the analysis of federal security policy, and the application of homeland security-related legislation. With prior academic training in business administration and history, Mr. Wheeler provides a unique perspective in the analysis of national security initiatives and the ramifications upon various sectors within society.

CHAPTER ONE
THE NATURE OF THE THREAT

Table Top: The Source of Terrorism

In your position as Associate Analyst for the Federal Bureau of Investigation (FBI), you are tasked to investigate, critique, and provide written reports on various topics that your supervisors require to establish and conduct tactical operations. Four days ago, an unidentified individual initiated a series of bombings in Sydney, Australia, targeting popular tourist destinations and claiming the lives of forty-three people, including five Americans. In the following days, the entire intelligence community was working diligently to determine how and why this event took place. Though no terrorist organization claimed responsibility for the event, it was not yet possible to rule out the involvement of any prominent or off-shoot group. The situation grew increasingly heated as Australian officials demanded retribution, the mass media offered conflicting, unsubstantiated causes for the event, and the U.S. public became noticeably concerned about subsequent events occurring upon American soil. The first real break in the case came yesterday, when security camera footage was obtained, allowing for a visual identification of the culprit, Harold Mitchell. Mr. Mitchell, a fugitive for the past twenty four hours, is a thirty-two-year-old Australian citizen, who does not possess a criminal record and has no known ties to extremist organizations. As you begin examining the myriad of files and records on this individual, you soon learn that he possesses a history of mental instability, specifically that he was diagnosed three years ago as a schizophrenic. In reviewing these documents, you ask yourself many probing questions; What were his motivations? Did he have a broad agenda other than murder? What do his targets and tactics symbolize? Is he part of a larger conspiracy that threatens the United States? Is this terrorism?

Introduction

The birth of the "Homeland Security Era" was ushered in on September 11, 2001 and represents a massive and historical movement, one that touches nearly every facet within society. While these efforts were initiated to confront a multitude of hazards and asymmetric threats, terrorism, specifically the heinous events of 9/11, provided the direct impetus for government action in this arena. Undoubtedly, a response to terror became imperative, as the United States and its international allies took appropriate measures to strengthen security and bolster preparedness to confront this burgeoning threat. As a large portion of the global community mobilized to execute military, intelligence, and law enforcement operations, it appears as if the historical context of terrorism was abandoned or misinterpreted. The enemy was collectively identified as select groups of Islamic fundamentalists, organizations such as al-Qaeda, Hezbollah, and Hamas. Nations grew wary of the tactics they employed, including hijackings and suicide bombings. Individuals became aware of their motives; to destroy the infidels and achieve paradise in the afterlife. Though partially correct, these notions purported by the mass media, pundits, and politicians ignore all other forms of radical organizations, activities, and ideologies. As a result, the public conceptualization of terrorism has been both dangerously narrowed and misled.

Therefore, to begin this comprehensive exploration into the arena of homeland security, it is vital that we establish a firm foundation in the historical context of terrorism. After all, this revolution in security measures has been primarily designed to confront the mounting threat that terrorism has imposed. This introductory chapter has been constructed to illustrate that such violent movements are not unique to recent history or the United States; they have occurred since the birth of the recorded history of man. In addition, this section will address the following issues:

- Defining terrorism
- Historical examples of terrorism
- Types of terrorism
- Tactics of terrorists
- The causes of terrorism
- The sociology and psychology of terrorism

Collectively, these topics offer the conceptual basis needed to engage in a detailed analysis of homeland security. This text will address auxiliary hazards such as natural disasters and human error; nevertheless, an understanding of the nature of the threat of terrorism proves vital in examining the topic of domestic protection.

Defining Terrorism

An arduous task that scholars, practitioners, and politicians have engaged in for decades is establishing a universally excepted definition of terrorism. After countless attempts, the term still remains as nebulous as ever. The debate surrounding the topic is political in nature, as nations are reluctant to accept a definition that may classify a religious or ethnic group as terrorists. In addition, terrorism is quite subjective, best characterized by the famous adage, "One man's terrorist is another man's freedom fighter." Depending upon the viewpoint utilized, violent acts may be seen as justified, furthering a noble cause, or as odious steps taken by an illegitimate force.

Terrorism appears to represent a notion that can be identified when it occurs, but difficult to affix a common meaning. This is not to say that attempts to define have been futile, as clarification is needed to prevent this buzzword from being utilized in scenarios where it does not apply. Therefore, the classifications created by scholars and political bodies must be identified and recognized.

One of the earliest attempts to define terrorism occurred in 1795 by the French government in the wake of political upheaval and mass executions taking place during the "Reign of Terror," led by Maximillian Robespierre. The term was conceptualized as "The systematic use of terror or unpredictable violence against governments, publics or individuals to attain a political objective. Terrorism has been used by political organization with both rightist and leftist objectives, by nationalistic and ethnic groups, by revolutionaries, and by the armies and secret police of governments themselves" (Weinberger 2003, 66). This classification represents one of the most comprehensive attempts to define terrorism, as it recognizes political motivation and all possible targets of terror. Though never gaining universal acceptance, it must be viewed as a remarkably lucid understanding of this specific form of violence, one that may be generally applied to the threats currently plaguing the global community.

In 1938, the League of Nations, the precursor to the United Nations, constructed the first international working definition of terrorism for the time, which viewed the notion as: "All criminal acts directed against a State and intended or calculated to create a state of terror in the minds of particular persons or a group of persons or the general public" (Weinberger 2003, 66). Due to the fracture of the League of Nations and worldwide conflict, this description never took hold, setting the stage for failure of future attempts in international political bodies. Since its inception, the United Nations has failed to agree upon standard terminology, with the closest effort coming in the form of a resolution that merely publicly condemned the use of terrorism.

The lack of a clear definition is not an issue exclusive to the international community; the U.S. government has also constructed multiple exceedingly vague descriptions. Turning to the most recognized documents, in the form of legislation, U.S. Law 104 302 from 1996 offers "A federal crime of terrorism is a crime calculated to influence or affect the conduct of government by intimidation or coercion or to retaliate against government conduct" (Weinberger 2003, 68). To add clarification to the statute, U.S. Law 100 204 from 1997 states, "The term terrorist activity means the organizing and participation in a wanton or indiscriminate act of violence with extreme indifference to the risk of causing death or serious harm to individuals not taking part in the hostilities" (Weinberger 2003, 68–69). These characterizations represent the most current legislative definitions of the term; however, government agencies have deviated from the prescriptions, establishing individual language of their own. For instance, the State Department employs Title 22 of the U.S. Code, which characterizes terrorism as "Premeditated, politically motivated violence perpetrated against non-combatant targets by sub-national groups or clandestine agents, usually intended to influence an audience" (Weinberger 2003, 68). Each of these classifications hold some semblance of validity, however, they also fail in providing detailed, all-encompassing terminology that can be applied across departmental and even national borders.

To accurately assess violent scenarios and their connection with fanatic activities, theorists have also devised many complicated methods to proximate terrorism. One of the most popular techniques utilizes twenty-six different variables to establish a complete meaning (Gupta 2001). No matter how thorough this approach may be, it still does not offer the universality needed to become widely accepted. In general, nearly all definitions of terrorism incorporate the following elements: it is intentional criminal violence, the perpetrator(s) is/are politically motivated, the act is meant to incite fear and to influence an audience. Each of these notions is valid and provides the basis for the construction of a comprehensive meaning. However, there are many other vital ideologies and means that represent terrorist activity. Primarily, such action includes a cruel use of force, focused upon neutrals and noncombatants (Gupta 2001). Historically, attacks upon military personnel have been characterized as a component of warfare, as it is expected that the armed services confront such violence. Although insurgent assaults upon U.S. and Coalition Forces during Operation Iraqi Freedom (2003–present), and the bombing of the U.S.S. Cole in 2000 have been deemed terrorist attacks, for the purposes of homeland security, these events must be viewed as military incidents.

Next, terrorism must be thought of as organized, calculated violence, not merely mischief or mayhem randomly conducted by a lone individual (Turk 1982, 66). Under a broad definition of the term, many different criminal activities may be included, misrepresenting the true meaning of terrorism. To avoid encapsulating armed robbery and assault, the attack must include the previous criteria, along with being strategically planned. Further, the number of participants involved is of no consequence, as one man, supported to some degree by an accomplice, carried out the Oklahoma City bombing of 1995, obviously considered a terrorist attack.

In addition, the motivations of terrorism need not be limited to political ideologies. Whereas all grand-scale violent activity is political in nature, as it impacts established governments in some form, the impetus behind the act may stem from religious or social grievances. Historical examples including the European-led Crusades and the uprisings in Northern Ireland during the twentieth century, both discussed later in this chapter, illustrate this notion. As a result, both religious and social ideologies must be factored into any comprehensive definition of terror.

A final component that needs to be added to the agreed upon elements of the term terrorism is the impact of the action itself. The incitement of fear, as previously noted, must be included; however, none of the attempted definitions mention any other consequence of attacks. According to Rakesh Gupta, professor of Social Sciences at Jawaharlal Nehru University in New Delhi, India, the fear that terrorists are able to cause are a direct result of their deprivation of an individual or group's right to the principles that Locke purported, a reference to life, liberty, and property (Gupta 2001). As a result, violent action that can be viewed as terrorism must occur on a scale that produces such significant loss.

Utilizing the framework provided in government documents, theoretical prescriptions, and widely held notions, the following definition of terrorism will guide us through the remainder of this text.

Terrorism is organized, politically, religiously, and/or socially motivated criminal behavior, meant to influence an audience, inflicted upon civilians or noncombatants, resulting in the incitement of fear and the deprivation of life, property, and/or freedom.

The History of Terrorism

To accurately investigate the arena of homeland security, terrorism, the primary cause and purpose of such efforts, must be placed in context. For onlookers, deluged by twenty-four-hour cable news and incessant warning, it appears as if we have reached a juncture in history never before witnessed. With the rise of globalization and advancements in technology, the tactics available to terrorists have altered significantly. However, the use of terrorism as a tool of violence and intimidation is absolutely not novel. The following historical examples, dating as far back as the Roman Empire, illustrate these facts and provide the needed framework to confront current crises.

The Sicarii, Zealots, and Assassins

Deemed by experts to be the first known terrorist organization, the Sicarii were Jewish extremists who opposed the Roman occupation of Israel and other Middle Eastern nations during the first century (Burgess 2003, 1). These individuals utilized coordinated covert actions, stabbing to death prominent Jewish citizens that were deemed sympathetic to Roman rule with daggers concealed beneath their clothing. Concurrently, the Zealots (also Jewish extremists) focused their attacks upon Romans and Greeks, carrying out executions in a similar manner (Burgess 2003, 1). Both groups were known to strike during the daytime in public areas with many witnesses, so as to inspire fear and discourage affiliation with Roman authorities. The utilization of such tactics came with the consequences of expected identification, probable capture, and possible execution. Though many Sicarii and Zealots lost their lives in the process, these attacks resulted in widespread panic throughout communities within the Middle East (Weinberger 2003, 64). (See box 1.1.)

Other scholars cite the Assassins as representing the first true historical example of a terrorist organization. This extremist sect of Shiite Muslims was known to habitually use hashish to reach a state of rapture, and then carry out their murderous plots. Targeting both Christian and Muslim political and religious leaders, the Assassins sought to ravage populations of divergent ideologies (Carr 2002, 52–53). Yet again, these individuals were both extremely organized and willing to sacrifice their lives for the common cause. (See box 1.2.)

Box 1.1   Terrorism Comparison: Sicarri and Zealots

Organized: Yes

Politically, religiously, and/or socially motivated: Politically and religiously

Inflicted upon noncombatants: Yes

Meant to incite fear: Yes

Deprivation of life, property, or freedom: Yes

Considered terrorism: Yes

Box 1.2   Terrorism Comparison: Assassins

Organized: Yes

Politically, religiously, and/or socially motivated: Religiously

Inflicted upon noncombatants: Yes

Meant to incite fear: Yes

Deprivation of life, property, or freedom: Yes

Considered terrorism: Yes

Herod The Great

The infamous biblical ruler during the time of Jesus in the region of Galilee, Herod The Great perpetrated numerous violent, terrorist-like acts upon his citizenry. Born of a wealthy Jewish family, loyal to the Roman Empire, circa 74 B.C., Herod was given the title of Prefect of Galilee at age sixteen. As an adult, he strengthened alliances with Rome and acquired military support to suppress all Jewish resistance. Along with troops provided by the empire, Herod marched upon Jerusalem to quell rebellion, a swift military victory, after which the king ordered the execution of a majority of the population to demonstrate wrath and solidify authority (Klein 2004, 15). Brutality begat brutality as Herod then sentenced over half of the members of the Sanhedrin (the Jewish court) to death for impinging upon his rule, relegating them afterward to confront religious affairs (15). The murderous penchant of the king was not solely imposed upon his subjects: he targeted his own kin, suspecting them of challenging his authority. Three of Herod's five sons, Alexander, Aristobulus, and Antipater were rumored to speak of killing their father and gaining control of all of Judaea. When learning of this suspected plot, the king turned the three over to Roman custody, demanding they be tried for treason. After a brief, farce of a trial, they were sentenced to death, which came in the form of starvation, as ordered by Herod (19). Finally, in his waning years of life, the king carried out his most vicious and well-known act, the Slaughter of the Innocents. Recounted in the Gospel of Matthew (although not substantiated or contradicted in other historical texts), Herod ordered preemptive vengeance after learning of the birth of the proclaimed "King of the Jews." Recognizing the direct challenge to his rule, Herod demanded the execution of all male children under the age of two in Judaea, resulting in the estimated deaths of 10,000 to 150,000 infants. (See box 1.3.)

Box 1.3 Terrorism Comparison: Herod the Great

Organized: Yes

Politically, religiously, and/or socially motivated: Politically

Inflicted upon noncombatants: Yes

Meant to incite fear: Yes

Deprivation of life, property, or freedom: Yes

Considered terrorism: Yes

Attila the Hun

Born in A.D. 406 to noble parents among the Huns, a nomadic sect hailing from the western reaches of China, Attila would eventually rise to infamy, leading many devastating incursions and sieges against the Roman Empire (Twiss 2002, 32). Becoming a military leader by his early twenties, Attila spawned an army of ruthless men,

---

Box 1.4   Terrorism Comparison: Attila the Hun

Organized: Yes
Politically, religiously, and/or socially motivated: Politically (to conquer lands and people)
Inflicted upon noncombatants: Yes
Meant to incite fear: Yes
Deprivation of life, property, or freedom: Yes
Considered terrorism: Yes

---

encouraging those under his command to pillage all conquered lands and maim those who resisted. The violence was so well known and feared that the Roman Empire paid an annual tribute to the Huns, with the promise of being spared. However, in A.D. 439, this uneasy treaty was broken, and the Huns initiated a series of invasions that would last for decades. Around this time, Attila led an attack upon the city of Naissus, leading to an extraordinary number of civilian deaths, so many it was rumored no one would enter the city for years afterward due to the intense lingering smell of death and decay (34). With the goal of controlling Constantinople, the eastern capital of the Roman Empire, Attila ordered sieges upon hundreds of villages, churches, and monasteries during the march. In one specific incident, the Huns encountered a nomadic tribe in Germany, led by Saint Ursula, whom Attila quickly admired. He proposed marriage, and when she refused, Attila killed her and ordered the massacre of all of her companions, totaling approximately 11,000 persons (37). This homicidal tirade swept through a majority of the European continent, including the territory boundaries of France, Hungary, and Italy, leaving nothing but death and destruction in the wake. (See box 1.4.)

The First Crusade

In November of A.D. 1095, Pope Urban II called for a massive European military journey to aid Christians in the Middle East and to liberate Jerusalem from Islamic control. With the promise that pilgrimage would absolve participants from all sins, the pope declared, "Let those who have long been robbers now be soldiers of Christ. Let those who once fought against brothers and relatives now rightfully fight against barbarians" (Carr 2002, 42). From the advent of the First Crusade, the thousands of knights led by European nobles, ransacked Jewish villages throughout the Rhineland, killing an untold number of innocent civilians (France 1997, 38). Filled with religious fervor, the soldiers advanced upon the Holy City, reaching its walls in July 1099. The Muslim and Jewish populations within the city were well guarded by the vast infrastructure of fortifications, requiring the approximately 13,000 crusaders to spend days constructing ladders, rams, and catapults. On July 15, the northern section of the wall was breeched, and the European forces swept through the city with brutal force (44). Muslims and Jews alike were targeted for death, as citizens of every gender and age fell victim to the invasion. In one instance, the crusaders set a

---

Box 1.5   Terrorism Comparison: The First Crusade

Organized: Yes

Politically, religiously, and/or socially motivated: Religiously

Inflicted upon noncombatants: Yes

Meant to incite fear: Yes

Deprivation of life, property, or freedom: Yes

Considered terrorism: Yes

---

synagogue ablaze, killing all those who sought shelter inside. Fleeing the city spared many, however, thousands upon thousands of civilians perished during the capture. (See box 1.5.) With the city in the possession of Christians, the crusaders celebrated, represented best by the words of Raymond of Aguilers:

> How they rejoiced and exulted and sang a new song to the Lord! For their hearts offered prayers of praise to God, victorious and triumphant, which cannot be told in words. A new day, new joy, new and perpetual gladness, the consummation of our labour and devotion, drew forth from all new words and new songs. This day, I say, marks the justification of Christianity, the humiliation of paganism, and the renewal of our faith. This is the day which the Lord hath made, let us rejoice and be glad in it, for on this day the Lord revealed Himself to His people and blessed them. (France 1997, 45)

Genghis Khan

This ruthless tribal leader and military tactician, born in Central Asia during the mid-twelfth century with the name Temujin, rose to prominence by conquering lands and building an empire that swept across continents. During childhood, an initial manifestation of Temujin's brutality was displayed when he slew his brother for attempting to pilfer food from the family (Klein 2004, 23). At the time, the Mongols were divided among many disparate tribes, with sparring between the groups being commonplace. As a result of his demonstration of superiority in warfare and the ability to suppress challenges from other clans, word of Temujin's power and bravery spread across Central Asia, with many tribes forging alliances and recognizing him as their leader. In circa 1195, the assembly of chieftains declared Temujin to be their Khan (leader), bestowing upon him the name of Genghis ("oceanic warrior") (24). For years after, Genghis Khan built a massive military force that relied upon cavalry, innovative weapons, and keen tactics to defeat their enemies. In 1207, Khan initiated a campaign intent upon conquering China, Manchuria, and Peking. Employing a vicious total war method, Khan ordered every territory to be pillaged and burned, so those lucky enough to flee would spread word of the devastation his army could cause. Those civilians taken capture by Khan's forces were subjected to execution by savage means, such as forced submerging into vats of scalding oil or being dragged by horse for miles (28). By 1221, lands stretching from the Mediterranean and Baltic Seas to the Pacific Ocean fell under the jurisdiction of Genghis Khan, either by

---

Box 1.6   Terrorism Comparison: Genghis Khan

Organized: Yes

Politically, religiously, and/or socially motivated: Politically

Inflicted upon noncombatants: Yes

Meant to incite fear: Yes

Deprivation of life, property, or freedom: Yes

Considered terrorism: Yes

---

surrender or conquest. Few times has history seen the widespread devastation and fear that resulted from Khan's rule. (See box 1.6.)

Torquemada

During the Middle Ages in Europe, fear within the Catholic Church began to spread regarding the threats posed by heretics, which resulted in the use of violence in an attempt to eradicate all opposition to the faith. In 1252, Pope Innocent IV officially sanctioned the use of torture and appointed the Dominican order of friars to lead what became known as the Papal Inquisition (Twiss 2002, 52). The most infamous manifestation of this power occurred 200 years later in the Kingdom of Castille, Spain. Tensions began brewing between the Jewish and Christian populations of the regions in the fourteenth century, with widespread violence ensuing following a bloody civil war. The Jews quickly became the arbitrary focal point for blame regarding all of the social ills occurring at the time. Facing the prospect of death or conversion of religion, many accepted the Catholic faith, becoming known as conversos (54). Underpinning friction remained, devoid of bloodshed, until 1478 when Dominican friar Tomas de Torquemada, an advisor to Queen Isabella, persuaded the monarch of the threats to the faith posed by conversos. Two years later, an edict from Pope Sixtus IV provided Spain with the authority to establish Inquisition tribunals to root out and punish heretics. On February 6, 1481, the Torquemada-led Spanish Inquisition carried out their first execution, as six conversos were burned alive (55). In years following, tribunals were established in nearly every major Spanish city and province. The accused were essentially faced with two choices, to admit guilt, offer the names of suspected heretics, and be sentenced with penance, or deny involvement and face certain torture and death. Great fear spread among the Jewish population, as individuals began to indict neighbors and acquaintances on false claims. Torquemada also ordered that those accused must forfeit all property, with the profits utilized to fuel the system and to supplement the wealth of Inquisitors. Whereas the fortunate accused faced public humiliation, such as being stripped of clothing and lashed during Sunday mass, thousands of others were subjected to imprisonment and unspeakable torture. Torquemada sanctioned the use of methods such as the rack, drawing-and-quartering, water torture, and hanging. When imposing the death sentence, done in front of spectators on public holidays, the deemed heretics were fastened to a pyre of wood, burnt alive, and quartered after death (Twiss 2002, 60).

Box 1.7   Terrorism Comparison: Torquemada

Organized: Yes
Politically, religiously, and/or socially motivated: Religiously
Inflicted upon noncombatants: Yes
Meant to incite fear: Yes
Deprivation of life, property, or freedom: Yes
Considered terrorism: Yes

Under his rule, the Spanish Inquisition claimed the lives of countless thousands of innocent civilians and virtually decimated the Jewish population in Spain. The system remained in place for nearly 300 years after his death in 1498; however, no single phase was as bloody or ruthless as the Spanish Inquisition under Torquemada. (See box 1.7.)

The Reign of Terror

The modern conceptualization of terrorism was first used by English philosopher Edmund Burke when describing the *regime de la terreur*, better known as the Reign of Terror, occurring during the French Revolution, from June 1793 to July 1794 (Martin 2003, 5). Led by Maximilien Robespierre, the radical Jacobin government sought to suppress any opposition to the dictatorship and solidify the grasp of the French Republic. The Jacobins, a powerful political party in favor of a centralized government, established the Revolutionary Tribunal, which authorized the arrest and oversaw the prosecution of suspected dissidents. Within a year's time, the makeshift court condemned nearly 40,000 people, ordering their execution by a novel weapon, the guillotine (Burgess 2003, 1). Much in the same manner as during the Inquisition, fear and panic spread across France as citizens were quick to name neighbors and business associates as disloyal to the Republic. Though lasting merely thirteen months, the Robespierre-led Reign of Terror left an indelible mark upon history. (See box 1.8.)

Box 1.8   Terrorism Comparison: the Reign of Terror

Organized: Yes
Politically, religiously, and/or socially motivated: Politically
Inflicted upon noncombatants: Yes
Meant to incite fear: Yes
Deprivation of life, property, or freedom: Yes
Considered terrorism: Yes

The Munich Massacre

Scholars point to the events that transpired on September 5, 1972, during the Summer Olympic Games, as the first example of modern terrorism; an infamous incident that would eventually be called "The Munich Massacre." On this day, eight members of the radical Palestinian organization known as Black September raided the apartment buildings occupied by Israeli athletes at the Olympic Village, in the host city Munich, Germany. The attackers, armed with rifles, handguns, knives, and explosives, captured eleven members of the team, killing two of them during the struggle. Within one hour's time, those fortunate enough to escape from adjoining rooms notified authorities, and West German law enforcement rapidly arrived at the scene. The eight members of Black September demanded the release of 234 Arab and German prisoners being incarcerated in Israel and West Germany, in addition to three airplanes for purposes of escape (Calahan 1995). Law enforcement established communication with the Israeli government, specifically Prime Minister Golda Meir, who indicated that the nation would never succumb to terrorist demands.

West German officials concluded that a rescue attempt was the only viable option, as the terrorists indicated that they were willing to die and kill for their cause, coupled with the fact that their demands would not be met. Law enforcement was able to isolate the attackers and hostages, transporting them by helicopter to the nearby Furstenfeldbruck Airport. With snipers and tactical units placed around the premises, the police ordered fire to be opened upon the terrorists as they moved a safe distance away from the helicopters. The initial sniper shots missed their targets, triggering an extended gun battle that lasted over an hour (Calahan 1995). At that time, West German officials ordered the tactical units to advance, forcing the terrorists to flee for cover. Recognizing the end was near, the attackers returned to the helicopters, throwing a grenade into one, killing five hostages, and opening fire in the other, killing the remaining four athletes (Calahan 1995). Shortly after, West German authorities were able to either capture or kill the eight terrorists, bringing an end to this tragic event. The Munich Massacre served as the first international public display of Islamic terrorism, due to the fact that it drew extensive media coverage. In addition, the event illustrated the symbolism that has accompanied proceeding attacks, as the carnage transpired at arguably the most important display of global peace, the Olympic Games. (See box 1.9.)

Box 1.9 Terrorism Comparison: the Munich Massacre

Organized: Yes

Politically, religiously, and/or socially motivated: Politically, religiously

Inflicted upon noncombatants: Yes

Meant to incite fear: Probable

Deprivation of life, property, or freedom: Yes

Considered terrorism: Yes

---

*   *   *

As this myriad of historical events illustrate, terrorism, as we have defined, is absolutely not new. Further, many of the motivations, practices, and consequences that have underlined current events have roots directly tied to history. For instance, the Sicarii,

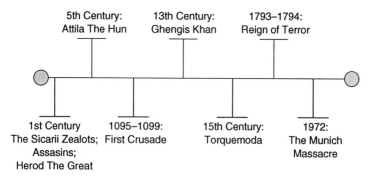

Figure 1.1   Timeline of Noted Terrorist Events.

Zealots, and Assassins all utilized covert actions and displayed a willingness to perish for their cause: tactics and beliefs that are seen in modern suicide bombings. Herod the Great, Attila the Hun, Genghis Khan, and Maximillian Robespierre all inflicted mass casualties and unthinkable brutality upon innocent civilians to incite fear and further their campaigns, similar to actions taken in the recent past by groups such as the Baathist regime in Iraq under Sadaam Hussein and the Taliban in Afghanistan. The First Crusade and the Spanish Inquisition serve to highlight the role of religious fervor in terrorist activity, while also underlining that Islam is not the only religion tied to unwarranted violence. In general, these examples provide the needed historical context and connections for any comprehensive discourse in protection and prevention measures.

As an ancillary note, the events utilized in this work clearly do not represent all of the terrorist activity that has occurred over the past two millennia. Readers may question why Hitler, Stalin, the Ku Klux Klan, and other murderous individuals and groups were excluded from the study. Undoubtedly, there are thousands of possible examples that exist in the annals of history; however, it is the duty of any practitioner or scholar of homeland security to access these events, analyze them, and construct comparisons between the past and the present. The events chronicled in this work represent a sample of this process, while providing the basis for a detailed examination of terrorism. Figure 1.1 provides a timeline of noted terrorist events.

Types of Terrorism

With a basic understanding of the environment in place, it is now necessary to classify the various forms of terrorist activity and the impact they have. Once again, there is no agreed upon format within which violent acts are to be distinguished; instead, experts have outlined a multitude of possible forms of terrorism, as seen in table 1.1.

Whereas the application of such classifications is needed, the summations currently established contain a great deal of overlap, thus requiring simplification and structure to produce a detailed and useful typology. Primarily, the inclusion of classifications centered on the tactics of terrorism are not beneficial due to the fact that individual groups can be placed in multiple categories. For instance, Aum Shinrikyo, the

Table 1.1   Previous Classifications of Terrorism

State sponsored	Right-wing	Left-wing	Nationalist
Anarchist	Islamic	Cyber	Biological
Chemical	Nuclear	International	Domestic
Revolutionary	Suicide	Megalomaniac	Separatist

organization that carried out the 1995 Tokyo Subway sarin gas attack, could be classified as right-wing, anarchist, religious, and chemical terrorists, as they either possessed such ideologies and motivations, or utilized such tactics. As a result, for our purposes, the following is a detailed, yet simplified, list of the forms of terrorism that characterize violent groups throughout the world.

State-Sponsored

This is a form of terrorism that is committed against enemies, both foreign and domestic, directed by nations, controlling parties, or individual leaders (Martin 2003, 33). State-sponsored is historically the most utilized type of terrorism, while also being the most capable of obtaining costly resources and personnel, due to ties to a nation's finances. In recent years, the world has not seen many incidents of state-sponsored terrorism, but these methods have been utilized by vicious dictators such as Adolf Hitler (Germany), Joseph Stalin (Russia), and Pol Pot (Cambodia). Nations have employed such treacherous tactics as they provide cost-effective means for waging war in a clandestine manner (Council on Foreign Relations 2005). Currently, the U.S. Department of State recognizes six state sponsors of terrorism (Iran, Cuba, North Korea, Libya, Syria, and Sudan), which officially places prohibitions on arms sales, economic assistance, and other privileges upon those nations (United States Department of State 2004, 85). A modern example of state-sponsored terrorism occurred in 1979, as the Iranian government utilized young militants to capture hostages at the American Embassy, triggering the infamous year-long standoff (Council on Foreign Relations, 2005).

Revolutionary Terrorism

This term is one that encompasses many of the previously conceptualized classifications of terrorism. Instead of distinguishing between left-wing, right-wing, nationalist, anarchist, separatist, and megalomaniac, revolutionary terrorism encompasses them all. As such, the term can be thought of as *terrorist activity employed by individuals or organizations that seek to overthrow a current political or social establishment, either domestic or international.* To distinguish between the subsets, left-wing groups seek to destroy democracies and establish communist or socialist rule, as seen in Russia's Bolshevik Revolution in 1917. Conversely, right-wing organizations aim to overthrow democracies and create fascist regimes, as was the case during the Nazi conquest, and illustrated today by sects of skinheads. Anarchists, on the other hand, generally utilize small, decentralized organizational structure, striving to destabilize any organized government with methods such as assassination, evidenced during the assassination of President William McKinley in 1901 by a Hungarian extremist (Council on Foreign Relations, 2005). Finally, megalomaniac forms are led by egotistical and self-righteous persons seeking to effect change and place a mark upon history, as was the case with Timothy McVeigh in the 1995 Oklahoma City bombing (Sprinzak 2001, 72–73). Though differences between these ideologies exist, they all share a common thread of utilizing terrorism to implement structural political changes. A strict definition of revolution is the overthrow of one government and its replacement with another. Clearly, all of the subsets previously mentioned characterize this term; therefore, it is appropriate to place them all under the umbrella of revolutionary terrorism. In addition, it is under this classification that the adage "One person's terrorist is another person's freedom fighter" comes into play. For example, the patriots of the American Revolution were viewed as terrorists by the British government in the 1770s. Whereas every form of terrorism is subjective in nature, distinguishing between unjust insurgent uprisings and needed revolution depends solely upon ones view of the situation and underlying causes. It is, and will continue to be, the duty of practitioners to engage in this debate and analyze terrorism worldwide.

Religious Terrorism

The final category of terrorism has arguably become the most recognized, feared, and frequent in modern times: religiously motivated violence. Under this premise, terrorist organizations base their mission and goals upon the notion that their faith is absolutely just, coupled with the belief that a higher power wishes them to extract vengeance upon all nonbelievers. This classification also presents the greatest threat to the global community, as susceptible victims do not reside in a single region or share common national bonds, as individuals of varying religions reside on nearly every continent in the world. In addition, the belief that "God" provides the justification of murder, theft, or torture makes this form of terrorism particularly dangerous. Religious-based violence requires a more intensive and time consuming indoctrination process to obtain participants, due to the fact that individuals must be transformed from devout in belief to possessing the desire to kill for the faith. However, religious terrorism has been rapidly growing worldwide, with nearly half of all known terrorist groups, as recently as 1995, being classified under this typology (Council on Foreign Relations, 2005). It is inaccurate to singularly identify Islamic fundamentalism as the lone occupant of this category; in truth, all extremist organizations that rely upon religion as their primary motivation for violence must be placed in this category. With this in mind, historical examples such as the Crusades and the Inquisition, along with contemporary events such as abortion office bombings must be viewed in the same vein as al-Qaeda or Hizbollah.

By using three broad, but detailed categories, students of homeland security are better able to establish context for current events and movements, while also drawing connections with historical occurrences. The tactics employed or underlying goals of the organization should not be included in the classification process; however, such discussion and analysis must occur once this segmentation has taken place. For purposes of organization and logical progression, the creation of state-sponsored, revolutionary, and religious forms of terrorism are most appropriate for homeland security operations.

The Tactics of Terrorism

The progression of the scope of terrorist attacks and capabilities directly coincide with advances made in technology, which offers a larger arsenal for perpetrators and increasing the number of targets for siege. Generally speaking, all terrorists utilize various tactics to demonstrate power, inflict harm upon current enemies, deter future resistance, vent frustrations, and strengthen the will and capacity of their organization. Needless to say, extremist groups have employed weapons of the times, from knives in early ages to chemical and biological arms today. Engaging in a discussion of particular weaponry is beyond the scope of this text; instead, we must focus on how these tools are utilized and which present the greatest threat to the global community. The following summarizes the common tactics of terrorism and includes a brief explanation of each.

Armed Robbery. Utilized primarily by groups to gain supplies, funds, or to incite fear among the general public. This represents the least dangerous and/or deadly tactic of terrorism (Price 1977, 56).

Kidnapping. Also known as "coercive bargaining." This method represents the taking of hostages of a particular nation or state and the issuance of demands to be met in exchange for their release. While historically not extremely successful, this tactic draws a great deal of media coverage to advertise the cause of the attackers. Examples include the string of airliner hijackings in the 1970's and 1980's, in addition to the Chechen rebels siege on a Moscow Theatre in 2002 (Price 1977, 56).

Assassination. For centuries, terrorist groups and nation states have engaged in organized targeting and murder of enemies, from leaders down to common civilians. This method is both effective and damaging due to the fact that governments can be thrown into turmoil if a president, prime minister, or monarch falls victim to assassination. In addition, it serves to draw significant attention to the group responsible. The assassination of Austrian Archduke Franz Ferdinand, which triggered the start of World War I, by the extremist group Black Hand is a notable example of this tactic (Price 1977, 47).

Random Targeting. Random targeting is currently one of the most utilized methods in the arsenal of terrorists. This tactic is employed in two general ways: (1) by attacking individuals and sites in an illogical fashion, spreading fear due to the fact that anyone could be a target, or (2) by selecting specific and symbolic persons and structures for attack (Turk 1982, 122). In terms of inciting panic amongst the populace, random targeting represents the most effective and utilized tactic. In addition, this method does not allow enemies to adequately anticipate future attacks, offering an additional benefit to terrorist organizations. Examples of random targeting include the myriad of bus bombings by Hamas and Hizbollah in modern Israel and recent al-Qaeda attacks such as the Madrid commuter train attacks of March 2004.

WMD. Acronym for Weapons of Mass Destruction, signifying modern armaments that possess the capabilities of producing catastrophic losses, both in terms of structural damage and loss of life. Included in this category are CBRNE: chemical, biological, radiological, nuclear, and explosive weapons. Terrorists may potentially acquire these arms from established or disbanded nations, or produce improvised versions of their own. To date, the only known modern terrorist attack utilizing WMD is the 1995 Tokyo subway bombing, in which the Aum Shinrikyo cult released sarin gas, killing twelve people.

Cyber. Technological advancements in recent decades have provided terrorists with an increased arsenal of effective tactics. Due to global connectivity and the reliance upon cyber networks and technology, attacks using computers have raised a serious threat to security worldwide. Malicious individuals can now use the cyber realm to pilfer funds, disable businesses and governments, and shut down critical infrastructure systems that rely upon computers for operation. This tactic is extremely beneficial due to the low costs of use and the fact that attacks can be carried out from remote locations. An example of this occurred in 2004 when a group of Romanian hackers infiltrated the controls of the life support systems within a research station in Antarctica, placing fifty-eight scientists in danger, but resulting in no fatalities (Poulsen 2004).

Suicide. This represents one of the most shocking tactics of terrorism, one that seems to be employed at a more frequent rate in recent years. To utilize this, organizations must recruit committed individuals who are willing to die for the cause, as they perish alongside victims during the attack. Examples of suicide terrorism include 9/11, Hamas attacks in Israel, and Chechen rebel bombings in Russia. There is a detailed discussion of suicide terrorism later in the chapter.

Innovative Methods. A final tactic that may be employed by terrorist organizations is broadly categorized as innovative methods. In essence, this represents the use of weapons created by the individuals themselves, or the development of novel methods, unsuspected by enemies. For example, terrorists in the Middle East have begun utilizing improvised explosive devices (IED) to attack targets. Conversely, the 9/11 attacks signify innovative methods, as the al-Qaeda hijackers used fully fueled jetliners as bombs. In addition, it appears as if there is no upper limit to this tactic of terrorism, as groups and individuals will constantly develop innovative means to execute attacks.

A fundamental understanding of the tactics of terrorism is required for all current and future practitioners of homeland security. In order to bolster domestic protection and preparedness, we must first be aware of the dangers that are present and the methods used to initiate attacks.

The Causes of Terrorism

With a conceptualization of the history, typology, and tactics of terrorism in place, it is now necessary to discuss how terrorism came into existence. According to scholars, the birth of terrorism was a direct result of the establishment of groups of political power and wealth within society. In modern times, this represents our fragmented party system, in a historical sense it represents the ruling elite. For terrorism to arise, both past and present major grievances must first exist between a cohesive subset of the overall population. To express these frustrations, social movements form in an attempt to usher in change and gain support, as a group in minority opinion generally initiates these measures (Crenshaw 1981, 383). Next, a barrier must exist between the group and the political process, meaning their interests cannot be fully represented for consideration (Gupta 2001). Finally, these organizations must become impatient with the lack of access and change, and make a rational choice to engage in violence to initiate reform. This three-step process is what we will call "The Progression of Terrorism," as illustrated in figure 1.2.

Figure 1.2 represents a macro-level view of the causes of terrorism; however, each stage involves many additional and differing events. For instance, within Stage 1, the grievances present must be deep-seeded and controversial, causing an immediate need to be heard. As the group attempts to obtain an audience, ranging from the very short term to decades in time, feelings of anger and helplessness may arise (Eqbal 1986, 5). Coupled with a general lack of access to the political system, the organization begins the path toward violence.

Next, in Stage 2, the barriers to entry may have come with either perceived or real violence at the hands of the party in power. Historically, incidents of terrorism have followed atrocities, such as occurred with the creation of a Jewish state in Palestine after the Holocaust (5). In addition, if the group determines that their options for peaceful action are either limited or nonexistent, they may begin to view the barriers as insurmountable, forcing violent action.

Once a group has made the rational choice to engage in violent behavior and employ terrorist methods, there are many different motivations that impact their choice in proceeding. First, for violence to occur, the group must be able to identify the target for their grievances and externalize their frustrations (5). As previously stated, terrorists seek to gain recognition and incite fear with their actions, which may force some groups to choose the most public form of attack possible. Next, the

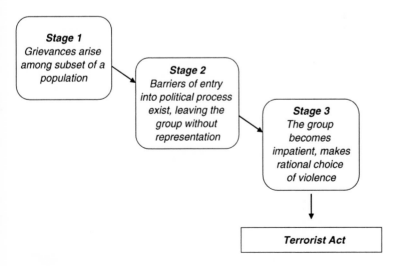

Figure 1.2   The Progression of Terrorism.

organization may seek to discredit or dislocate the operation of the government that denied them access, leading them to consider the targeting of bureaucratic structures. The use of terrorism may also be an attempt to create a reaction from the government, which will lend additional publicity, and possibly sympathy, to the group's agenda. Finally, the use of these measures may serve to solidify the internal cohesion of the organization, to justify the cause, and to demonstrate power (Crenshaw 1981, 383).

Scholars have asserted that the spread of violence in recent decades is primarily the result of globalization and reduced trade barriers in the wake of the Cold War. Due to the reliance upon an interconnected global marketplace, the borders of nearly every nation have become increasingly porous, allowing for the rapid flow of products and people, making the tracking of dangerous individuals extremely difficult. In addition, the end of the Cold War depolarized the globe, allowing for the spread of Western principles and values, in addition to capitalism. For those nations and peoples that have not benefited from this growth, a large anti-Western sentiment has intensified, resulting in attacks upon the United States, Great Britain, and Spain (Schrader 2002). These events, coupled with the intricacies of the progression of terrorism, illustrated in figure 1.2, represent the most notable causes for the increase in insurgent violence.

What Makes a Terrorist?

The final section of this introductory chapter seeks to explore the mindsets of terrorists, specifically the psychological and sociological factors that contribute to the spread of violent actions in support of ideology. Included in this section is a discussion pertaining to arguably the most incomprehensible tactics of terrorists, suicide attacks. A conceptualization of such intricacies is vital for both homeland security and foreign policy purposes.

Generally speaking, psychologists have not been able to devise a single, universally applicable terrorist profile. In addition, experts have concluded that a vast majority of terrorists do not meet the established criteria to be labeled as psychopaths, or mentally ill in any way (Stahelski 2004). Instead, many scholars have turned to the field of sociology, seeking answers as to how an individual becomes a terrorist. Sociologists and psychologists have reached a consensus that terrorist organizations utilize cult-like conditioning methods to recruit individuals, desensitize the person, and turn them into cold-blooded assassins. Studies have shown that some terrorists are the product of a broken home environment, growing up without a parent, and that they may avoid connection with stable conventional social groups, such as in schools or at work (Stahelski 2004). In addition, a large number of violent fanatics come from an affluent background and are highly educated. Because terrorism is, in many cases, an extreme exhibition of political, social, and/or religious concerns, the wealthy and educated are more inclined to engage in decisive action, challenge those perceived to be at fault, and turn to violence if necessary (Turk 1982, 126). Further, in terms of modern terrorists, individuals join organizations due to their immediate social network, namely close friends. A study recently conducted by Marc Sageman, adjunct professor of psychology at the University of Pennsylvania, revealed that 68 percent out of a sample of 400 known Islamic terrorists entered a fundamentalist movement because their close friends were already members, whereas 20 percent joined due to family ties (Dingfelder 2004, 21). Dr. Sageman also concluded that nearly 70 percent of these individuals established such ties while living as expatriates in foreign lands for the purposes of schooling or employment. During their stay, these individuals were drawn to religious centers and formed strong bonds with other expatriates. As Sageman commented on these figures, "There is no evidence of brainwashing, they simply acquired the beliefs of their friends" (21).

Keeping in mind information regarding why individuals become terrorists, we must now examine how organizations generally function. First, terrorist groups have progressed from extremely vertical organizations with defined hierarchy to being much more horizontal in nature; members are well trained and an overarching strategy is developed allowing autonomous cells to be formed, each possessing the capability to operate without detailed orders (Gupta 2001). In general, terrorist groups are directed by an extremely charismatic leader, one that can effectively illustrate the perceived ills in the world, identify enemies, and recruit the personnel needed for attacks. Under the guidance of this person, each potential member is indoctrinated in a subconscious, unseen five-step process as developed by Anthony Stahelski, represented in figure 1.3.

Within Phase 1, individuals are indoctrinated and trained in remote, isolated environments. The depluralization process occurs as individuals are stripped of all other previous associations, relationships, and identities, forcing the member to be totally dependent on the organization for self-esteem and a sense of affiliation. This entire process can be completed quickly or it could take years, depending upon the subject in question (Stahelski 2004). Next, deindividuation occurs as a person gives up identity, morals, and beliefs that are deviant to the group. During this phase, the individual either consciously or subliminally accepts the values and views of the leader, becoming one faceless part of the overall group (Stahelski 2004). Phase 3 is quite similar to deindividuation, except that this process is then extended outside of the organization as a means to establish a cohesive front in the face of enemies. Within this phase, members disavow all relationships, attitudes, or notions regarding

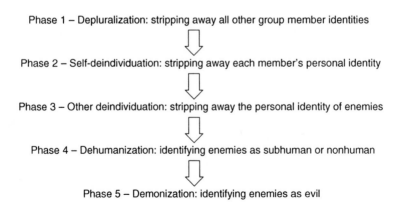

Figure 1.3 The Five Phases of Social Psychological Conditioning.
Source: Stahelski 2004.

the identified opposition, which is then replaced with the ideals that the enemy is homogenous (Stahelski 2004). Next, the group conditions members to view themselves with all positive values, such as being responsible, intelligent, brave, and to think of the enemies in negative terms, such as being disloyal, murderous, and amoral. The leaders of the group then portray the opposition as nonhuman, comparing them to animals, vermin, and insects (Stahelski 2004). This imagery allow for the progression of the terrorist mindset, as individuals will have a far less difficult time inflicting pain upon entities that are viewed as nonhuman. Finally, within Phase 5, the leaders convey notions that the enemy is also absolutely evil and the cause for all ills throughout the world. In addition, many historical examples illustrate the fact that terrorist organizations have thought of enemies as literally representing the devil, for example, Osama bin Laden calling the United States "Great Satan" (Stahelski 2004). By establishing this imagery and engraining such notions into the minds of followers, terrorist leaders are able to cultivate militants who are not only willing to kill, but also those who feel it is just and they will experience a reward for these actions. The five phases of social psychological conditioning represent a detailed depiction of how many terrorist organizations function in cult-like fashion and are able to transform members from peaceable activists to murderers. However, this model does not represent the only way in which fanatic groups operate, recruit, or indoctrinate. As stated at the beginning of the section, there is no universally applicable terrorist profile; therefore, practitioners must have an understanding of basic principles and processes, while also recognizing the existence of diverse methods and mindsets.

Suicide Terrorism

To conclude this chapter, the omnipresent threat of suicide attacks must be examined. This form of terrorism has drastically increased in number during the last twenty years, from an average of three per year during the 1980s, to approximately fifty per year since the dawn of the new millennia in 2000. Further, whereas accounting for only less than 5 percent of terrorist incidents since 1980, suicide attacks were responsible for 48 percent of terrorism-related deaths, without factoring in 9/11 (Pham 2005, 132). Arguably the most incomprehensible form of terrorism, suicide attacks evoke opinions that the perpetrators must be desperate, crazed, or somehow forced into this action. Political leaders have insisted that poverty is the primary factor that drives individuals to suicide terror, and that economic relief in Middle East and Eastern European regions would solve this issue. For example, President George W. Bush stated in 2002 that:

> We fight poverty because hope is the answer to terror . . . We will challenge poverty and hopelessness and lack of education and failed governments that too often allow conditions that terrorists can seize. (Atran 2003, 1536)

This line of thought may provide a palatable answer to tough questions: nevertheless, research has demonstrated that individuals engaging in this form of terrorism are not poor, uneducated, or irrational. Studies of suicide terrorism in Palestine, conducted by psychologist Ariel Merari, illustrated that a vast majority of bombers were in their early twenties, deeply religious, and strongly connected to a social group that advocated these methods (Atran 2003, 1537). Generally speaking, these individuals were indoctrinated in an environment that viewed these actions as heroic and just, as approximately 70 to 80 percent of Palestinians supported suicide attacks as of 2002 (1537). Those that have been properly trained by charismatic leaders view their act of suicide as martyrdom, meaning honorably dying for the cause. While difficult to conceptualize, terrorist organizations that employ suicide attacks perceive themselves engaged in a war, and are willing to perish in an attempt to defeat their enemies. As a result, suicide bombers in places such as Palestine, Chechnya, Iraq, and Israel must be viewed as rational, however fanatical their views may be.

Terrorist organizations utilize such tactics due to its low cost, high potential death counts, exaggerated incitement of fear, and the media coverage that is obtained (Sprinzak 2001, 72–73). In addition, it is extremely difficult for nations to establish effective homeland security policies that possess the ability to prevent suicide terrorism. Because there are thousands of vulnerable targets, many potential attackers, and deficient methods of detecting bombs attached to humans, it is virtually impossible to end suicide terrorism (Atran 2003, 1535). While the world witnesses the growth of this form of terrorist activity, the use of women and children as bombers, and the increasingly gruesome results of attacks, homeland security officials must recognize the element of futility in attempting to mitigate individual incidents. Since a suicide bomber is unfortunately likely to be successful if they are willing to give up their life, we must instead seek to disrupt the terrorist organizations themselves, while also increasing security around sensitive targets. If these groups are disrupted, it is unlikely that as many individuals will receive the needed indoctrination, the supplies, or the coordination to execute massive suicide attacks. This recognition of our limitations in preventing such attacks, coupled with our initiatives to increase security and dispel the organizations responsible, will allow homeland security practitioners to confront the mounting threat of suicide terrorism.

Conclusion

This introductory chapter confronted a multitude of topics to provide a comprehensive viewpoint of terrorism. Beginning with establishing a concrete definition that will be applied throughout, the chapter offers the needed historical context of such events, illustrating the fact that the impetus for homeland security is not a new issue. By understanding the history, typology, tactics, sociology, and psychology of terrorism, those engaged in protection and preparedness efforts will be better equipped to conceptualize what threats we are protecting against. While homeland security also includes incidents resulting from natural disasters and human error, terrorism represents the basis for the large movement beginning after 9/11. As a result, this chapter provides the information and analysis needed to form the framework for our detailed exploration into the arena of homeland security.

Case Study: Suicide Terrorism

Introduction

Though suicide terrorism has occurred for hundreds of years, these tactics are more prevalent in the present time than ever before in history. Examples of such acts can be found throughout the world today, most visibly in nations located in the region of the Middle East. However, suicide terrorism has been on a steep and swift incline in Russia in the past decade, carried out by rebels from the breakaway republic of Chechnya. These attacks and the Russian government response illustrate many important public policy issues. By analyzing the timeline of these acts, government reply, and lingering ramifications, it becomes clear that the phenomenon of suicide terrorism is a vital issue for many nations.

Background

The plight of the Chechen people and the violent movement that has resulted is unlike many conflicts the world witnesses today. When the subject of suicide bombings is brought up, images of Arab and Palestinian individuals are immediately conjured. It is unlikely that a year will pass without such an attack in Israel or Iraq being reported by the mass media. As a result, we as a global community have become very aware of suicide bombing tactics used as a religious or social instrument. However, this is not the case in the Chechen/Russian paradigm; this conflict has been a result of Russian control and dominance of Chechnya. Many in this occupied territory hold a deep-seeded sense of nationalism, and, quite frankly, an intense hatred for the Russian government. These are some of the many reasons that Chechen rebels fight so vigorously, using any means necessary, to cause chaos in the area in an attempt to gain true independence.

The situation concerning the Chechen attacks present very unique and dangerous problems for the Russian nation and its government specifically. This case study will offer a timeline of suicide bombings in that area of Eastern Europe and the fallout that has resulted. However, focus will be placed on a recent conflict between Chechen rebels and Russian forces, which ended in the death of hundreds of civilians. Though no suicide bombing tactics were used in this incident, this case will draw connections and seek to explore how the history of such attacks and the threat of those in the future have influenced the reaction and policies of the Russian government.

Timeline of Events

- June 7, 2000: A Chechen suicide car bomber kills two Russian special police officers near Grozny.
- July 2–3, 2000: Chechen rebels attack five law enforcement bases, one of which killed fifty-four people.
- December 27, 2002: Suicide bombers attack Russian government headquarters in Gronzy, taking approximately eighty lives.
- May 14, 2003: Sixteen killed, one hundered and forty-five wounded in suicide bombing at a festival in the town of Iliskhan-Yurt.
- June 5, 2003: Woman suicide bomber blows up a bus near Russian/Chechen border, killing eighteen.

- July 5, 2003: Seventeen killed after a duo of suicide bombers stage attack at a concert in Moscow.
- August 1, 2003: Chechen suicide bomber attacks a military hospital in Mozdok, killing fifty.
- December 9, 2003: Five killed in central Moscow as a result of suicide bombing.
- August 31, 2004: Female suicide bomber kills nine and wounds fifty-one people outside the Moscow subway station.

The conflict between the Russian government and Chechen rebels has greatly escalated within the past few years. Relatively small-scale acts, carried out by a single person or small group of individuals, appear to have become the modus operandi for this guerrilla faction. These attacks could materialize anytime, anywhere within the Russian borders, leaving law enforcement agencies with very few options for action. As a result, the response of the Russian government to such sieges has become much more hard-line, illustrating the effect suicide attacks can have on public policy.

To properly explore this notion, it is useful to analyze one of the more recent and most publicized events. On October 23, 2002, forty Chechen rebels occupied the House of Culture, a prominent theatre in Moscow. The armed insurgents took hostage the crowd of approximately 700 civilians, demanding the withdrawal of Russian forces from the breakaway republic of Chechnya. The terrorists, half of whom were women, were armed with high-powered weapons, had strapped explosives to their bodies, and also installed additional bombs throughout the theatre.

On a videotaped message, released to the media, the Chechen rebels announced their willingness to die for their cause. Within the first day they did release some hostages: those of Muslim heritage, a few children, and a man with a heart condition. On October 26, Russian Special Forces introduced a morphine aerosol to neutralize the terrorists and stormed the building shortly after. All Chechen rebels were killed, shot in the head at point blank range, as they were essentially walking bombs. Two hostages died as a result of gunshot wounds from terrorist fire, and approximately 120 others perished as a result of exposure to the gas utilized.

The worldwide media covered this event from beginning to end, producing live video feeds of the horrific situation. In the days following the siege, Russian president Vladimir Putin publicly apologized for the loss of so many civilians, but emphasized that hundreds were rescued, the terrorists were killed, and such hard-line action was necessary. He vowed to take "measures adequate to the threat" in all future cases. What has resulted was a tighter grip of Russian control over the republic of Chechnya. Terrorist acts committed by Chechen rebels have continued in the years following (ex. Beslan School Hostage Crisis, 2004), and the reaction of the Russian government has been increasingly impatient and lethal.

Discussion Questions

1. In what ways has the use of Chechen-led suicide bombings aided the creation of this new Russian policy and reaction to the Moscow Theatre and other events?
2. Is the policy, coupled with its manifestation in force, a correct or necessary remedy?

3. What are the ramifications for the public image of the Russian government, both regionally and globally?

4. Could the use of suicide bombings within the United States have a similar effect on our public policy?

5. Compare/Contrast the Moscow Theatre siege with that of the 1993 events in Waco, TX.

6. Could the U.S. government take the same form of aggressive action if a similar incident occurred within our boarders? What would be the possible ramifications?

Key Terms and Definitions

dehumanization. Phase 4 of Stahelski's five phases of social psychological conditioning in which enemies are identified as subhuman or nonhuman.

demonization. Phase 4 of Stahelski's five phases of social psychological conditioning that entails identifying enemies as evil.

depluralization. Phase 1 of Stahelski's five phases of social psychological conditioning that entails the stripping away of all other group member identities.

other-deindividuation. Phase 3 of Stahelski's five phases of social psychological conditioning that includes the stripping away of the personal identity of enemies.

religious terrorism. Religiously motivated violence based upon the belief that one's religion is singularly just and that a higher power wishes them to extract vengeance upon all nonbelievers.

revolutionary terrorism. Terrorist activity employed by individuals or organizations that seek to overthrow a current political or social establishment, either domestic or international.

self-deindividuation. Phase 2 of Stahelski's five phases of social psychological conditioning in which each member's personal identity is stripped away.

state-sponsored terrorism. A form of terrorism that is committed against enemies, both foreign and domestic, directed by nations, controlling parties, or individual leaders.

terrorism. Organized, politically, religiously, and/or socially motivated criminal behavior, meant to influence an audience, inflicted upon civilians or noncombatants, resulting in the incitement of fear and the deprivation of life, property, and/or freedom.

References

Atran, Scott. 2003. Genesis of suicide terrorism. *Science Magazine* 299, March 7: 1536.

Burgess, Mark. 2003. A brief history of terrorism. *Center for Defense Information.* July 2, 2003: 1.

Calahan, Alexander B. 1995. *Countering terrorism: The Israeli response to the 1972 Munich Olympic Massacre and the development of independent covert action teams.* Marine Corp Command and Staff College. April 1995.

Carr, Caleb. 2002. *The lessons of terror.* Random House, Inc., New York: 42–53.

Council on Foreign Relations. 2005. *Types of terrorism.* Obtained from <http://www.terrorismanswers.org/terrorism>. Accessed on August 3, 2005.

Crenshaw, Martha. 1981. The causes of terrorism. *Comparative Politics* 13, no. 4: 383.

Dingfelder, Sadie F. 2004. Fatal friendships. *Monitor on Psychology* 25, November: 21.

Eqbal, Ahmad. 1986. Comprehending terror. *MERIP Middle East Report* 140, May–June: 5.

France, John. 1997. The capture of Jerusalem. *History Today* 47, no. 4, April: 38–45.

Gupta, Rakesh. 2001. Changing conceptions of terrorism. *Strategic Analysis: A Monthly Journal of the IDSA* 35, no. 9.

Klein, Shelley. 2004. *The most evil dictators in history.* Barnes and Noble Books, New York: 15–28.

Martin, Gus. 2003. *Understanding terrorism: Challenges, perspectives, and issues.* Sage Publications, California: 5–33.

Pham, J. Peter. 2005. Killing to make a killing. *The National Interest* Fall: 132.

Poulsen, Kevin. 2004. South Pole "cyberterrorist" hack wasn't the first. *Security Focus.* <http://www.securityfocus.com/news/9356>.

Price, H. Edward, Jr. 1997. The strategy and tactics of revolutionary terrorism. *Comparative Studies in Society and History* 19, no. 1: 47–56.

Schrader, Holger. 2002. Patterns of international terrorism. *American Diplomacy* 7, no.1.

Sprinzak, Ehud. 2001. The lone gunman. *Foreign Policy* November–December: 72–73.

Stahelski, Anthony. 2004. Terrorists are made, not born: Creating terrorists using social psychological conditioning. *Journal of Homeland Security* March.

Turk, Austin T. 1982. Social dynamics of terrorism. *Annals of the American Academy of Political and Social Science* 463: 122–126.

Twiss, Miranda. 2002. *The most evil men and women in history.* Barnes and Nobel Books, New York: 32–60.

United States Department of State. 2004. *Patterns of global terrorism 2003.* Counterterrorism Office. April: 85.

Weinberger, Jonathan. 2003. Defining terror. *Seton Hall Journal of Diplomacy and International Relations* Winter/Spring: 66.

CHAPTER TWO
WHAT IS HOMELAND SECURITY?

Table Top Scenario: Rethinking Homeland Security

As a result of some very public embarrassments covered extensively by the 24-hour news media, the Department of Homeland Security (DHS) has come under increased political pressure. At a recent press conference, the secretary of the DHS warned citizens of emerging threats and suggested that Americans stage mock evacuations of homes, offices, towns, and cities to better prepare themselves in case of a terrorist attack. What resulted in the following days was a sense of panic among the public, chaotic scenes of people fleeing buildings, and massive traffic jams as millions of citizens stage practice evacuations simultaneously. Immediately afterward, reporters, pundits, and comedians hit the television airwaves to critique and satirize these seemingly foolish statements and the concern they caused. To make matters worse, two days later, the General Accounting Office (GAO) released a comprehensive report that revealed various managerial and operational failures that have occurred within the DHS in the past six months. The report cited serious transitional and integration difficulties, highlighted by the absence of information sharing between segments within the organization. In addition, it was revealed that three months earlier, the DHS raised the Threat Level from "Elevated" to "High" based on unsubstantiated intelligence.

In responding to these issues, the president directed the secretary of the DHS to conduct a thorough analysis of the organization and to construct a report detailing possible means of reform. To begin this process, the secretary informed the top brass at the DHS that the department needed to get "back to the basics." He presented a list of questions that required a reexamination of the entire organization, including its mission, responsibilities, resources, and structure. They were as follows: What is homeland security? What is the department's primary function? Who provides oversight and accountability? What legislation and policy initiatives offer the basis for operation? What is the status of interagency communication and coordination? Does the current structure contribute to or detract from organizational unity? What are our goals? How do we define success?

Introduction

With a detailed conceptualization of the history, typology, and psychology of terrorism in place, it is necessary to shift focus to the broad arena of homeland security.

Undoubtedly, the events of September 11, 2001, drastically altered the way in which society views the threats within a rapidly expanding interconnected world. In the wake of these catastrophic attacks, the U.S. federal government engaged in the single largest bureaucratic overhaul since 1947, when Harry Truman reconfigured the nation's armed forces, creating the Department of Defense (DoD; Haynes 2004, 369). The movement toward heightened protection and preparedness has had a significant impact upon law enforcement, state and local governments, and domestic and foreign policy. This chapter begins by drawing clear distinctions between the operations of homeland defense and homeland security, concepts that comprise the foundation of policy within this area. Next, a history of homeland security will be given, beginning with pre-9/11 recommendations and ending with the current status of the DHS. Further, this chapter will discuss the importance of state and local government participation in these initiatives. Finally, an analysis of the legislative branch's role in the arena of homeland security will be provided. Taken together, these issues represent a broad understanding of the nature of homeland security and its effect upon federal policy.

Homeland Defense versus Homeland Security

The necessary starting point for any discussion centered on the protection of a sovereign nation is defining and differentiating between homeland defense and homeland security. These terms, while seemingly similar and often used interchangeably, hold a vast amount of distinct qualities. The divergence between defense and security involves separate political actors, operational alternatives, bureaucratic agencies, and legislative decrees. Clear boundaries drawn between these terms provide a true understanding of the nature of homeland security.

To date, the federal government has failed to devise an agreed upon definition of homeland defense, thus creating a sense of ambiguity relating to the term. However, the May 1999 U.S. Army Training and Doctrine Command (TRADOC) White Paper "Supporting Homeland Defense" offers the most descriptive classification of this phrase. According to the publication, homeland defense represents the protection of our territory, population, and critical infrastructure by deterring and defending against foreign and domestic threats, supporting civil authorities for crisis and consequence management, and helping to ensure the continuance of critical national assets (Department of the Army 1999, 1).

Historically, the Army and Navy performed the functions of homeland defense. Throughout the 1800s, Congress appropriated increased funding to the military for the construction of fortifications and the monitoring of domestic ports. These initiatives were altered by the passage of the Posse Comitatus Act of 1878, which prohibits military forces from engaging in domestic law enforcement activities, unless explicitly authorized by the Constitution or an act of Congress (U.S. Congress 1878). This legislative decree was initiated in direct response to the aggressive and violent actions taken by Federal Troops in southern states during the period of Reconstruction following the U.S. Civil War. As a result of the Posse Comitatus Act, homeland defense efforts were then aimed toward the use of military force overseas to protect the nation.

A recent example of military law enforcement on domestic soil came on May 15, 2006, when President Bush addressed the nation detailing his immigration reform plan, which subsequently propelled Posse Comitatus into the immigration debate. Of the five points President Bush presented, the first point: The president stated, "One way to help this transition is to use the National Guard. So, in coordination with governors, up to 6,000 Guard members will be deployed to our southern border" (The White House 2006). Is this action a violation of Posse Comitatus? No, it is not. The National Guard has been used in a similar role at least two times in recent history. The Guard helped with the emergency response efforts after the 9/11 attacks, and assisted the evacuation and clean up efforts after Hurricane Katrina devastated New Orleans. The statute responsible for this particular role of the National Guard is the Stafford Act, under Title 42 of the U.S. Code, Section 5121. First passed in 1988 as an amendment to the Disaster Relief Act of 1974, the Stafford Act "authorizes the use of active duty personnel either upon the request of a governor or by the President's own call when he believes the primary responsibility for dealing with an emergency of national significance lies with the Federal government" (Silliman 2005). In addition, the Stafford Act allows the president to declare a major disaster area, and deploy the military for up to ten days to preserve life and liberty.

A final element relating to Posse Comitatus has recently been made by the congressionally appointed Gilmore Commission and focuses upon potential legislative reform. This highly regarded group of scholars, military personnel, and industry leaders has found that under Supreme Court rulings, military operations concerning U.S. security and borders may not necessarily be subject to Posse Comitatus oversight. Hence, the group has recommended that Congress reexamine governing statutes in this area and establish strict Rules of Engagement standards to appropriately differentiate between military operations and law enforcement functions of the armed forces, as certain elements of domestic intelligence are gathered through military operations for homeland defense purposes.

The domestic role of the military continued to erode until the post–World War II era. With the proliferation of nuclear and ballistic armaments during the Cold War, the United States was faced with the threat of strikes within its borders. As a result, the U.S. and Canadian forces joined to create the North American Air Defense Command (NORAD), which monitors the skies in the hopes of intercepting incoming threats. With this exception, the military continued to play a minimal domestic role in protection efforts, transforming homeland defense to civil defense. With the growth of terrorism since the 1960s, federal law enforcement agencies have taken the lead in civil defense initiatives. However, the military has continued to be utilized for forward deployment to confront threats before they manifest within our borders (Garamone 2001, 1).

The progression of homeland defense as a concept was quickly altered by the 9/11 attacks. It became clear that the use of traditional law enforcement, coupled with military operations, could not provide adequate protection in this new age of terrorism. With the movement toward formal bureaucratic organization of these efforts came a new term that encompassed a new mission: *homeland security*. As defined by the federal government, homeland security represents a concerted national effort to prevent terrorist attacks within the United States, reduce America's vulnerability to terrorism, minimize the damage, and recover from attacks that do occur (Office of Homeland Security 2002, 1). These notions are rather vague and markedly different from the characterization of homeland defense. Homeland security does not delineate operational actors or options; it is an all-inclusive effort that requires the input and assistance of every government entity, both civilian and military. While the military provides a vital service to bolster protection and preparedness, the use of armed forces does not specifically fall within the parameters of this term. Although some activities pertaining to homeland security may occur abroad, it can be stated that operations generally occur within the United States and involve civilian law enforcement personnel. The concept has remained relatively nebulous; however, this broad definition has served as the cornerstone for all activities in the field, from the creation of the Office of Homeland Security (OHS) to the current configuration of the DHS.

Of further importance, the current incarnation of homeland security includes activities that confront threats posed both by terrorism and natural disasters, known as an "All-Hazards" approach. This viewpoint has served as the framework for the creation of bureaucratic entities, such as the DHS, that are responsible for domestic protection. Though a majority of funding and policy support has been directed toward antiterrorism operations, the dangers posed by natural disasters still represent a real and credible threat to the welfare of the nation. The importance of "All-Hazards" was clearly demonstrated in August 2005 with the catastrophic events triggered by Hurricane Katrina, a topic that will be discussed later in the chapter.

Although the military does not possess a pronounced presence in domestic law enforcement activities, their role in homeland security remains vital in terms of response to natural disasters. Primarily, the National Guard, under the immediate control of individual states, is mobilized in times of severe weather events. The statute responsible for this particular role of the National Guard is the Stafford Act, under Title 42 of the U.S. Code, Section 5121. First passed in 1988 as an amendment to the Disaster Relief Act of 1974, the Stafford Act "authorizes the use of active duty personnel either upon the request of a governor or by the President's own call when he believes the primary responsibility for dealing with an emergency of national significance lies with the Federal government" (Silliman 2005). In addition, the Stafford Act allows the president to declare a major disaster area, and deploy the military for up to ten days to preserve life and liberty.

In addition, State and Commonwealth officials have the power to authorize these reservist troops into action when deemed necessary. For instance, the National Guard has played an important role in the wake of Hurricane Katrina: they were mobilized for purposes of rescue, relief, and law enforcement. However, the executive branch of the federal government, specifically DoD, has the legal authority to deploy these units to overseas combat arenas. This is evidenced by the fact that nearly 40 percent of the forces serving in Iraq and Afghanistan as of 2005 belong to the Army and Air National Guards (Walters 2005, 24). Though vital to the success of military engagements worldwide, a principal duty of the Guard is response to domestic disasters such as hurricanes, floods, wildfires, and other dangerous storms.

In addition, federal armed forces can and have been compelled to respond to catastrophic events within U.S. borders. Under laws governing these actions, the governor of the state affected must make a formal request to the president of the United States for the deployment of troops to needed areas. Under the president's orders, DoD may then become the coordinating body for rescue and recovery efforts, gaining operational control of the National Guard and other law enforcement personnel (Barnes and Walsh 2005, 28). Such actions occurred in the aftermath of Hurricane Katrina, as the Army's 82nd Airborne Division from Fort Bragg, North Carolina, were sent to New Orleans for search and rescue purposes. Since 9/11, the Pentagon has established the Northern Command to develop detailed plans for military response to terrorist attack and natural disasters and to oversee all domestic operations. Under these powers, the Northern Command, located in Colorado Springs, Colorado, has expanded the training of the National Guard to assist state and local law enforcement and first responders (29). These actions have sparked a heated debate among elected officials and military leaders regarding the role of the military in domestic affairs. However, with the presence of the Northern Command and the power of state officials to request the aid of federal troops, the armed forces continue to play a major role in the recovery from dangerous events.

Drawing such distinctions between homeland defense and homeland security does not mean that the two concepts are mutually exclusive; rather, they both function to accomplish the same goal, the continued security of the United States. Whereas the military confronts threats abroad and law enforcement engages in domestic protection, recent policy initiatives have resulted in furthering the cooperation of these contrasting entities. The most notable collaborative effort between the armed forces and executive agencies has been *Operation Liberty Shield*. This effort has united the Departments of Homeland Security, State, Justice, and Defense to establish detailed strategies to address issues such as border security, transportation screening, health preparedness, and enemy detainment. Utilizing a single framework, each organization has been charged with a specific area of operation, the sum of which seeks to result in a concerted effort to confront terrorist threats. Through the use of increased information sharing and intelligence dissemination, Operation Liberty Shield has reportedly increased the strategic planning capabilities of the federal government, actions that further efforts in homeland security (Department of Defense 2005).

The Birth of Homeland Security

Undoubtedly, 9/11 provided the critical impetus needed for domestic protection to gain centerstage in policy discussions; however, elected officials had been analyzing emerging threats and possible solutions prior to 2001. The bombings that occurred at the World Trade Center in 1993, in Oklahoma City in 1995, and at the Atlanta Olympics in 1996 directly exposed the nation's vulnerability to attack. With a significant increase in global terrorist activity abroad in the late 1990s, several federal commissions were created to investigate the preparedness of the United States and to provide recommendations to bolster such efforts. The most notable was the *US Commission on National Security in the*

21st Century, commonly referred to as the Hart–Rudman Commission. Established in 1998 by the DoD, the commission produced three reports, detailing specific global threats and the lack of substantial counterterrorism capabilities within the United States. In their final report, titled "Roadmap for National Security: Imperative for Change," released January 31, 2001, the commission surmised that the nation's security community was severely ill-equipped to confront pending danger. The panel advised a wide sweeping reorganization of federal agencies, personnel, and Congressional oversight capabilities. Specifically, the Hart–Rudman Commission recommended the creation of a National Homeland Security Agency, a Cabinet-level department that would serve as the umbrella organization for existing entities involved in homeland security activities, such as the Coast Guard, Customs Service, and Border Patrol (Lathrop and Eaglen 2001, 4). Though seemingly prophetic in their analysis and advice, the commission's findings failed to gain the attention of a majority of lawmakers until the aftermath of the most deadly terrorist attack in the history of the United States.

In the days following 9/11, the federal government swiftly moved to create a plethora of reactionary policy initiatives. Congress quickly passed Public Law 107–38, providing $40 billion for emergency appropriations, of which approximately $10 billion was directed toward homeland security efforts (Haynes 2004, 371).

To formally organize these initiatives, President George W. Bush signed Executive Order 13228 on October 8, 2001. The decree officially established the OHS, charged with creating and administering a detailed national strategy to secure the United States from future terrorist attacks. In addition, the directive also founded the Homeland Security Council (HSC) to be the primary coordinating and advising body for domestic protection efforts (The White House 2001). Shortly thereafter, former governor of Pennsylvania Tom Ridge was appointed director of OHS and chairman of the HSC.

In the months following the establishment of the OHS, lawmakers began to discuss the creation of a new executive agency focused upon homeland security, based on the findings of the Hart–Rudman Commission. It quickly became apparent that the integration of multiple agencies, coupled with the creation of new specialized security organizations, required a dramatic governmental restructuring and billions of dollars in additional funding. On May 2, 2002, Senator Joseph Lieberman introduced legislation proposing the establishment of the Department of National Homeland Security, which would be the centerpiece for handling terrorist threats, natural disasters, and emergency planning (Haynes 2004, 372).

One month later, President Bush announced a similar proposal, with one important difference. The legislation requested by the president called for the creation of the DHS, a cabinet-level organization, much in the same vein as that proposed by Senator Lieberman, which would possess one striking divergence. The Bush administration sought a department that was devoid of arguably cumbersome management constraints. Specifically, the proposed organization would not be required to participate in the civil service system, providing management with increased flexibility. With such a structure in place, DHS personnel would have been increasingly accountable for their actions and could be disciplined or dismissed with relative ease. The civil service system that governs employment within all other federal departments has been known to make it extremely difficult to hire workers, to redistribute resources, and to punish ineffective staff (O'Beirne 2002, 20). In the administration's view, civil service reform was needed to ensure the establishment of an organization that was truly agile and able to meet new and developing threats.

Although the president's proposal garnered the support of many, lawmakers could not reach the necessary agreement for these provisions to be included in the proposed bill. On November 2, 2002, Congress passed the Homeland Security Act of 2002, which was signed into law by President Bush on November 25, 2002 (U.S. Congress 2002). The legislation officially created the DHS, shifting twenty-two agencies and over 170,000 employees under its control.

The DHS

In March 2003, the newly formed department began formal operations. Led by recently confirmed Secretary Tom Ridge, the DHS began the process of agency integration and organizational formatting. To spur the transition from disparate agencies charged with national security operations under various jurisdictions to a central clearinghouse for such initiatives, the DHS first solidified its mission and strategic goals, provided in box 2.1.

With these core concepts firmly in place, DHS's next task was to establish an organizational structure that promoted coordination and cohesion, while allowing for the merger of long-standing agencies and newly established departments. The top brass within the administration chose to divide the organization into four distinct subsets, called directorates. These divisions, each led by an undersecretary, were charged with providing functional authority for national protection and preparedness efforts and to correct the vulnerabilities revealed by the 9/11 attacks. In its original form, the four directorates were organized as seen in box 2.2. Aside from the agencies within these divisions, the DHS also claimed jurisdiction over the U.S. Coast Guard and the U.S. Secret Service, both reporting directly to the secretary of Homeland Security.

This configuration of the DHS provided the organizational basis for all agency operations until 2005. In July of that year, Secretary Michael Chertoff announced a major restructuring as a means of improving its agility and effectiveness. Based upon the results of the legislatively mandated Second Stage Review by auditors both internal and external to the agency, DHS leadership sought to align the department to better manage risk, vulnerability, and consequence; prioritize guiding policies by a risk-based approach; and create strategies that would allow for a proactive increase in domestic security (Office of Press Secretary 2005, 1). This novel structuring of the DHS was officially implemented in late 2005, in the wake of organizational difficulties exposed during Hurricane Katrina, a topic that will be discussed later in the chapter.

These alterations focused primarily on eight functional areas and included the creation of multiple offices, the establishment of new leadership positions, and the fragmentation of existing segments. A discussion of each of these areas is provided below, followed by a graphical depiction in figure 2.1 of the current organization of the DHS.

Centralize and Improve Policy Development and Coordination. The reorganization created a new Directorate of Policy, led by an undersecretary, to serve as the lead for

---

Box 2.1   Mission and Strategic Goals of the Department of Homeland Security

DHS Mission

We will lead the unified national effort to secure America. We will prevent and deter terrorist attacks and protect against and respond to threats and hazards to the nation. We will ensure safe and secure borders, welcome lawful immigrants and visitors, and promote the free-flow of commerce.

DHS Strategic Goals

- Awareness. Identify and understand threats, access vulnerabilities, determine potential impacts and disseminate timely information to our homeland security partners and the American public.
- Prevention. Detect, deter, and mitigate threats to our homeland.
- Protection. Safeguard our people and their freedoms, critical infrastructure, property, and the economy of our nation from acts of terrorism, natural disasters, or other emergencies.
- Response. Lead, manage, and coordinate the national response to acts of terrorism, natural disasters, or other emergencies.
- Recovery. Lead national, state, and local and private sector efforts to restore services and rebuild communities after acts of terrorism, natural disasters, or other emergencies.
- Service. Serve the public effectively by facilitating lawful trade, travel, and immigration.
- Organizational Excellence. Value our most important resource, our people. Create a culture that promotes a common identity, innovation, mutual respect, accountability, and teamwork to achieve efficiencies, effectiveness, and operational synergies.

Source: Department of Homeland Security 2004a, 4–8.

Box 2.2   Directorates of the Department of Homeland Security

Border and Transportation Security (BTS)

- The U.S. Customs Service (formerly under the Department of Treasury)
- The Immigration and Naturalization Service (part) (formerly under the Department of Justice)
- The Federal Protective Service
- The Transportation Security Administration (formerly under the Department of Transportation)
- Federal Law Enforcement Training Center (formerly under the Department of Treasury)
- Animal and Plant Health Inspection Service (part)(formerly under the Department of Agriculture)
- Office for Domestic Preparedness (formerly under the Department of Justice)

Emergency Preparedness and Response

- The Federal Emergency Management Agency (FEMA)
- Strategic National Stockpile and the National Disaster Medical System (formerly under the Department of Health and Human Services)
- Nuclear Incident Response Team (formerly under the Department of Energy)

- Domestic Emergency Support Teams (formerly under the Department of Justice)
- National Domestic Preparedness Office (formerly under the Federal Bureau of Investigation)

Science and Technology

- CBRN Countermeasures Programs (formerly under the Department of Energy)
- Environmental Measurements Laboratory (formerly under the Department of Energy)
- National BW Defense Analysis Center (formerly under the Department of Defense)
- Plum Island Animal Disease Center (formerly under the Department of Agriculture)

Information Analysis and Infrastructure Protection

- Federal Computer Incident Response Center
- National Communications System (Formerly under Department of Defense)
- National Infrastructure Protection Center (Formerly under Department of FBI)
- Energy Security and Assurance Program (Formerly under Department of Energy)

Source: Department of Homeland Security 2004a, 4–8.

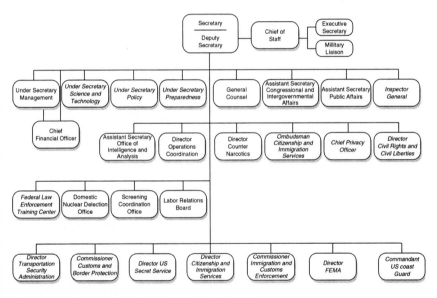

Figure 2.1 Current Organizational Chart of the DHS.
Source: Department of Homeland Security 2005b.

the coordination of all DHS policies and regulations (Office of Press Secretary 2005, 2). The Directorate assumed these functions previously occurring within the Border and Transportation Directorate, and now manages the development and implementation of department-wide policy, while also crafting long-term strategic planning. In addition, the Office of International Affairs, the Office of Private Sector Liaison, the Homeland Security Advisory Council, the Office of Immigration Statistics, and Senior Asylum Officer were also transferred to this Directorate during the reorganization (2).

Strengthen Intelligence Functions and Information Sharing. In late 2005, the DHS created the Office of Intelligence and Analysis, led by a Chief Intelligence Office that reports directly to the secretary of Homeland Security, for the purpose of administration and operation in information gathering and dissemination (Office of Press Secretary 2005, 2).

The Office assumed personnel from the former Directorate of Information Analysis and established the goals of collecting and synthesizing all relevant intelligence, establishing heightened coordination with members of the Intelligence Community, effectively advising senior officials, and sharing information with state, local, and private sector affiliates (2).

Improve Coordination and Efficiency of Operations. The reorganization also created the position of director of Operations Coordination to administer the Homeland Security Operations Center (HSOC) and to lead all the collaborative activities of the DHS. As the point of contact for these activities, the director also oversees operations involving multiple offices within the organization, coordinates disaster management activities, and facilitates the transition of raw intelligence into immediate action (Office of Press Secretary 2005, 2).

Enhance Coordination and Deployment of Preparedness Assets. During this process, the Information Analysis and Infrastructure Protection (IAIP) Directorate was reorganized as a new Directorate for Preparedness. Led by an undersecretary, the division also includes: an assistant secretary for Cyber Security and Telecommunications who serves as the central authority for assessing and responding to threats facing these assets; a chief medical officer to coordinate a response to biological attacks; an assistant secretary for Infrastructure Protection; training elements of the Office of State and Local Government Coordination and Preparedness (OSLGCP); the U.S. Fire Administration; and the Office of National Capital Region Coordination (Office of Press Secretary 2005, 2). The Directorate serves as a consolidation of DHS functions of grant administration, first responder training, citizen awareness, public health, and infrastructure and cyber security (2).

Improve National Response and Recovery Efforts. The reorganization also redefined the mission of FEMA, by stating that the agency must focus all of its efforts on the proven values of response and recovery. In addition, to ensure effective and efficient communication during disasters, the DHS has been adjusted to ensure that FEMA reports directly to the secretary of Homeland Security (Office of Press Secretary 2005, 2).

Integrate Federal Air Marshals Service (FAMS) into Aviation Security Efforts. FAMS, originally under the jurisdiction of the Immigration and Customs Enforcement bureau, was logically transferred to the Transportation Security Administration (TSA) in 2005, as they share a common mission (Office of Press Secretary 2005, 3).

Merge Legislative and Intergovernmental Affairs. During the reorganization, the Office of Legislative and Intergovernmental Affairs was established to serve as a single point of contact for communication and coordination with federal, state, and local officials (Office of Press Secretary 2005, 3).

Assign Office of Secretary to Management Directorate. To create more efficient administration practices, the Office of Secretary was transferred under the Management Directorate, now controlling all information systems, security accreditations, contractual activities, and resource oversight (Office of Press Secretary 2005, 3).

As a result of deficiencies in control and communication experienced in the few years since the DHS was created, the 2005 realignment represents an important step in achieving organizational excellence. By structuring the department along functional areas based on a risk management methodology, the organization has eliminated overlapping segments and created a more simplified bureaucracy. The passage of time will allow for adequate assessment of the success of the reorganization; however, the streamlined approach intuitively allows for heightened coordination of homeland security activities. Future practitioners within the field must be intimately aware of the novel structure of the DHS, how it impacts functionality, and the vital components contained within.

DHS in Action

Since its inception, the DHS has engaged in a myriad of operations ranging from the creation of detailed national plans to responses to catastrophic incidents within the United States. This section begins with a discussion of notable organizational activities that represent the bulk of the output for the newly created bureaucracy. In addition, a summary of victories and deficiencies will be chronicled as a means of offering a general background into the history of the department. With these facts in mind, current and future practitioners will be better equipped to analyze the role of the DHS in government-wide homeland security operations.

Strategic Planning and Public Information

Since its creation, one of the primary roles of the organization falls within the realm of planning and awareness. As the central coordinating authority for homeland security efforts, the DHS has crafted multiple National Strategy documents that detail specific threats facing the nation and steps that must be taken to increase preparedness. Beginning in July, 2002, the original OHS produced the *National Strategy for Homeland Security*, detailing critical mission areas such as Intelligence and Warning, Border and Transportation Security, Domestic Counterterrorism, Infrastructure Protection, and Emergency Response, in addition to the roles and responsibilities of various government agencies (Office of Homeland Security 2002). In the years since the release of this seminal document, the DHS has also produced the *National Strategy for Physical Protection of Critical Infrastructure and Key Assets, the National Strategy for Secure Cyberspace, the National Response Plan, the National Strategy for Maritime Security, and the National Strategy for Pandemic Influenza*. These documents represent important strides in planning for homeland security operations and serve to adeptly inform government agencies, policymakers, and the general public.

In addition, the organization has established valuable information sources: the most prominent being the website, Ready.gov. This website offers generalized overviews of the threats facing the nation and steps that citizens can take to ensure preparedness, including best practices of building emergency supply kits and creating family response plans. The creation of National Strategy documents and public information tools therefore represent a series of important strides made by the organization.

The Homeland Security Advisory System (HSAS)

The HSAS represents one of the primary public service tools that the DHS possesses. The system is a five-step graphical and color-coded guide meant to direct law enforcement and inform citizens, and is displayed on prominent government websites and cable news broadcasts. Unveiled on March 12, 2002, the threat level has consistently rested upon "Elevated," represented by yellow color-coding. However, since its inception, the advisory has been raised to "High," represented by orange color, five times on a nation-wide basis and twice for specific geographical areas. When DHS officials, in consultation with the HSC, decides upon altering the advisory, federal, state, and local governments are forced into action, deploying additional police and emergency response units in an effort to better detect, deter, and respond to terrorist attacks.

Although the system appears to be a clear and concise method of communicating threats to disparate levels of government and the general public, the implementation of the tool has been riddled with difficulties. First, the DHS has failed to establish detailed protocols and procedures in coordinating with federal, state, and local agencies to implement heightened security in times of threat-level adjustments. Many national and state leaders have expressed frustration with the system, stating that generally they first learn of a change in level from the mass media (General Accounting Office 2004, 4). In addition, the DHS has failed to provide guidance as to the specific threats facing localities, where additional protection is needed, and what steps should be taken to bolster the security of vulnerable targets. As a result, state and municipal authorities have been forced to direct additional staff and resources in the form of increased police patrols and security personnel, costing anywhere from a few hundred to over a million dollars a day (6). Also, many small localities that generally face little danger of terrorist attack have been forced to take such measures during nation-wide alerts. Such occurrences represent unfunded mandates, as there are few avenues available for lower levels of government to recoup the costs resulting from an increased advisory. Conversely, on the federal level, many agencies have stated that when increased threats are announced, little to no additional security measures are put in place due to the large force that is constantly utilized and the lack of information regarding detailed threats provided by the DHS.

However, in the recent past, the DHS has abandoned the use of nation-wide alerts, choosing instead to focus upon specific localities or targets, such as mass transit in the wake of the London attacks in July 2005. These tactics have led to increasing credibility for the system and the better conveyance of threats facing the nation. Although marred with difficulties since inception, the HSAS represents one of the most effective tools created by the DHS to disseminate information to federal, state, and local decision makers, in addition to the general public.

Response to Natural Disasters

One of the primary functions and strategic goals of the department is response to threats facing the nation, both natural and manmade. Although terrorism provided the impetus for the homeland security movement and remains a perpetual topic of concern, thankfully, the DHS has yet to face response operations due to malicious attack; hurricanes occurring in the Gulf Coast region during the summers of 2004 and 2005 represent the only catastrophic incidents in which the department has responded.

The summer of 2004 provided the first major test for the DHS in responding to disasters, coming in the form of four major hurricanes, Charley, Frances, Ivan, and Jeanne, all striking the state of Florida and causing extended damage to the eastern seaboard. Starting with Hurricane Charley at the beginning of August, in each instance, the DHS ordered over 1,000 FEMA personnel to Florida to lead immediate response efforts. Within hours of being declared an emergency site, DHS officials coordinated the movement of ice, meals-ready-to-eat, and canned goods, while also working in conjunction with state and local leaders to provide messages over public broadcast mediums to affected citizens. In addition, the DHS deployed community relations staff to access damage throughout the state and make funds available for municipal and personal recovery (Department of Homeland Security 2004b). The short-term response of FEMA was generally viewed as adequate and timely, signaling a high level of effectiveness of operations. However, a few pointed complaints regarding the agency's actions resulted in the wake of Hurricane Frances; primarily that the organization declared Miami-Dade County a disaster area, awarding millions to residents, even though damage in the area was minimal (Kestin and O'Matz 2004, 1). Apart from these specific concerns, federal officials and the general public were satisfied with the actions of the DHS during these times of crisis; feelings that would not be present one year later.

On August 29, 2005, Hurricane Katrina made landfall in southeastern Louisiana, directly impacting the city of New Orleans, resulting in massive damage and hundreds of deaths. In the days before landfall, DHS Secretary Michael Chertoff directed FEMA to pre-position search and rescue and relief resources in the region in an attempt to mitigate the predicted destruction. Upon initiation of the disaster, the agency was responsible for the successful evacuation of hundreds of New Orleans residents and for the deployment of some food and water. However, once the massive flooding of the city began, the emergency grew too large for the planning and management capabilities of the organization. FEMA Director Michael Brown conveyed notions that neither he nor his staff was aware of the need for food, water, and medical attention for refugees displaced within the Superdome, even though they were well chronicled by the mass media (CNN 2005). Such thinking signaled the lack of communication and coordination within the agency, a primary criticism of the management of this disaster. Further, elected officials in the region have issued pointed accusations, claiming that FEMA turned away individuals and organizations seeking to provide air support, medical assistance, and relief supplies for refugees in the area, stating that they were not authorized to engage in such operations (Gaouette et al. 2005, 1). In addition, political leaders from many other states conveyed their willingness to lend support to response efforts; however, they too were turned away in the days shortly following Katrina. For example, in the days leading up to Hurricane Katrina, New Mexico Governor Bill Richardson offered to send resources to the Gulf Coast, including hundreds of National Guard troops. Instead of recognizing the need and immediately approving the deployment, the request was held up within the DHS due to the fact that state officials failed to properly fill out paperwork, resulting in a delay of five days (2). These allegations point to the poor management of the disaster on the part of the DHS, specifically FEMA, as they followed procedures by the book instead of recognizing the need for flexibility in the face of a catastrophic event. The organizational failures during Hurricane Katrina forced the resignation of Director Brown, resulted in a stark tarnishing of the agency's image, and raised serious concerns about the department's ability to respond to catastrophic events.

Organizational Victories

One of the major strides made in recent years by the DHS has been the detention and arrests of suspected terrorists and their affiliates. Most notably, law enforcement officials were able to disrupt a terror cell, with ties to al-Qaeda, in suburban Buffalo, New York, in September 2002. Also, in 2004, New Jersey prosecutors filed charges against Yehuda Abraham, who was laundering funds for terrorists seeking the purchase of shoulder-fired missiles to target commercial airlines (Kady II 2003, 749–772). All told, approximately 850 individuals have been arrested in connection with terrorist activities or conspiracies since 2001. Though these victories have been attributed to multiple agencies, DHS played a vital role in the gathering of intelligence and the coordination of operations. As a result, the disruption of multiple cells and plots should be viewed as a success for the department.

The next area in which the DHS has experienced success concerns public relations and trust: this is an area in which the department has produced a fair share of gaffes; nevertheless, some strides have also been made. Most notably, programs such as Ready.gov, a website that teaches individuals how to create emergency plans and prepare for threats, have effectively communicated important messages to citizens (Kilian 2003, 1). The use of these informative tools has allowed the DHS to gain public attention and trust. When Secretary Tom Ridge announced that the public should prepare themselves for a possible chemical attack by purchasing duct tape and plastic to cover windows and doors, citizens responded and heeded the recommendation. Though this incident was a public relations blunder for the department, it served to illustrate the fact that the public trusted the department and followed their advice (Frum 2003, A14). These instances highlight the fact that citizens were and are willing to listen to the DHS and act according to instructions, something that is absolutely necessary during a crisis.

Next, funding has been a major area of success for the DHS since its inception. The monetary support for the department has increased dramatically in each fiscal year since 2001. In addition, there appears to be no sign whatsoever that financial assistance for the DHS will significantly decrease in the near future. Although the department has failed somewhat in utilizing these funds properly, the fact that they have been able to secure and increase support signals a major victory.

Finally, the DHS has succeeded in enhancing the area of air security. The department has provided a great deal of support for the TSA and other similar organizations. Over 50,000 individuals have been hired as airport screeners, along with a significant increase in air marshal personnel. As a result, airports and airlines have become a fortified infrastructure, representing another victory for the DHS.

Organizational Deficiencies

Existing agencies that now make up the DHS, including the Secret Service, FEMA, and the U.S. Customs and Border Protection (CBP), each held differing cultures, practices, and values prior to their inclusion. This has created significant organizational issues, as it has proven to be an extremely difficult task to coordinate and unify their collective efforts. These deficiencies have been echoed in a recent review issued by the GAO, stating that the DHS has failed to develop detailed and measurable goals, dedicated needed personnel, or obtain the leadership support that would hasten the integration process (General Accounting Office 2005, 9). In addition, the GAO has surmised that due to the complexity, existing organizational challenges, and the serious consequences that could result in failure, the DHS possesses many threats to effectiveness (Haynes 2004, 369).

These failures have also been witnessed by the general public thanks to the mass media, reaffirming a sense of dysfunction within the DHS. The use of the color-coded threat system and seemingly unwarranted elevations has created a source of confusion on the part of citizens. The lack of detail department officials have provided to the public in terms of mounting threats has caused widespread concern in regards to the coordination of the agency.

Shortly after the department's creation, Mitch Daniels, Director of the Office of Management and Budget (OMB), stated, "because al-Qaeda doesn't have a three-foot-thick code of federal regulations to read through, this department is going to need to be nimble" (O'Beirne 2002, 24). This quote, from one of the prominent figures in the Bush administration, signaled a call for innovation at DHS. As world events have demonstrated, the U.S. must be prepared for attacks from country-less vigilantes, a situation that requires an imaginative yet controlled agency to confront an ever-evolving dynamic. The demand for innovation necessitates commitment on the part of both administrators and staff. It appears as if the lack of coordination has quelled an entrepreneurial spirit in which, staff members are encouraged to develop new concepts to confront security issues. Such a lack of creativity signals that the culture within the organization does not value such characteristics. Early in 2005, Chief Technology Officer Lee Holcomb stated that a culture of innovation and collaboration would be established within DHS, fueled by the introduction of novel information technology (IT) (Cone 2005, 22). However, since the Science and Technology Directorate has received approximately $1 billion annually, approximately 3 percent of overall funding, it is difficult to achieve advancements within this area. When broken down, the actual funds directed solely for research and development is $431 million, an amount that is drastically low and unable to support pioneering discoveries (Issues in Science and Technology 2004, 17). Innovation, both in the functioning of the organization and the development of new technology, is undoubtedly essential to the sustained success of DHS; however, the organization has failed to fully commit to or exhibit such values.

A final area in which DHS has displayed numerous failures is in regard to agency integration efforts. Experts have stated that the department faces many obstacles as a result of the differing agencies that are now under its control, each coming to the table with varying values and practices. The integration effort requires a combination of organizations that focus on domestic law enforcement and those that confront national security and intelligence issues. Many feel that because these roles are so different, a unified culture will be difficult to achieve (Sloan 2002, 124). In addition, there have been numerous instances in which DHS has experienced turf wars with the Central Intelligence Agency (CIA) and the DoD, public battles that have damaged the image of the organization. The department also has faced strained relationships with state and local law enforcement, as these lower levels have viewed ambiguous directives from DHS as unfunded mandates. Once the decision is made to raise the threat level, state and local agencies are forced to increase security measures, tactics that cost a great deal of money. These notions signal the fact that the DHS has failed in achieving collaboration as a result of leadership difficulties and the lack of a unified culture.

The Role of the Legislative Branch

In addition to the prescribed functions and resulting structure, the Homeland Security Act of 2002 also provided the necessary means of oversight and control. Whereas obviously accountable to the president as an executive agency, DHS relies upon Congressional action to approve key policy initiatives, confirm the secretary and undersecretaries, and to provide annual budgetary allotments. In the House of Representatives, the Committee on Homeland Security and the Appropriations Subcommittee on Homeland Security are the bodies that possess jurisdiction. In addition, within the Senate, the Judiciary Committee, the Commerce, Science, and Transportation Committee, and the Appropriations Subcommittee on Homeland Security execute the mandatory oversight. The participation of the legislative branch in homeland security policy formation and the operations of the DHS provides the appropriate check, ensuring that the executive agency be held answerable for their activities.

Government-Wide Homeland Security Activities

Since its inception, the DHS has conducted a vast majority of domestic security activities; however, many other agencies have also contributed significantly toward these ends. To better define and categorize operations, the federal government has listed six areas of functions that comprise the sum of homeland security. First, *intelligence and warning* activities are among the most vital means to decipher threats and prevent disasters, and are primarily carried out by the DHS (Waters 2005, 1). Second, *border and transportation security* comprise operations to monitor, screen, and deter unauthorized persons or devices from entering the country. These activities are controlled by the DHS, specifically the TSA, the CBP, and the Bureau of

Immigration and Customs Enforcement (ICE) (1). A third function of homeland security is *domestic counterterrorism*, which mainly relates to FBI-initiated law enforcement activities to investigate and detain suspected terrorists. Fourth, the *protection of critical infrastructure and key assets* signifies the monitoring and securing of complex systems (such as electrical grids, transportation, and communication), federal buildings, and national landmarks. A majority of these activities are carried out by the DoD and law enforcement agencies. A fifth component is *emergency preparedness and response*, which are measures taken to manage the consequences of future attacks or natural disasters. Jurisdiction for this area belongs primarily to the DHS and the Department of Health and Human Services (DHHS). The final activity that is included in homeland security operations is the *defense against catastrophic threats*, which denotes the research and development of technology and theory to mitigate the possible use of WMDs. Such measures are executed by multiple agencies including the DHS, DoD, and DHHS (2).

The classification of various facets of homeland security activities reveals areas of policy focus and the true government-wide nature of such operations. Whereas the DHS has become the focal point of bureaucratic action within the field, the participation of multiple agencies remains crucial to the safekeeping of the nation.

Funding for Homeland Security

Due to the fact that homeland security funding is spread over 200 federal appropriation accounts, involves multiple governmental agencies, and has included numerous supplemental payments, tracking the movement of these funds has been a complex task (Waters 2005, 2). One thing, however, is clear: homeland security initiatives have received significantly increased funding since 2001. Beginning with the emergency appropriations after 9/11 and ending with the president's proposed budget for the fiscal year 2006 (FY2006), funding in this area has nearly tripled. Specific figures are provided in table 2.1.

Whereas these numbers illustrate the powerful and steady growth of homeland security financing, it is also important to understand how these funds are being disbursed. For FY2005, 37 percent of the $49.1 billion allotted for this purpose has

Table 2.1 Total Federal Resources Allocated for Homeland Security, 2001–2006 (in billions) (Waters 2005, 2)

	2001	2002	2003	2004	Est. 2005	Est. 2006
Discretionary budget authority						
Regular appropriations	15.0	17.1	32.2	36.5	43.0	42.2
Supplemental appropriations	3.6	12.3	5.9	0.1	0.6	0
Fee-funded activities	0.7	2.0	2.6	3.2	3.3	5.4
Mandatory spending	1.5	1.7	1.8	1.9	2.2	2.2
Gross budget authority	20.7	33.0	42.5	41.7	49.1	49.7

been dedicated to border and transportation security activities, and 31 percent went toward the protection of critical infrastructure and key assets. Further, 17 percent was directed to emergency preparedness and response, 8 percent to domestic counterterrorism, 7 percent to the defense against catastrophic threats, and 1 percent to intelligence and warning operations (Waters 2005, 2).

Since the unprecedented increases in funding of domestic protection, the DHS has received the lion's share of appropriations. Of these funds, the BTS directorate has received at least 50 percent annually. In FY2005, approximately $10 billion has been provided to the agencies involved in border security and control, and nearly $6 billion has been given specifically to the TSA for operations. These figures do not include the myriad of additional costs for protection of other modes of transportation or administrative expenses. Overall, this directorate represents the largest financial obligation for the DHS. Table 2.2 displays funding figures for the DHS since 2001.

The BTS directorate is and has been very well funded, but some other areas of the organization have not received the monetary support needed. The most significant examples of intraorganizational underfunding include first responders and research and development. First, for FY2005, programs supporting state and local first responders have been allocated $3.1 billion (Department of Homeland Security 2005d). Though seemingly a large investment, this expanding area is in great need of financial support, and even this amount does not provide enough. The DHS has claimed first responder initiatives to be a major focus, but because so many personnel and resources are needed, they have not been provided the financial backing for adequate operation.

Next, DHS efforts in the area of research and development have not received sufficient funding since the organization was established in 2002. For FY2005, less than $1 billion has been allocated to these initiatives, which represent approximately 3 percent of the organization's total budget. This is clearly not enough for such an important area of operation, which includes providing grants to business and universities. Research and development activities present many promising opportunities for the DHS, developing technology and tactics that could improve effectiveness and efficiency at dramatically lower costs. This is another area where the organization must place more financial emphasis.

Table 2.2 Funding for the Department of Homeland Security (in billions) (Waters 2005, 6)

	2001	2002	2003	2004	Est. 2005	Est. 2006
Border and Transportation Security (BTS)						
Border and Immigration Enforcement	5.5	8.5	8.0	8.0	8.7	9.7
TSA and Air Marshals	1.6	3.7	5.9	5.3	6.1	6.3
Subtotal (BTS)	7.1	12.2	13.9	13.2	14.8	15.9
Emergency preparedness and response	0.1	1.3	0.2	1.0	2.6	0.1
State and local grant programs	0	0.2	6.5	3.3	3.1	3.4
Coast Guard	2.5	2.6	3.6	3.3	3.7	3.9
Science and technology	0	0.2	0.5	0.8	1.0	1.3
Other	0.9	1.3	1.4	2.2	2.3	2.6
Total (DHS)	10.7	17.7	23.1	23.8	27.6	27.1

State and Local Government in Homeland Security

Although the focus of this discussion has been on federal departments and policies, the other levels of government have also played a crucial role in homeland security efforts. Whereas the DHS is charged with the broad task of domestic preparedness, most of the operational activities, specifically law enforcement and emergency response, lie in the hands of state and local agencies. The department is responsible for monitoring and directing the activities to subordinate agencies, though possessing only 7 percent of law enforcement personnel involved in homeland security operations (Lehrer 2004, 71–85). As a result, the federal government heavily relies upon state and local government for policy support and operational contributions.

At the time the DHS was formally organized, one of the primary auxiliary duties that required action was the establishment of a specialized office to synchronize federal, state, and local efforts. These objectives were decreed by President Bush through Homeland Security Directive/HSPD-8, issued on December 17, 2003. The order called for the DHS to "establish policies to strengthen the preparedness of the United States to prevent and respond to threatened or actual domestic terrorist attacks, major disasters, and other emergencies by requiring a national domestic all-hazards preparedness goal, establishing mechanisms for improved delivery of Federal preparedness assistance to State and local governments, and outlining actions to strengthen preparedness capabilities of Federal, State, and local entities" (The White House 2003).

In responding to this call, the organization created the OSLGCP, independent of the four major directorates. This agency assumed the responsibilities of providing support to lower levels of government and the extensive network of first responders in terms of funding, coordinated training, exercises, equipment acquisition, and technical assistance (Office of State and Local Government Coordination and Preparedness 2005). To accomplish these tasks, the OSLGCP gained jurisdiction of the Office for Domestic Preparedness (ODP), and established the Offices of Community Preparedness, and State and Local Government Coordination.

A majority of the strides made in the involvement of disparate levels of government have been a result of the efforts conducted by the ODP. Originally established in 1998 by the Department of Justice, the ODP has become the primary staple of grant supervision, training, and exercises since its move to the DHS in 2003. Since its inception, the office has provided over $7 billion in grants to states and localities, trained nearly 600,000 first responders, and managed approximately 400 coordinated exercises (Office for Domestic Preparedness 2005). In arguably its most important function, the ODP provides competitive grant funding under the Homeland Security Grant Program (HSGP), contributing funding for six major external organizations, shown in box 2.3.

The OSLGCP, particularly the ODP, has made significant strides in involving and supporting subordinate levels of government in homeland security activities. With large amounts of grant funding, training, and exercises, state and local governments have been able to purchase equipment, obtain personnel, and involve communities to achieve heightened domestic protection. However, some of the actions taken by the

---

Box 2.3   Programs Funded by the Office for Domestic Preparedness

State Homeland Security Grant Program (SHSGP). The SHSGP provides funds to enhance the capability of state and local units of government to prevent, deter, respond to, and recover from incidents of terrorism involving the use of chemical, biological, radioactive, nuclear, and explosive (CBRNE) weapons and cyber attacks.

Urban Area Security Initiative (UASI). UASI addresses the unique equipment, training, planning, and exercise needs of large, high-threat urban areas. Funding is provided for select urban areas and nonprofit organizations.

Law Enforcement Terrorist Prevention Program (LETPP). The LETTP provides support to state and local law enforcement agencies to help detect, deter, and prevent terrorism. Funds may be used to enhance terrorism prevention activities in the following areas: information sharing; target hardening; threat recognition; intervention to interdict terrorists; and interoperable capabilities.

Citizen Corps. Citizens Corps is a grassroots initiative that encourages citizens to play a role in hometown security through personal preparedness and community-based action. Funding helps support over 1,200 local Citizens Corps Councils that coordinate Citizens Corps programs nationwide.

Emergency Management Performance Grants (EMPG). The EMPG program supports comprehensive emergency management at the state and local levels and encourages the improvement of mitigation, preparedness, response, and recovery capabilities for all hazards.

Metropolitan Medical Response System (MMRS). The MMRS provides funds to designated localities to plan, train, conduct exercises, and purchase equipment and pharmaceuticals to improve readiness and respond to catastrophic incidents, both terrorist acts and natural disasters.

Source: Office for Domestic Preparedness 2005.

DHS have been viewed as unfunded mandates, meaning that the federal government has placed increased obligations upon the lower levels without providing adequate monetary support. The basis of these notions lies within law enforcement activity, specifically the need for supplemental staff during times of amplified threat or special events. When the terror threat level is raised, landmarks are suspected targets, or a large gathering such as a sporting event occurs, state and local agencies must increase the number of officers on the ground. With heightened security comes increased costs, representing hundreds of millions of dollars, most of which is not supported by the federal government. As a result, though DHS has made a great deal of progress in terms of the inclusion of state and local government, areas in which improvement is necessary remain.

Higher Education in Homeland Security

To respond to the newfound threats facing the nation and the subsequent growth in the field of homeland security, colleges and universities quickly began development of curricula to meet this emerging demand. Soon after, faculty and students began to play a vital role by conducting cutting-edge research to spark innovation in prevention and preparedness measures. As a result, within a few short years, the higher education community has become a primary figure in homeland security efforts. All indications point toward the fact that federal funding for these tasks and the need for individuals with scholarly experience in this field will only continue to grow. Though there have been significant increases in funding and policy support for academic activities within this field, the federal government must take additional steps to heighten the participation of colleges and universities, as they provide a valuable service to the nation.

In capitalizing on the expertise of higher education, DHS created a formal program within the organization's Science and Technology directorate, which deems certain universities as "Centers of Excellence." Along with the prestigious title, the chosen institutions that receive these competitive awards are also provided with upward of eighteen million dollars for research activities (Department of Homeland Security 2005c). Currently, the department has named five "Centers of Excellence" and has charged each with specific areas of exploration. In November 2003, the University of Southern California was presented with the first such award and was given the responsibility of researching the economic impact of terrorist attacks. Next, in April 2004, Texas A&M and the University of Minnesota were named expert institutions in the fields of agricultural and food security. In January 2005, the University of Maryland received the honor and was charged with researching the social and behavioral aspects of terrorism. Finally, in December 2005, Johns Hopkins University obtained the distinction, with a mission to examine protection, deterrence, and response issues related to high consequence events related to WMDs (2005). Currently, the department is planning for the establishment of three more centers in the near future.

While the "Centers of Excellence" program has effectively solicited the participation of faculty throughout the nation, the department has also recently increased efforts to foster student involvement. The DHS Scholars and Fellows Program was established to train and mentor future practitioners in areas such as disaster mitigation, emergency response, and prevention through the use of technology. Currently, the department funds 174 undergraduate and graduate students across the nation (2005). These individuals, in institutions in thirty-eight states, receive tuition waivers, stipends, and internship opportunities.

The funding of university research, the establishment of "Centers of Excellence," and the creation of the Scholars and Fellows Program represent the positive strides of the federal government to utilize the expertise of higher education to confront emerging threats. The partnership between public institutions and universities are in no way a recent practice. Academics were called upon to aid in the development of the atomic bomb in the Manhattan Project during the 1940s and to assist the invention of cutting-edge weapons during the Cold War (Carnevale 2005, 33). Just as this symbiotic relationship proved to be beneficial during those times, homeland security efforts will be greatly enhanced by the continued involvement of higher education.

The Private Sector in Homeland Security

In recent decades, the federal government has become increasingly reliant upon the private sector for purposes of research and development and the delivery of services. This trend of devolution has continued with the growth of homeland security as private industry has quickly responded to the national effort. The primary mechanism used to foster this relationship has been competitive grant funding for the research and development of innovative technologies and practices. To lead the effort of engaging businesses, DHS created the Homeland Security Advanced Research Projects Agency (HSARPA), modeled after DoD's famous and effective Defense Advanced Research Projects Agency, as the clearinghouse and coordinating body for these activities. The department has also identified key private sector initiatives including border protection and monitoring, biological protection, surveillance systems and sensors, and information analysis (Knezo 2003, 6).

Further, the DHS has also actively sought "innovative and unique" concepts and technologies from the private sector by issuing unsolicited proposals from businesses for the purposes of contracting (Littlejohn 2004, 1). Although the proposals must be evaluated according to Federal Acquisition Regulations, the willingness of the department to entertain novel applications further signals the benefits of public–private partnerships. Undoubtedly, engaging industry for the advancement of homeland security is a vital step in ensuring heightened protection and preparedness. Due to the fact that the private sector controls a vast majority of critical infrastructure systems and possesses the resources and manpower to engage in extensive research and development, the DHS must continue to encourage their active involvement.

Conclusion

The growth of homeland security within the United States represents one of the most wide-sweeping bureaucratic movements in history. The events of 9/11 forced this nation and the entire global community to be cognizant of the threat that this new age of terrorism poses. Many vital policy initiatives have been created to reorganize government institutions and strengthen law enforcement capabilities to respond to these dangers. Immense progress has been made, however, improvements are needed to solidify coordinated domestic preparedness efforts. This chapter has introduced key legislation, organizations, terms, and goals relating to homeland security. With an understanding of these core concepts and events in mind, a detailed inspection of the many facets that comprise homeland security may be pursued.

Case Study

FEMA and the DHS Reorganization

Emergency management within the United States dates as far back as the 1930s during President Franklin Roosevelt's New Deal initiatives. During that time, agencies such as the Reconstruction Finance Corporation and the Bureau of Public Roads were established to respond to and provide funds for recovery from natural disasters. Further attention was given to such efforts during the Johnson and Nixon administrations due to a series of damaging hurricanes, floods, and earthquakes that required federal intervention. Additional organizations such as the Federal Disaster Assistance Administration were created to handle such situations that arose virtually on a yearly basis (Department of Homeland Security 2005e). It was not until 1979, when President Carter issued an executive order that merged over 100 disaster-related national entities, that FEMA was formed. At this time, with the nation focused on the nuclear threat posed by the USSR during the Cold War, the newly created organization also assumed the civil defense responsibilities previously held by the DoD (Department of Defense 2005). As a result, FEMA became the federal arm for all disaster preparation and response, whether occurring naturally or as a result of malicious human intention. In the following decades, the organization was tasked to respond to hundreds of incidents, including Love Canal, Three Mile Island, the Loma Prieta Earthquake, and Hurricane Andrew. Due to the level of ineffectiveness displayed by the organization, as will be discussed later, President Clinton appointed James Lee Witt as FEMA director, marking the first instance of leadership by an individual possessing emergency management experience. Witt engaged immediately in a series of reforms that streamlined the response process, strengthened preparation for disasters, and deemphasized the focus upon improbable nuclear threats. Centered on the strategic goals of mitigation, preparedness, response, and recovery, FEMA became an independent agency that was extremely effective and admired (Adams 2002, 24). Then, in November 2002, the organization was officially placed under the control of the DHS, created in direct reaction to the terrorist threat demonstrated by 9/11. As lead agency for the Emergency Preparedness and Response Directorate of the DHS, FEMA has maintained similar operational tactics and actions; however, the organization has been compelled to confront the issues of preparation and response to events that may be triggered by extremist organizations. These factors highlight the fact that FEMA is currently responsible for the management of all hazards, either natural disasters or terrorist attack.

In its history, the organization has experienced times of both disappointing performance and extremely successful operations. Specifically, FEMA has been widely praised for their response during the flooding of the Mississippi in 1993 and the Oklahoma City bombing in 1995; however, as previously stated, they received stark and pointed criticism for efforts during Hurricanes Andrew and Katrina. Throughout this time, the organization has maintained a mission that values national preparation for disasters and recovery from ones that do occur, relying on core competencies of coordination between all levels of government, assisting communities, individuals, and businesses in recovery, and reducing the risk of future events, either natural or manmade. By examining the history of FEMA, it is clear that the agency has reached heights of effectiveness when a majority emphasis is placed upon natural disasters, not malicious attack. A series of reforms of the 1990s responded to criticisms that included the organization's focus on preparation for nuclear attack by the Soviet Union. Many lawmakers and federal officials expressed opinions that these operations significantly detracted from the FEMA's ability to confront frequently occurring natural disasters. In turn, similar sentiments are currently surfacing regarding the emphasis placed upon terrorist attack, as one of many possible causes of recent dysfunction. Conventional disaster management rationale dictates that in preparing for all disasters and not focusing upon ones such as terrorism, there are commonalities such as resource issues, response capabilities, and preparedness strategies that pervade throughout each (Abernathy and Weiner 1995, 45). Whereas many emergency management leaders claim that FEMA's placement within the DHS was both necessary and logical, others, including former director James Lee Witt, have levied sentiments that the reorganization has resulted in the stagnant, ineffective operation of the agency.

Discussion Questions

1. Referring to the Case Study and the previous discussion of Hurricane Katrina, what role, if any, did the DHS have in impacting FEMA's response capabilities?
2. FEMA experienced extremely similar deficiencies during Hurricane Andrew in 1992, in the form of poor communication, inaccurate information, and slow response. As a result, what is the heart of the issue in this case, FEMA's placement in DHS or the inability of government agencies to respond to catastrophic events? Why?
3. By focusing largely on the issue of terrorism, is the DHS mission and operation incompatible with that of FEMA, which has historically focused upon natural disasters?
4. In your opinion, will the DHS and FEMA be able to achieve full integration and a unified mission? If not, what then should be the solution?
5. Due to the failures of FEMA in Hurricane Katrina, should the agency be moved out of the jurisdiction of the DHS? If so, what effect will this have on both organizations?

Key Terms and Definitions

Department of Homeland Security. Officially created by the Homeland Security Act of 2002, this mega agency is charged with preventing and deterring terrorist attacks and protecting against and responding to threats and hazards to the nation.

Executive Order 13228. Issued on October 8, 2001, this decree by President George W. Bush established the OHS and the HSC.

homeland defense. The protection of our territory, population, and critical infrastructure by: deterring and defending against foreign and domestic threats, supporting civil authorities for crisis and consequence management, and helping to ensure the continuance of critical national assets.

homeland security. A concerted national effort to prevent terrorist attacks within the United States, reduce America's vulnerability to terrorism, and minimize the damage and recover from attacks that do occur.

Homeland Security Directive/HSPD-8. Issued on December 17, 2003, by President George W. Bush, calling for the establishment of policies to strengthen the preparedness of the United States to prevent and respond to threatened or actual domestic terrorist attacks, major disasters, and other emergencies by requiring a national domestic all-hazards preparedness goal, the establishment mechanisms for improved delivery of federal preparedness assistance to state and local governments, and the outlining of actions to strengthen preparedness capabilities of federal, state, and local entities.

Operation Liberty Shield. A federal effort that has united the Departments of Homeland Security, State, Justice, and Defense to establish detailed strategies to address issues such as border security, transportation screening, health preparedness, and enemy detainment.

Posse Comitatus Act of 1878. Post-Reconstruction legislation that prohibits military forces from engaging in domestic law enforcement activities, unless explicitly authorized by the Constitution or an act of Congress.

The Office of State and Local Government Coordination and Preparedness (OSLGCP). A major office within the DHS that includes the ODP, the Office of Community Preparedness, and the Office of State and Local Government Coordination. The OSLGCP provides support to lower levels of government and the extensive network of first responders in terms of funding, coordinated training, exercises, equipment acquisition, and technical assistance.

United States Commission on National Security in the 21st Century (also known as the Hart–Rudman Commission). A pre-9/11 commission that recommended the creation of a National Homeland Security Agency, a cabinet-level department that would serve as the umbrella organization for existing entities involved in homeland security activities, such as the Coast Guard, Customs Service, and Border Patrol. These findings provided the basis for the current configuration of the DHS.

References

Abernathy, Ann Marie and Weiner, Leslie. 1995. Evolving federal role for emergency relief. *Forum for Applied Research and Public Policy* 10, no. 1: 45–48.

Adams, Shawn. 2002. A beginner's guide to learning emergency management. *Risk Management* 49, no. 5: 24–26.

Barnes, Julian E. and Walsh, Kenneth T. 2005. A uniform response? *U.S. News and World Report* 139, no. 12: 28–29.

Carnevale, Dan. 2005. A degree you hope you never need. *The Chronicle of Higher Education* February 18: 33.

CNN. 2005. The disaster response: "Magnificent" or "embarassment"? November 14. <http://www.cnn.com/2005/WEATHER/09/02/katrina.response/index.html>.

Cone, Edward. 2005. Portal power: Dept. of Homeland Security getting it together. *CIO Insight* January 5: 22.

Haynes, Wendy. 2004. Seeing around corners: Crafting the new Department of Homeland Security. *The Review of Policy Research* May: 369–372.

Department of the Army. 1999. *U.S. Army Training and Doctrine Command (TRADOC), Supporting Homeland Defense, White Paper.* Department of the Army, Norfolk, Virginia U.S., May: 1.

Department of Defense. 2005. Homeland defense: Operation Liberty Shield. <http://www.defenselink.mil/specials/homeland/liberty.html>.

Department of Homeland Security. 2004a. Securing our homeland: U.S. Department of Homeland Security strategic plan. Washington, D.C.: 4–8.

———. 2004b. Massive federal response underway for Hurricane Frances. <http://www.reliefweb.int/rw/rwb.nsf/db900SID/SODA64L2VL?OpenDocument>.

———. 2005a. DHS organization: History: Who became part of the department. <http://www.dhs.gov/dhspublic/interapp/editorial/editorial_0133.xml>.

———. 2005b. Department of Homeland Security organization chart. <http://www.dhs.gov/interweb/assetlibrary/DHS_OrgChart.pdf>.

———. 2005c. Homeland Security Centers of Excellence: Partnering with the nation's universities. <http://www.dhs.gov/dhspublic/display?theme=43&content=4276>.

———. 2005d. DHS budget in brief: Fiscal year 2005. <http://www.dhs.gov/interweb/assetlibrary/FY_2005_BIB_4.pdf>.

————. 2005e. FEMA history. <http://www.fema.gov/about/history.shtm>.

Frum, David. 2003. Beyond duct tape: The best defense is a strong offense. *The Wall Street Journal* February 22: A.14.

Gaouette, Nicole, Miller, Alan C., Mazzetti, Mark, McManus, Doyle, Meyer, Josh, Sack, Kevin. 2005. Put to Katrina's test. *The L.A. Times* September 11: 1–16.

Garamone, Jim. 2001. A short history of homeland defense. Armed Forces Press Service. <http://www.defenselink.mil/news/Oct2001/n10252001_200110252.html>.

General Accounting Office. 1992. *Organizational culture: Techniques companies use to perpetuate or change beliefs and values.* GAO, Washington, D.C., February.

————. 2004. *Homeland security advisory system: Preliminary observations regarding threat level increases from yellow to orange.* Washington, D.C., February 26: 4–6.

————. 2005. *Department of Homeland Security: A comprehensive and sustained approach needed to achieve management integration.* GAO, Washington, D.C., March: 9.

Gilmore Commission. 2003. *Forging America's new normalcy: Securing our homeland, preserving our liberty.* RAND Corporation. Arlington.December 15.

Issues in Science and Technology. 2004. Defense, homeland security dominate Bush's FY2005 R&D budget. *Issues in Science and Technology* 20, no. 3, Spring: 17.

Kady II, Martin. 2003. Homeland security. *The CQ Researcher Online* 13, no. 31: 749–772.

Kestin, Sally and O'Matz, Megan. 2004. FEMA gave $21 million in Miami-Dade, Where storms were like "A severe thunderstorm." *The Sun Sentinel* October 10: 1.

Knezo, Genevieve J. 2003. *Homeland security and counterterrorism research and development: Funding, organization, and oversight.* CRS Report for Congress. Congressional Research Service, Washington, D.C., June 20: 6.

Kilian, Michael. 2003. Ridge urges Americans to be ready, not afraid. *Chicago Tribune/Knight Ridder Tribune Business News* February 20: 1.

Larson, Eric and Peters, John. 2001. *Overview of the Posse Comitatus Act. Preparing the U.S. Army for homeland security: Concepts, issues, and options.* RAND Corporation: 243–245.

Lathrop, Charles and Eaglen, Mackenzie M. 2001. *The Commission on National Security/ 21st Century: A Hart–Rudman Commission Assessment.* The Institute of Land Warfare. April 6: 4.

Lehrer, Eli. 2004. The homeland security bureaucracy. *The Public Interest* no.156: 71–85.

Littlejohn, J. Michael. 2004. Doing business with homeland security. *ASHRAE Journal* 46, no. 12, December: 1.

O'Beirne, Kate. 2002. A bureaucracy with a difference? *National Review* 54, no. 13, July 15: 20–22.

Office for Domestic Preparedness. 2005. Program highlights. <http://www.ojp.usdoj.gov/ odp/about/highlights.htm>.

Office of Homeland Security. 2002. *National strategy for homeland security.* July. <http://www. whitehouse.gov/homeland/book/nat_strat_hls.pdf>.

Office of Press Secretary. 2005. Homeland Security Secretary Michael Chertoff announces six point agenda for Department of Homeland Security. The Department of Homeland Security, July 13: 1–3.

Office of State and Local Government Coordination and Preparedness. 2005. SLGCP fact sheet. <http://www.ojp.usdoj.gov/odp/docs/slgcpfactsheet.pdf>.

Silliman, Scott. 2006. *Using the military during national emergencies.* Duke University. May 24. <http://www.dukenews.duke.edu/2005/10/sillimanoped_print.htm>.

Sloan, Stephen. 2002. Organizing for national security: The challenge of bureaucratic innovation in the war against terrorism. *Public Administration Review* 62, Spring: 124–125.

U.S. Congress. 1878. *The Posse Comitatus Act.* 45th Cong., 3d. Government Printing Office, Washington, D.C.

U.S. Congress. House. 2002. *The Homeland Security Act.* H.R. 5005. 107th Cong., 2d sess. Government Printing Office, Washington, D.C.

Walters, Jonathan 2005. Whose guard is it, anyway? *Governing* 18, no. 12, September: 24.

Waters, Mike. 2005. *Federal funding for homeland security.* Congressional Budget Office, Economic and Budget Issue Brief. July 20: 1.

The White House. 2001. Executive Order 13228. October 8, 2001. Government Printing Office, Washington, D.C.

———. 2003. Homeland Security Presidential Directive/Hspd-8. <http://www.whitehouse. gov/news/releases/2003/12/20031217-6.html>.

———. 2006. President Bush addresses the nation on immigration reform. <http://www. whitehouse.gov/news/releases/2006/05/print/20060515-8.html>.

Trebilcock, Craig T. 2000. The myth of Posse Comitatus. *Journal of Homeland Security.* October.

CHAPTER THREE
PUBLIC POLICY ISSUES

Table Top Scenario: The Ambiguity of Public Policy

As clerk for Supreme Court Chief Justice John Roberts, you are responsible for researching all relevant data regarding each case that falls before the High Court. Today, you have been directed to prepare a brief for Chief Justice Roberts relating to an approaching national security-based lawsuit, *Khamid vs. Gates and Gonzales*. Turning to the case history, you quickly decipher the intriguing and complicated path that has compelled the Supreme Court to adjudicate the matter. In January 2004, a joint task force that included representatives from the FBI, CIA, and DoD was successful in apprehending two purported terrorists: Amil Khamid, a U.S. citizen living in St. Louis, Missouri, and Umar Rahal, a Syrian nationalist operating in war-torn Iraq.

The investigation of these men began in late 2002, when the FBI received an anonymous tip of suspicious activity from a resident in Khamid's apartment complex. After weeks of rudimentary visual surveillance, law enforcement determined that the man might indeed pose a threat to national security. In April 2002, the FBI obtained a warrant to wiretap Khamid's landline and cellular phone, while also monitoring all of his Internet activity. Under the powers of the USA PATRIOT Act, law enforcement did not inform the suspect of the wiretaps at any time. In addition, with the same authority, the FBI gained access to Khamid's consumer records, detailing all of the purchases and/or rentals he ever made. After a year and a half of surveillance, law enforcement had recorded hours of conversations between the suspect and Umar Rahal, a known terrorist who had orchestrated dozens of bombings in Iraq and Syria. On these tapes, Khamid and Rahal laid out details for massive coordinated attacks in the United States and Iraq, targeting transportation systems and military installations. In January 2004, Khamid chartered a flight to Syria and then traveled to Iraq to meet Rahal. Upon crossing the border between the nations, U.S. Army forces apprehended Khamid, who was in possession of hundreds of pounds of C4 explosives and multiple automatic weapons. He was taken into custody by the military, and held as a prisoner of war. After weeks of interrogation, Khamid divulged all information regarding the plot, including the whereabouts of Rahal, who was quickly detained. Held in a military brig for approximately two months, Khamid was then transported to the United States to stand trial for a myriad of serious crimes, including treason.

A short trial then took place in St. Louis, and the jury convicted Khamid, sentencing him to death. During that trial and subsequent appeals, his attorneys claimed law enforcement illegally obtained conversations and purchase records, directly challenging the constitutionality of vital provisions of the USA PATRIOT Act. In addition, Khamid purported that in Iraq, military forces wrongly held him as a prisoner of war while also engaging in coercive measures, including the withholding of food and water. Due to the contentious nature of these events, and the claims of illegal seizures and torture, the Supreme Court chose to hear the case.

Upon internalizing these facts, you list a series of questions that will serve as the basis for your investigation into constitution law and international conventions. Included are the following. Did law enforcement violate the powers of the USA PATRIOT Act? Does the Constitution, prior legislative statutes, or judicial precedents support delayed notification of warrants? Can military forces hold a U.S. citizen as a prisoner of war? Was Khamid tortured and were the Geneva Conventions violated? Clearly this will prove to be an extremely difficult task for you and for the court.

Introduction

To continue this exploration into the field of homeland security, it is important to confront vital issues of public policy, both domestic and foreign. Undoubtedly, many legislative initiatives and strategic plans have been put into place on every level of bureaucracy, drastically altering the way in which our nation confronts this pressing topic. Clearly, public policy plays a vital role in every avenue of homeland security, and consequently, they are interwoven and explicitly addressed in every chapter of this text. This section provides a unique analysis of significant events in U.S. policy; ones that are reoccurring in the discussion of homeland security and that are key for the effective operations of future practitioners. Divided into two sections, domestic and foreign, Chapter Three addresses the following:

- Domestic Policy
  - The USA PATRIOT Act
  - Continuity of Operations
- Foreign Policy
  - Policy Alternatives
  - Diplomacy and Military Action
  - Enemy Combatants
  - Ethical Treatment of Prisoners

Within the discussion of these policy initiatives, a detailed history of the legislative record, various viewpoints of stakeholders, and relevant court cases will be presented. By examining the most poignant issues in homeland security policy, the audience will draw connections between domestic and international efforts, while also gaining an intimate knowledge of prevailing law and legal precedent.

Civil Liberties versus Security

This chapter also contains the discussion of topics that have a common underlying theme, the balance between liberty and security. Scholars, politicos, and journalists have all devoted countless hours fueling this debate and exploring whether or not recent policy initiatives have increased domestic protection at the expense of basic, unalienable rights. This text does not assume a particular position on these issues; instead, it will lay the foundation for knowledgeable practitioners and students to examine whether the U.S. government has followed a course of action that is cognizant, consistent with Constitutional rights, and respectful of both vital principles. Therefore, throughout the reading of this chapter, it is necessary to become familiar with the history, details, and implementation of each policy, while continuing to ascertain how the scales of liberty versus security have been tipped.

Domestic Policy

The USA PATRIOT Act

The age of the "War on Terror" has witnessed the creation of vital policy initiatives, the passage of numerous bills, and the judgment of the Supreme Court on cases relating directly to homeland security. Perhaps the most prominent and heavily debated form of government action within this realm is the USA PATRIOT Act.

In the weeks following the 9/11 attacks, various law enforcement and intelligence gathering agencies began to disseminate information regarding a lack of communication that prevented the nefarious al-Qaeda plot from being uncovered. According to reports, the FBI, the CIA and the National Security Agency (NSA) had all been independently monitoring the movements of suspected terrorists within U.S. borders. Specifically, in the months leading up to that fateful day, the al-Qaeda sleeper cell was the focus of over seventy separate FBI investigations (Cooper et al. 2004, 19). However, the data collected on these individuals remained within each organization, never reaching top-level administrators so that it could be shared with other agencies. This failure to "connect the dots" and decipher gathered intelligence became the impetus for Congress to take action and establish the USA PATRIOT Act.

The Uniting and Strengthening America by Providing Adequate Tools Required to Intercept and Obstruct Terrorism Act (the USA PATRIOT Act) became federal policy by a swift and concerted effort on the part of the federal government. The bill, H.R. 3162 (an incorporation of H.R. 2975 and S. 1510) was introduced on October 23, 2001, by sponsor Congressman James F. Sensenbrenner, Jr. (R-WI) and cosponsor Congressman Michael G. Oxley (R-OH). It passed in the House by a vote of 357:66 on October 24, and also in the Senate by a vote of 98:1 the following day. The lone nay vote came from Senator Russell Feingold, a democrat from Wisconsin. On October 26, 2001, the act was signed into law by President George W. Bush (U.S. Congress 2001). As a result of the speedy manner in which Congress chose to present, debate, and implement this policy, little controversy initially surrounded its inception.

This legislation was created to strengthen the abilities of government agencies to collect and share information regarding ongoing investigations of terror plots, capabilities that would help to prevent future attacks upon this nation. The Act incorporated many detailed legal prescriptions, with the primary focus of increased intelligence capabilities. Below is a summary of the most prominent provisions of the act, followed by a detailed discussion, organized by functional category (U.S. Congress 2001).

Section 203   Authority to share grand jury information
Grand jury records may be shared with law enforcement if they are ordered by court, approved by defendant, requested by federal attorney, or if it directly relates to an ongoing investigation pertaining to national security.

Section 212   Authority to share electronic, wire, and oral interceptions
Internet service and cable providers may disclose consumer information if they believe it is vital to national security.

Section 213   Authority for delaying notice of the execution of a warrant
The judge issuing a warrant may allow for delayed notification if there is a risk of: endangering the life or physical safety of an individual; the party involved may flee; the party involved may destroy evidence; the party involved may influence or tamper with witnesses.

Section 310   Financial Crimes Information Network (FinCEN)
Moves FinCEN under the Department of Treasury and charges the unit with leading investigations into all terrorist-related financial crimes and creating and maintaining a government-wide accessible database pertaining to suspicious financial activity.

Section 312   Special due diligence for correspondent accounts and private banking accounts
Each U.S. financial institution that conducts business with foreign entities must establish specific procedures to collect customer information, analyze transactions for suspicious activity, and report discrepancies to FinCEN.

Section 313   Prohibition on U.S. correspondent accounts with foreign shell banks
U.S. financial institutions may not conduct business with foreign companies that do not have a physical presence in a country.

Section 326   Verification of identification
Financial institutions must verify a person's ID, keep detailed records regarding their account, and cross-reference each person with databases of known terrorist identities.

Section 356   Reporting of suspicious activities by securities brokers and dealers
The secretary of the Treasury must consult with the Securities and Exchange Commission and the Federal Reserve to establish procedures for the monitoring and disclosing of suspicious activity.

Sections 501, 626   Request for production of consumer records
Senior officials within the FBI may request the production of books, records, papers, documents, and consumer activity pertaining to purchases of individuals suspected of terrorist activity. The request must be either approved or denied by a U.S. magistrate judge.

Section 504   Coordination with law enforcement
Formally allows officers who conduct surveillance to share information with other federal law enforcement agencies.

Section 507   Disclosure of educational records
The attorney general may request an order from federal courts to obtain educational records of students, present or former, under suspicion of terrorist activity. This expands the term "educational institution" to include vocational and technical entities such as flight schools.

Investigative Capabilities

Specifically, Title II of the Act established the manner in which surveillance tactics shall be put into action. First, the Act amended Rule 6 of the Federal Rules of Criminal Procedure, allowing federal agencies access to grand jury information involving foreign intelligence, an action that was previously barred (U.S. Congress 2001, Sec. 203). Next, it revised and updated the Foreign Intelligence Surveillance Act of 1978 (FISA), stating that law enforcement officials can obtain warrants to investigate novel forms of communication, including e-mail, Internet traffic, cellular phones, and voice messaging systems (2001, Sec. 206). These court-ordered warrants provided for roving wiretaps, in which law enforcement tracks all communication of a person of interest, no matter where they reside or travel. Also, the Act stated that federal courts could authorize a delay in the notification of a warrant if law enforcement demonstrated that notice could compromise the integrity of an ongoing investigation (2001, Sec. 213). These aforementioned provisions comprise some of the most important aspects within the USA PATRIOT Act that relate to the increased intelligence capabilities of government agencies.

Monitoring Financial Transactions

In recent years, the federal government has become increasingly concerned with the flow of funding for numerous terror cells throughout the world. In the wake of 9/11, it became quite clear that foreign nationals and possibly even foreign governments were supplying the finances needed to support terrorists and the purchase of equipment to carry out their plots. As a result, federal lawmakers took action to monitor these transactions, with the hope that investigations would lead to the thwarting of future dastardly schemes. Therefore, the Act also incorporated various statutes that addressed the financing of terrorist operations, many of which modified the Bank Secrecy Act of 1970. Title III allowed law enforcement agencies to monitor financial transactions of organizations, individuals, and institutions to detect fraud and/or money laundering. Agencies such as the FBI and CIA were provided with jurisdiction over all transactions that occurred domestically, in addition to foreign organizations that conduct any form of business within the United States. Next, the Act created the ability of law enforcement to obtain warrants to investigate, make arrests, and seize any asset of suspected entities if deemed to be appropriate (2001, Title III). As the tracking of assets and financial transactions may provide government agencies with additional information regarding the operation of terror cells, these specific provisions greatly bolstered their investigative abilities.

Obtaining Transactional Records

A final aspect of this legislation that must be addressed lies in Title V of the Act, which aimed at removing obstacles to investigate terrorism. One of the most important components is contained within both Sections 501 and 626, which allowed the FBI to request and obtain transactional records of organizations and individuals. This includes access to all forms of communication, financial records, and consumer reports, with the exception of activities explicitly protected by the first amendment to the U.S. Constitution (U.S. Congress 2001, Sec. 501). This was considered third party information in that the FBI could obtain such records from credit card companies, corporations, and libraries without notification or consent of the individual in question. In a manner of speaking, this provision is connected to the monitoring of financial transactions, as the Bureau has the capability to track exactly what an individual may purchase, rent, or lease. By taking such initiatives, law enforcement may be able to detect patterns and possible threats by observing the activities of a person through the businesses and institutions that they come in contact with. This facet of the legislation provided yet another tool for government agencies in their efforts to mitigate terrorist plots.

Further Congressional Action

By the end of 2005, there had been four major efforts made by various Representatives and Senators to amend the USA PATRIOT Act and curb some of the contentious provisions. Three of the four bills introduced by notable politicians, including Senators Lisa Murkowski (R-AK), Ron Wyden (D-OR), Bernie Sanders (I-VT), and Representatives Dennis Kucinich (D-OH), Jerrold Nadler (D-NY), and John Conyers, Jr. (D-MI) either failed to reach the floor for vote or were rejected. However, on June 15, 2005, the House voted 238:178 in favor of an amendment introduced by Senator Sanders that blocked funding for the FBI and the Justice Department to conduct third-party searches of library records (U.S. Congress 2005c). Though not directly altering the USA PATRIOT Act in any way and representing a minor adjustment in the implementation of the law, the Sanders amendment signifies a growing concern within the halls of Congress.

To continue, many provisions included within the Act were set to sunset (expire) on December 31, 2005. In July of that year, Congress passed a bill called USA PATRIOT Improvement and Reauthorization Act of 2005, which addressed many controversial sections of the Act. Specific provisions, including Sections 206, 213, 215, and 505 were amended to generally require increased burden of proof and judicial oversight for the execution of searches and the obtainment of third-party records (U.S. Congress 2005b). With increased reporting, monitoring, and oversight, lawmakers found a compromise on many of the sections, which balanced civil liberties and security concerns.

However, other sections set for sunset could not be agreed upon. These are found in Title II of the Act, primarily concerned with increased surveillance capabilities of law enforcement, including roving wiretaps and the monitoring of novel forms of communication. Once again, the apprehension of Congress was displayed as weeks of intense debate ensued regarding whether or not to extend, revoke, or amend these sections. Instead of allowing sunset, the House and the Senate passed H.R. 4647, which rescheduled the deadline for February 3, 2006 (U.S. Congress 2005a). The reauthorization of the USA PATRIOT Act will undoubtedly prove to be a highly contested matter, one that will illuminate where politicians, and by proxy, the American public, stand on this issue.

The Judiciary and the USA PATRIOT Act

Since inception, the USA PATRIOT Act has been the subject of two notable lawsuits, each affecting the legislation in different ways. First, ***Humanitarian Law Project vs. Ashcroft*** (CV 03–6107 ABC (MCx)) challenged the constitutionality of Section 805 of the Act, which expands the definition of "material support" for terrorism to include providing expert advice or assistance to extremist groups (U.S. Congress 2001, Sec. 805). The plaintiffs in the case were five organizations and two U.S. citizens that sought to offer advisory services to the PKK and LTTE, foreign groups that represent the interest of Kurdish and Sri Lankan refugees. These groups have been formerly classified as terrorist organizations by the U.S. government, making it illegal under the Act for U.S. companies to conduct business with them.

The plaintiffs filed suit, claiming that Section 805 of the USA PATRIOT Act was vague and in violation of the First and Fifth Amendments (United States District Court, Central District of California 2004, 12). On January 23, 2004, U.S. District Judge Audrey Collins ruled that Section 805 and the term "expert advice or assistance" was impermissibly vague, and summarily granted the plaintiffs enjoinment for the enforcement of this provision. However, she refused to grant a nationwide injunction of the matter, meaning that the ruling would only be applied to this particular case (United States District Court, Central District of California 2004, 36). While this case represents the first judicial stand against the USA PATRIOT Act, the ruling has had little lasting effect on its implementation.

A second court case that addressed issues relating to the Act was ***John Doe, ACLU vs. Ashcroft*** (04 Civ. 2614 (VM)), which challenged the constitutionality of Section 2709 of the Electronic Communications Privacy Act, which was amended by the USA PATRIOT Act. Under this law, the FBI has the authority to obtain National Security Letters (NSL), a form of administrative subpoena, which compels communication organizations (Internet Service Providers, telephone companies) to release customer records that are relevant to investigations relating to terrorism or national security, without notifying the customer in question (United States District Court, Southern District of New York 2004, 1). The ACLU claimed that the law violates the First, Fourth, and Fifth Amendments, and provides a vast amount of unchecked power to the executive branch. On September 29, 2004, U.S. District Court Judge Victor Marrero ruled in favor of the ACLU, stating that without judicial oversight and notification of a subpoena, Section 2709 was in violation of the First and Fourth Amendments (United States District Court, Southern District of New York 2004, 2–4). This case impacted the USA PATRIOT Act due to the fact that the ability of the FBI to obtain NSLs for terrorism and other investigations was significantly curtailed. However, these issues were rectified by the passage of the aforementioned H.R. 3199, which provided for increased judicial oversight, immediately diminishing the impact of the ruling.

Although no single court case has arisen that challenges the overall constitutionality of the USA PATRIOT Act, the legal proceedings previously mentioned signify the important role that the judiciary plays in the arena of homeland security. This policy initiative has possessed an explosive and controversial history, one that directly impacts the security of the United States. No matter the outcome of future debates, it is clear that both Congress and the courts will have a direct say in how the USA PATRIOT Act is implemented.

Support for the USA PATRIOT Act

Many government agencies have been quick to fully support the USA PATRIOT Act, heralding it as a vast improvement to the responsiveness of law enforcement. An organization that is a key beneficiary of the Act and the powers included is the Department of Justice, which in July of 2004 released a progress report detailing the many benefits that have resulted. Specifically, the department stated that the Act has "expanded laws governing the investigation and prosecution of terrorism within the parameters of the Constitution and our national commitment to the protection of civil rights and civil liberties" (U.S. Department of Justice 2005). In addition, the powers granted in the Act have led to the arrest of 310 individuals connected to terrorist plots, leading to 179 convictions.

The Department of Justice also claims that Section 203, which allows agencies access to sensitive grand jury records, has been extremely beneficial to national security. The organization stated that this provision has been utilized to revoke visas, prevent reentry into the country, and track financial transactions of suspected terrorists. Also, in 2002, the Attorney General established specific guidelines for the use of these powers, as an attempt protect civil liberties by preventing the collection of information of innocent civilians. In addition, the department has asserted that Title III of the Act, which focuses upon financial tracking of terrorists, has uncovered multiple nefarious plots (U.S. Department of Justice 2004).

The department also has argued that Section 501, which allows for the obtainment of third party purchasing records, has permitted law enforcement to track the movement of suspected terrorists, providing clues as to the possibility of mounting threats. Many of the measures of surveillance provided in the USA PATRIOT Act previously have been utilized in criminal cases involving organized crime and drug traffickers, a fact that the Department interjected in support of its use for terrorist activities. Finally, the organization insisted that judicial review and consent are required for these investigative actions, which forces a check to the power of governmental agencies (U.S. Department of Justice 2005). The Department of Justice has emphatically and convincingly supported the Act by providing detailed cases in which it has aided the disruption of terrorist plots while keeping in mind the protection of civil liberties. Further, according to various measurements, U.S. citizens have made it known that they widely favor the USA PATRIOT Act. In a 2004 Pew Research Center nationwide survey, when asked to describe attitudes regarding the steps taken by the government to reduce the threat of terrorism, seventy-one percent responded very/fairly well as opposed to twenty-five percent responding not too well/not well at all (*Polling Report* 2005a). Also, in a 2004 Fox News/Opinion Dynamics Poll, when asked to state if the USA PATRIOT Act was good or bad for America, fifty-four percent stated it was a good measure as opposed to twenty-eight percent that viewed it as bad (*Polling Report* 2005b). While additional polls and measurements have been conducted, a vast majority appears to indicate the general support of society for this legislation.

Opposition to the USA PATRIOT Act

Although many individuals have viewed the USA PATRIOT Act as a legislative success, there remain a large number that strictly oppose the initiative and the many provisions contained within. These individuals are primarily concerned with the expansion of governmental authority and possible threats to civil liberties as a result of the Act. The group that has led the charge against the Act, the American Civil Liberties Union (ACLU), has taken many steps to inform and persuade the public to be cognizant of the possible abuses of power that the legislation may have produced. The ACLU has taken part in many court cases, either as primary party or as friend of the court, in an effort to end many of the provisions included in the Act. The issues involved in these cases include religious/ethnic profiling, misuse of warrants, closed immigration hearings, and habeas corpus violations (Baker 2003, 547). This organization has also extensively lobbied Congress in efforts to amend the legislation in a manner that poses no threats to civil rights. These attempts have thus far been unsuccessful, but the group has remained vigilant in their efforts.

The ACLU has also publicly announced their concerns regarding the Act and the resulting powers granted to law enforcement. First, the organization views the increased surveillance capabilities of agencies as a source of unchecked authority. Their primary assertion is that Titles II, III, and V are in direct violation of the Fourth Amendment to the U.S. Constitution, which protects against illegal searches and seizures. In their view, the obtainment of grand jury records and roving wiretaps provide agencies with the ability to conduct searches without any standard of suspicion (American Civil Liberties Union 2003). Since only one judge must sign the order for warrants, the ACLU claims that judicial review is virtually nonexistent. In addition, the organization insists that the delayed notification of warrants, found in Title II, poses a massive threat to liberties. Procedural notification forces law enforcement to operate in the open and without this, the group claims that government agencies essentially have a blank check to search whatever they want, whenever they want. Finally, the ACLU maintains that the provisions found in Section 501, which allows for third-party records to be obtained, violates both the First and Fourth Amendments

(American Civil Liberties Union 2003). The group argues that because targeted individuals are not provided with notice of these searches, and some of the records may be an exercise of free speech, that these provisions should be deemed unconstitutional. The ACLU has raised many other concerns regarding the Act, but the aforementioned arguments represent the most vital assertions made by a powerful voice in opposition.

Other interest groups have also joined the ACLU to voice their concerns with the Act. The American Library Association (ALA) has attempted to curb law enforcement attempts to obtain third-party records, which reveal literature that individuals have solicited. Much in the same way as the ACLU, the ALA claims that this provision violates the First and Fourth Amendments, and therefore, libraries should not be forced to release these records. The group has also lobbied Congress to pass the Freedom to Read Amendment, which would block Department of Justice funding for these searches, an initiative that was voted down in the House of Representatives in 2004 (Jordan 2004, 10).

Finally, individuals in both the media and the general public have also voiced their displeasure with the legislation. Many have adopted the opinion that increased intelligence gathering capabilities of law enforcement provides the opportunity for government to directly violate civil liberties. By allowing the CIA to have a role in domestic surveillance and transforming the focus of law enforcement to the arena of information gathering, these individuals have claimed that the government is likely to abuse this newfound power (Martin 2004, 7). They also maintain that such data analysis and record tracking would result in numerous "false-positives" in which innocent citizens would become the focus of investigations. These arguments serve to highlight the central theme involved in the opposition to the USA PATRIOT Act. Whether it is the ACLU, the ALA, or the mass media, many citizens are of the opinion that the legislation provides far too much power to the federal government, which allows for civil liberties to be compromised in the process.

Continuity of Operations

Since the advent of long-range nuclear weapons and the Cold War, planning has been needed to ensure the seamless transition of the essential function of federal government to a location outside Washington, D.C., in case of a catastrophic disaster. Following the end of the Cold War, less attention had been given to these issues at the federal level, but the tragic events of 9/11 and Hurricane Katrina have sparked a renewed interest in planning for worst case scenarios. The issue of continuity is not only present in the public sector but must also be addressed in the private sector in order to maintain a functioning economy.

Planning at a government-wide level is critical because much of the recovery from an incident from an all-hazards perspective might include the maintenance of civil authority, and infrastructure repair. Continuity of operations planning (COOP) presumes the existence of an ongoing, functional government to fund, support, and oversee actions taken at all levels of government. Policymakers must consider that the number and types of potential interruptions are almost unlimited, and that effective COOP planning must provide, in advance of an incident, a variety of means to assure contingent operations.

Issued by FEMA in July 2004, Federal Preparedness Circular 65 addresses how the administrative agencies of the federal government will address the Continuity of

Operations Program. As stated in Federal Preparedness Circular 65 (Federal Emergency Management Agency 2004, 2):

> COOP planning is simply a "good business practice"—part of the fundamental mission of agencies as responsible and reliable public institutions. For years, COOP planning had been an individual agency responsibility. The changing threat environment and recent emergencies, including localized acts of nature, accidents, technological emergencies, and military or terrorist attack–related incidents, have shifted awareness to the need for COOP capabilities that enable agencies to continue their essential functions across a broad spectrum of emergencies. Also, the potential for terrorist use of weapons of mass destruction has emphasized the need to provide the President a capability which ensures continuity of essential government functions across the Federal Executive Branch.

The DHS plays a critical role in the COOP process. As outlined in Federal Preparedness Circular 65 (Federal Emergency Management Agency 2004, 3):

- Ensuring the performance of an agency's essential functions and operations during a COOP event
- Reducing loss of life
- Executing, as required, successful succession to office in the event
- A disruption renders agency leadership unable, unavailable, or incapable of assuming and performing their authorities and responsibilities of office
- Reducing or mitigating disruptions to operations
- Ensuring that agencies have alternate facilities from which to continue to perform essential functions during a COOP event
- Protecting essential facilities, equipment, vital records, and other assets
- Achieving a timely and orderly recovery from an emergency and reconstitution of normal operations that allows resumption of essential functions for both internal and external clients
- Ensuring and validating COOP readiness through a dynamic, integrated test, training, and exercise program to support the implementation of COOP plans.

Planning for and implementing a COOP scenario is a daunting challenge for all federal agencies and requires a coordinated effort among government agencies. As policymakers address issues across the spectrum of homeland security, solutions are needed to ensure the operation of government functions.

The balancing of privacy and Constitutional rights with security concerns has become a major concern for policymakers in the emerging homeland security context. Without giving consideration to civil liberties, the core democratic values of America's foundation will be lost. Building upon the previous discussion of the USA PATRIOT Act, this section will examine issues dealing with suspected terrorists that are being addressed by the U.S. legal system and international community.

Foreign Policy

Public policy questions in the homeland security arena are not solely based on domestic concerns but also must include the international dimension. Concerns regarding privacy and civil liberties do not pertain only to American citizens; they have a far-reaching importance across the globe. This section will focus on policy and legal questions that impact international relations and rights guaranteed to perceived "enemies" of the United States. Two key concepts will be discussed here: diplomacy versus military action and the definition of an enemy combatant. Both of these issues are of paramount concern to policymakers when dealing with terrorism and other threats to national security.

Foreign Policy Alternatives

To properly begin the exploration of foreign policy as it relates to domestic protection, overarching alternatives must be identified and discussed. Thus, the following represents eight general security-related international relations strategies available to a nation, which form the framework for current and future operations abroad.

Diplomacy/Constructive Engagement. Diplomatic measures are the primary steps taken by government entities when addressing terrorist threats. Meant to quell future aggression, bureaucrats actively engage foreign governments to reach mutually agreeable outcomes. Such policy measures have been demonstrated by the U.S. inclusion of multiple nations to dethrone the Taliban in Afghanistan, the overthrow of Saddam Hussein's rule in Iraq, and many other aspects of the War on Terror. The media plays an integral role in these efforts, as they can act as in intermediary between nations and terrorist organizations. However, the media involvement has acted as a double-edged sword, as irresponsible reporting may fuel the agenda of the opposition (Perl 2005, 8).

Economic Sanctions. Economic sanctions have been utilized to confront enemy regimes for decades. Such action can either be unilateral, where one nation establishes the policy, or multilateral, where a coalition of governments impose a sanction. Generally speaking, economic sanctions have been implemented by the United States against nations such as Cuba and Iran, when it has been determined that a particular country has participated in terrorist activity or other atrocities. However, statutes regarding the use of this policy have been altered in recent years. The United States now possesses the capability to impose sanctions upon nongovernmental entities, both foreign and domestic, that are believed to be supporters of terrorism (Perl 2005, 9).

Economic Inducements. Another form of policy that may be utilized to confront terrorism is to provide financial assistance to foreign governments to reduce poverty and create a positive image of the United States. Many experts believe that the seeds of terrorism are sown as a result of poor economic conditions, coupled with the lack of opportunity. However, it is unclear if such measures are effective, as other factors also drive individuals to violence (Perl 2005, 11).

Covert Action. Governments also rely upon covert action as a means of fending off terrorist attacks. Law enforcement, military, and intelligence agencies comprise the groups charged with such efforts. Operations towards these ends include communication monitoring, infiltration of suspected organizations, seizures, and detainments. Covert action seeks to uncover the strategy, structure, strengths, and weaknesses of menacing groups (Perl 2005, 11).

Rewards for Information Program. Many policies regarding terrorism are supplemented with offerings of rewards. The motivating factor behind this method is that greed will drive individuals to reveal details about their associates. Such measures have historically produced many positive results. The United States currently employs such policy, with bounties being offered for top al-Qaeda leaders (Perl 2005, 12).

Extradition/Law Enforcement Cooperation. Another tactic utilized to combat terrorism is law enforcement cooperation and extradition. Closely tied to diplomacy, these measures seek to develop relationships with foreign governments and establish intelligence sharing practices. Currently, the United States has agents from the FBI located in over fifty countries, monitoring terrorist activity. Diplomatic relations are also vital once suspects are apprehended and extradition is sought. There are many political and legal nuances that are involved in this process, but it still remains a vital tool to bolster security (Perl 2005, 12).

Military Force. The use of military force is generally recognized as one of the final and most decisive acts to combat terrorism. Such initiatives may be utilized for pre-emptive purposes or in retaliation for aggression. When implemented by superpowers, military action is undoubtedly one of the most effective policies to thwart terrorist operations. However, the use of such force also possesses many negative ramifications. Civilians may fall as casualties of war, troops may be deployed for extended periods of time, and campaigns are extremely costly (Perl 2005, 12).

International Conventions. A final policy initiative that nations may utilize is international conventions. Also closely tied to diplomacy, these conventions represent agreements between sovereign nations to attempt to bring offenders to justice through prosecution or extradition. The United Nations has played host to many such agreements in the recent past (Perl 2005, 13).

International Homeland Security Operations: Diplomacy and Military Action

As discussed throughout this text, the concept of homeland security is new and evolving within the American experience. One area in which this is apparent is the use of military force outside the borders. An explanation of the civil and military divide was provided previously. This section further explores the role diplomacy and military action play in the U.S. effort in the War on Terror.

Following the 9/11 attacks, the United States launched military strikes against the Taliban government and al-Qaeda forces in Afghanistan. In March 2003, the United States and its allies engaged in a preemptive war against Iraq in an effort to prevent future terrorist attacks. These military actions garner most of the news headlines; much work is also being conducted on a diplomatic level to help defend the nation against terrorism.

A system of international laws and customs have evolved since the end of World War II, which help govern the appropriate use of military force and conduct during war. Both the Geneva Conventions and Hague Conventions set agreements that outline the rules of war. With the creation of the United Nations, the global community has been brought together to address issues on a diplomatic level before the use of military force.

In the expanding global economy, the United States has increasingly felt a sense of duty and obligation to stabilize the balance of power around the globe. The recent actions in Iraq have helped to illustrate a difference in the approach to foreign policy between the United States and the nations of Europe. As the European Union evolves and grows, the potential power base in Europe may expand exponentially. This multi-nation coalition changes the post–World War II paradigm of traditional superpowers and the post–Cold War standing of the United States. One must consider the emerging shift in power that may occur with the rise of the European Union when examining the future of international relations at both the diplomatic and military levels.

Following World War II, Europe has tended to work diplomatically to build relationships with former enemies, whereas the United States has sought leeway within the framework of international law (Valsek 2003, 17). From a European perspective, recent U.S foreign policy seems to be grounded more in a display of military power than reliance on the system of international law to resolve conflicts (17). Though this European perception exists, much has changed on the global scene, which constitutes a shift in U.S. foreign policy. Given that the War on Terror does not follow the traditional course of military action (nation versus nation) new paradigms must be explored before creating a framework for the international rule of war. In developing this new framework, the international community must consider the following (18–19):

- *Non-state actors are playing a larger role.* The United Nations was established to regulate relations between countries. With the emergence of terrorist organizations who operate within many different nations, the role of the international community in defining war has become less clear.
- *The problem of failing or failed states.* A definition of state-sponsored terrorism was provided in chapter one of this text, which helps shed some light on this emerging problem. To complicate the matters of state-sponsored terrorism, nations with limited or no central governments have become havens for terrorist organizations. If a nation does not or cannot control a section of its territory, should it be held responsible for the actions of terrorist organizations based there?
- *The technological nature of the threat is changing the definition of self defense.* With the collapse of the Soviet Union and change in the balance of power, especially involving WMDs, the global environment has experienced a shift in power away from the traditional "superpowers" to smaller nation-states. Established international law (U.N. Charter Article 51) allows for a nation to respond to a well-established threat prior to being attacked.
- *Humanitarian law is challenging state sovereignty.* The major question here is, "Does sovereignty protect nations from abusing its own citizens?" The apparent answer is no, but Article 2 of the U.N. Charter states, "no other state or international organization may scrutinize what is happening inside a state except with the full consent of the territorial state." This statement leaves room for interpretation and challenges the international community to examine the existing rules of military engagement.

    With these emerging issues in mind, policymakers within the homeland security arena must pursue a new means of defining the rules governing war as it applies to the terrorist threat. Organizations and customs exist in the international community that can be utilized in pursuing new standards. However, a dialogue must be opened with countries from around the world in order to build a robust system that can combat terrorism without increasing the reliance on American military forces.

Enemy Combatants

Throughout the history of the United States, the legal community and court system has addressed protecting the rights of civilians from military court trials as opposed to state and federal courts. There are legal questions surrounding how to define an enemy combatant and right to trial debates date back to the American Civil War with the quest to define the difference between a "prisoner of war" and an "enemy combatant." One of the major legal issues discussed in this area relates to the civil rights afforded to detainees. The U.S. Supreme Court has defined the concept of an enemy combatant through a series of decisions that provide the basis for the current interpretation of detainees from the global War on Terror. We will now explore the cases that set the legal precedent in the United States for the application of enemy combatant status in three lawsuits filed by detainees in 2004 in the U.S. Supreme Court.

The first case that established the distinction of enemy combatant versus prisoner of war stemmed from the U.S. Civil War, *Ex parte Milligan*. In this case, Milligan, who was a Confederate, was tried by court martial in which he was convicted and sentenced to be hanged (Rotunda and Nowak 2005, 2). Milligan filed for a writ of habeas corpus and appealed to the U.S. Supreme Court on the basis that he was a civilian and citizen of a state that had not joined the rebellion, and as a civilian he was not subject to the jurisdiction of a court martial. In its ruling, the court found, "It is not easy to see how he can be treated as a prisoner of war, when he lived in Indiana for the past twenty years, was arrested there, and had not been, during the late troubles, a resident of any of the states in rebellion." The court interpreted this case to limit the power of military courts in states not invaded and not engaged in rebellion and where federal courts were open.

It was not until World War II that the court issued its next decision pertaining to enemy combatants. In the Nazi Saboteurs case (*Ex parte Quirin*), the U.S. military captured Nazi spies landing in the United States and President Roosevelt established a military tribunal to try the suspects for violations of the rules of war. One of the suspected saboteurs, Hans Haupt, was a U.S. citizen and among the six suspects executed. The Quirin case narrowly interpreted Milligan and held that although civil courts were functioning this does not insulate combatants from military jurisdiction, even if the suspect is a U.S. citizen (Rotunda and Nowak 2005, 2). In this case, the court defined "unlawful belligerents" or "unlawful combatants" as: "distinguishing characteristics of lawful belligerents is that they carry arms openly and have a fixed emblem. Persons who take up arms and commit hostilities without having the means of identification prescribed for belligerents are punishable as war criminals" (3). This definition is important because as described in the Quirin case, members of terrorist organizations would be classified as "unlawful combatants."

The Quirin case also concluded that the president, through executive power, can wage war and punish war criminals. This right was confirmed by Congress through a declaration of war and permitted war crimes to be prosecuted by military commissions. Although Haupt was a U.S. citizen, the Supreme Court held that regardless of citizenship, he had engaged the United States and violated the laws of war. The Querin case is important because it states that trial by military commissions does not offend the constitution. In this case, the Supreme Court gave great deference to executive authority, and Congressional recognition of that authority.

The third in the series of cases that helped establish legal precedence for the classification of enemy combatants also comes from World War II. The U.S. military commission in China tried German soldiers who had engaged in military action against the United States after the surrender of Germany but before the surrender of Japan. In *Johnson vs. Eisentrager*, the court found that since Germany was no longer at war with the United States that these soldiers were now "unlawful belligerents" (3). The court went on the say that these prisoners had no right to test the legality of their detention by the U.S. military.

Now that a legal precedence has been established through an examination of case law, we will shift our focus to the 2004 detainee cases questioning the status of suspected terrorists as "enemy combatants" in the current War on Terror. Following the 9/11attacks, the legal issues related to enemy combatants once again came to the forefront as the perpetrators of these attacks were not part of a military force, but were civilians. The United States responded to these attacks with military action against the Taliban regime of Afghanistan in October 2001, which led to the capture of numerous Taliban and al-Qaeda officials. These captors were transported to the U.S. Naval base at Guantanamo Bay in Cuba.

The first case that questions the status of enemy combatants involves citizens of Australia and Kuwait who were captured by American military forces in Afghanistan. In *Rasul vs. Bush* the petitioners claimed that they "are not nationals of countries at war with the United States and they deny that they have engaged in or plotted acts of aggression against the United States" (4). The court held it did have jurisdiction over detainees held at Guantanamo Bay and a distinction exists between nationals of who the nation is at war with and nationals who are not at war with the United States. Along with these distinctions, the court articulated that the case differed from the Eisentrager case because the petitioners in Rasul had not been convicted by a U.S. military commission, but had been detained without ever being charged or convicted of any wrongdoing (4). Though these important distinctions were established in Rasul, the court did not indicate the relevant procedures for non-citizens during their hearings.

The next case, *Hamdi vs. Rumsfeld*, deals with an American citizen who was captured in Afghanistan as an enemy combatant against the United States. Hamdi was originally sent to Guantanamo Bay, but upon learning he was an American citizen, he was transferred to a naval brig in Norfolk, Virginia. This case produced no majority decision, but a plurality opinion was authored by Justice Sandra Day O'Conner. This case does provide a definition of the term "enemy combatant" as found in Justice O'Connor's findings, "part of or supporting forces hostile to the United States or coalition partners in Afghanistan and who engage in an armed conflict against the United States there" (7). Based on this definition, the court would only answer the question before it, "whether the detention of citizens falling within this definition is authorized." In *Hamdi*, the court held yes, based on an act of Congress that authorized the use of military force by the president against "nations, organizations, or persons" he deemed "planned, authorized, committed, or aided" in the 9/11 attacks (8). *Hamdi* holds that enemy combatants must be given a "meaningful opportunity to contest the factual basis for detention before a neutral decision maker."

It is important to note that Hamdi was a U.S. citizen and the court clearly states that their decision was narrow. This case holds that U.S. citizens should receive a status hearing, with minimal due process. In her findings, Justice O'Conner cited Army Regulation 190–8 as a guide, "it is notable that military regulations already provide for such process in related instances, dictating that tribunals be made available to determine the status of enemy detainees who assert prisoner of war status under the Geneva Convention" (United States Supreme Court 2003, 32). Therefore, the ruling in the Hamdi case does not require all detainees to get a status hearing. Only U.S. citizens are guaranteed access to a status hearing. Justice O'Connor's ruling goes on to state that the burden of proof is on the detainee to prove that he or she is not an enemy combatant. The U.S. government, outside of the Hamdi ruling, granted status hearings for everyone held in Guantanamo, Bay.

The case involving Jose Padilla, an American citizen, has garnered international media attention as it involved a plan to detonate a "dirty bomb" in the United States, and it brought the enemy combatant debate to the forefront of legal issues within the homeland security arena. Padilla was arrested in relation to a warrant in connection with a grand jury investigation into the 9/11 attacks on May 8, 2002, at Chicago's O'Haire International Airport after traveling to Egypt, Saudi Arabia, Afghanistan, Pakistan, and Iraq. Padilla's attorney filed to dismiss the material witness warrant on May 22. While this motion was still pending, President George W. Bush ordered Secretary of Defense Donald Rumsfeld to detain Padilla as an "enemy combatant" in military custody. The president based his decision on Congress' authorization of military force in Afghanistan and held that it was, "consistent with U.S. law and the laws of war for the Secretary of Defense to detain Mr. Padilla as an enemy combatant." Padilla was transferred by DoD officials to a naval brig in Charleston, South Carolina.

The Department of Justice charged Padilla with crimes after receiving a favorable ruling from the 4th U.S. Circuit Court that allowed the government to hold him without charge. These charges were brought by the government after the defendant sought Supreme Court review. Ironically, this has led to criticism that the government was attempting to evade a status review.

The Supreme Court heard the case, *Rumsfeld vs. Padilla*, in April 2004, but on June 28, 2004, the court determined that the case had been improperly filed because the petition had named the secretary of defense, and not the commanding officer of the naval brig, as Padilla's custodian. Padilla remained in custody. On September 9, 2005, the 4th U.S. Circuit Court of Appeals ruled that President Bush did indeed have the authority to detain Padilla without charges. The ruling cites the joint resolution by Congress authorizing military action following the 9/11 attacks, as well as the June 2004 ruling concerning Yaser Hamdi. Attorneys for Padilla, plus a host of civil liberties organizations, contended that the detention was illegal.

On November 22, 2005, Padilla was officially indicted on charges that he "conspired to murder, kidnap and maim people overseas" (U.S. Department of Justice). There was no mention of the original allegations put forward by the U.S. government three years ago: Padilla's alleged plot to use a dirty bomb in the United States. The indictment did not mention that Padilla ever planned to stage any attacks inside the country or Padilla's connection to al-Qaeda or ties to the terrorist group. Instead, the indictment laid out a case involving five men who helped raise money and recruit volunteers in the 1990s to go overseas to countries including Chechnya, Bosnia, Somalia, and Kosovo. Padilla, in fact, appears to have played a minor role in the conspiracy. He is accused of going to a jihad training camp in Afghanistan, but the indictment offers no evidence he ever engaged in terrorist activity. In studying the Padilla case, one must remember that in the legal system the proof required to hold someone is much lower than the proof required to successfully try and convict them. Therefore, it does not necessarily mean that he was not in fact part of a dirty bomb plot, only that the prosecutors did not believe there was enough evidence to prove the charge beyond reasonable doubt.

These six Supreme Court cases provide a legal standing for detaining enemy combatants and outlines the necessary procedures for determining an individual is unlawfully engaged in military action against the United States. The case study in this chapter will explore another complex case involving a U.S. citizen and his legal pursuit for clarification as an enemy combatant.

Ethical Treatment of Prisoners

Closely connected to the issue of detaining enemy combatants is the treatment prisoners receive while held in custody. Debates have been held in many countries around the globe for defining torture and the ethical treatment of prisoners. The Geneva Conventions define the international standard for the treatment of prisoners of war (see box 3.1), but the question of how to define an enemy combatant is not as widely understood. This discussion has not been completed at the national level within the United States and remains a major public policy–level question in the homeland security arena.

Box 3.1   Prisoners of War as Defined by the Geneva Convention

1. Prisoners of war must be humanely treated at all times. Any unlawful act that causes death or seriously endangers the health of a prisoner of war is a grave breach of the Geneva Conventions. In particular, prisoners must not be subject to physical mutilation, biological experiments, violence, intimidation, insults, and public curiosity (Convention III, Art. 13).
2. Prisoners of war must be interred on land, and only in clean and healthy areas (Convention III, Art. 22).
3. Prisoners of war are entitled to the same treatment given to a country's own forces, including total surface and cubic space of dormitories, fire protection, adequate heating and lighting, and separate dormitories for women (Convention III, Art. 25).
4. Prisoners of war must receive enough food to maintain weight and to prevent nutritional deficiencies, with account of the habitual diet of the prisoners. Food must not be used for disciplinary purposes (Convention III, Art. 26).
5. Prisoners of war must receive adequate clothing, underwear, and footwear. The clothing must be kept in good repair and prisoners who work must receive clothing appropriate to their tasks (Convention III, Art. 27).
6. Prisoners of war must have adequate sanitary facilities, with separate facilities for women prisoners (Convention III, Art. 29).
7. Prisoners of war must receive adequate medical attention (Convention III, Art. 30).
8. Prisoners of war must receive due process and fair trials (Convention III, Art. 82 through Art. 88).
9. Collective punishment for individual acts, corporal punishment, imprisonment without daylight, and all forms of torture and cruelty are forbidden (Convention III, Art. 87).

Prohibitions against torture are discussed in Article 75 Section 2 of the Geneva Conventions as:

> The following acts are and shall remain prohibited at any time and in any place whatsoever, whether committed by civilian or by military agents: (a) violence to the life, health, or physical or mental well-being of persons, in particular: (i) murder; (ii) torture of all kinds, whether physical or mental; (iii) corporal punishment; and (iv) mutilation; (b) outrages upon personal dignity, in particular humiliating and degrading treatment, enforced prostitution and any form or indecent assault; (c) the taking of hostages; (d) collective punishments; and (e) threats to commit any of the foregoing acts. (Geneva Conventions)

The Geneva Conventions go on to state that detainees need not be charged or convicted in order to be held as prisoners of war. In fact, the conventions allow detainment of civilians who find themselves on the battlefield whether they are actively engaged in combat or not. The definition provided by the Geneva Convention helps set a context and a basis for U.S. policymakers when addressing the issue of torture and the legal and ethical treatment of the prisoners of the War on Terror.

Along with the definition provided by the Geneva Conventions, the United Nations adopted the Universal Declaration of Human Rights in 1948. Article 5 of this Declaration states, "No one shall be subjected to torture or to cruel, inhuman or degrading treatment or punishment" (UN Declaration of Human Rights). As a means of monitoring and preventing the practice of torture, the United Nations Convention against Torture and Other Cruel, Inhuman or Degrading Treatment or Punishment (UNCAT) was established in 1987 (UN). UNCAT is an international human rights instrument, which intends to prevent torture and other similar activities pertaining to civilians, military personnel, and prisoners. This agreement helped create the UN Committee against Torture, whose goal is to bring together heads of state to examine the duties of national leaders in a preventive role.

In examining cases such as the 2004 Abu Ghraib prison scandal in Iraq one can see the intricacies facing both policymakers and soldiers detaining prisoners. It was through this scenario that American citizens became widely aware of torture-related issues. Personnel of the U.S. Armed Forces, CIA officers, and contractors involved in the occupation of Iraq stood accused of numerous instances of abuse and torture of prisoners held in the Abu Ghraib prison since 2003.

An internal criminal investigation by the U.S. Army began in January 2004. Subsequent reports from the mass media and graphic pictures showing American military personnel in the act of abusing prisoners made the public aware of the attrocities commited by U.S. forces in Iraq. Following this investigation, the DoD removed seventeen soldiers and officers from duty, and seven soldiers were charged with dereliction of duty, maltreatment, aggravated assault, and battery. Between May 2004 and September 2005, seven soldiers were convicted in court martials, sentenced to federal prison time, and dishonorably discharged from the military.

Soldiers at Guantanamo Bay, Cuba, and other locations are actively engaged in the collection of intelligence to prevent future terrorist attacks. Chapter five of this text discusses the need for intelligence gathering and analysis within the context of homeland security. Whereas the need for highly reliable actionable intelligence is paramount, the means of collecting that data needs to follow an established, legal, and ethical process, which is acceptable to the citizens of the United States. As a democracy, America holds certain ideals in high regard. It is important for the discussion of torture and treatment of prisoners, whether they be classified as prisoners of war or enemy combatants, to include the values of American society and to reflect the qualities of American principles. The issues that are facing the nation in this area are great and require delicate consideration and agreement from the American people as well as the international community.

Conclusion

Public policy plays a monumental role in the growth and success of homeland security efforts, as such initiatives provide the framework within which government entities, private corporations, and individual citizens operate. Domestic policies such as the USA PATRIOT Act and Continuity of Operations, coupled with foreign policies such as the ethical treatment of prisoners and enemy combatants, interact to form the approach taken by the federal government in engaging the War on Terror. Further, politicians, observers, and future practitioners must all be cognizant of how such initiatives affect the delicate balance between civil liberties and security. Though citizens generally have been willing to accept reform for the promise of heightened protection, society is far from willing to relinquish time-honored rights and privileges. Due to this impetus for improved methods of securing the homeland and the need for debate regarding how the movement affects the core values of the nation, an active, open, public debate about relevant public policy will remain vital to current and future operations within this arena.

Case Study: The Abu Ali Case

As discussed earlier in this chapter, government action (legislative, administrative, military) and international cooperation is necessary to effectively address the evolving terrorist threat. One example of where these areas intersect is the recent case involving an American citizen, Ahmed Omar Abu Ali, with alleged ties to the terrorist group al-Qaeda, captured in Saudi Arabia and charged with conspiracy to assassinate President George W. Bush. Abu Ali was born in Houston, Texas, raised in Falls Church, Virginia, and made contact with al-Qaeda while studying at the Islamic University in Medina, Saudi Arabia, in 2001.

According to U.S. District Court documents, Abu Ali was arrested in Saudi Arabia on June 11, 2003, and detained in a Saudi Arabian prison without charges or access to legal counsel (United States District Court, Eastern District of Virginia, 2005, 2). Three other Americans were arrested in the same time period as Abu Ali, but were all extradited to the United States within a month. On June 16, 2003, FBI agents executed a search warranted issued by the U.S. District Court for the Eastern District of Virginia with the instructions to look for weapons, cellular phones, and documents connecting Abu Ali with the other three individuals arrested in Saudi Arabia. At approximately the same time as the raid on Abu Ali's apartment, FBI officials visited the prison in which

Abu Ali was detained and observed an interrogation in which he confessed to joining "a clandestine al-Qaeda cell" and that "al-Qaeda told him he must conduct terrorist operations or return to the United States and establish an al-Qaeda cell" (4).

Defense lawyers argued that Abu Ali gave a false confession after being whipped and beaten by the Saudi security force known as the Mubahith. In petitions filed by Abu Ali's legal counsel, allegations that his "fingernails had been removed" and of "hidden things that could not be seen and were even worse" (12). Prosecutors denied that Abu Ali was ever mistreated while in Saudi or American custody. They presented video testimony from Abu Ali's Saudi interrogators who said he confessed immediately after being confronted with evidence obtained from other al-Qaeda members. On July 28, 2004, a petition was filed in the U.S. District Court for a writ of habeas corpus requesting a ruling if Abu Ali was illegally detained in Saudi Arabia and asking for his release or to obtain his release and have him appear in a U.S. court for further proceedings (13).

Abu Ali testified about his detention and alleged torture at a pretrial hearing, but he did not testify at trial. Instead, he relied on the testimony of a doctor and a psychiatrist who said his account was consistent with being tortured. Prosecution witnesses provided contrary evidence to the Abu Ali's claims of torture on two occasions, the pretrial hearing and the trial itself. It is important to understand that if any evidence of torture was present and confirmed, the U.S. government would not and could not move forward with prosecution. On November 22, 2005, in the U.S. District Court, a jury found Abu Ali guilty of nine charges related to his involvement in terrorist activities. Abu Ali was found guilty on the following charges (United States District Court for the Eastern District of Virginia, 2005).

1. Conspiracy to provide material support and resources to a designated foreign terrorist organization (al-Qaeda).
2. Providing material support and resources to a designated foreign terrorist organization (al-Qaeda).
3. Conspiracy to provide material support to terrorists.
4. Providing material support to terrorists.
5. Contribution of services to al-Qaeda.
6. Receipt of funds and services from al-Qaeda.
7. Conspiracy to assassinate the president of the United States.
8. Conspiracy to commit air piracy.
9. Conspiracy to destroy aircraft.

Timeline of Events in the Abu Ali Case

- 2003: Arrested and held in Saudi Arabia.
- February 2005: Returns to the United States.
- October 31, 2005: Trial begins in Federal Court.
- November 22, 2005: Convicted on nine counts including plotting to assassinate the president of the United States, providing support to al-Qaeda, and planning to hijack an airplane.
- February 2006: Sentencing scheduled.

Key Terms and Definitions

ACLU vs. Ashcroft. A 2004 court case that challenged the constitutionality of Section 2709 of the Electronic Communications Privacy Act, and, by proxy, the USA PATRIOT Act. This provision allows of the obtainment of NSL, authorizing the release of third-party documents from communication companies. On September 29, 2004, U.S. District Court Judge Victor Marrero ruled in favor of the ACLU, stating that without judicial oversight and notification of a subpoena, Section 2709 was in violation of the First and Fourth Amendments.

continuity of operations. Plans and measures that are established to ensure that the U.S. government would be able to continue in case of catastrophic events.

diplomacy: The art and practice of conducting negotiations between accredited persons representing groups or nations.

enemy combatant. An individual who was part of or supporting Taliban, al-Qaeda, or associated forces that are engaged in hostilities against the United States or its coalition partners. This includes any person who has committed a belligerent act or has directly supported hostilities in aid of enemy armed forces.

Geneva Conventions. Four treaties formulated in Geneva, Switzerland, that set the standards for international law for humanitarian concerns. The Conventions were first adopted in 1864 and last revised in 1949.

Hague Conventions. Of 1899 and 1907. They provide regulations for the commencement of hostilities and conduct of belligerents and neutral powers toward each other and other nations, and outlawing the use of certain types of weapons in warfare.

Humanitarian Law Project vs. Ashcroft. A U.S. court case that challenged the constitutionality of Section 805 of the USA PATRIOT Act, which expands the definition of "material support" for terrorism to include providing expert advice or assistance to extremist groups.

National Security Letters (NSL). A form of administrative subpoena, which compels communication organizations (Internet service providers, telephone companies) to release customer records that are relevant to investigations relating to terrorism or national security, without notifying the customer in question.

torture. The infliction of severe physical or psychological pain or grief as an expression of cruelty, a means of intimidation, deterrent, revenge, or punishment, or as a tool for the extraction of information or confessions.

USA PATRIOT Act. A legislative initiative passed by Congress in the wake of 9/11 that drastically bolstered the capabilities of domestic law enforcement in various ways, including communication, searches and seizures, and surveillance. This Act has become on of the most heavily contested policies enacted during the age of the War on Terror.

writ of Habeas Corpus. Issued by a judge ordering a prisoner to be brought before the court; generally ordering that a prisoner be brought to the court so it can be determined whether or not he is being imprisoned lawfully.

References

American Civil Liberties Union. 2003. Surveillance under the USA PATRIOT Act. <http://www.aclu.org/SafeandFree/SafeandFree.cfm?ID=12263&c=206>.

Baker, Nancy V. 2003. National security versus civil liberties. *Presidential Studies Quarterly* 33, no. 3: 547–567.

Cooper, Matthew, Shannon, Elaine, and Novak, Viveca. 2004. Probing the memo. *Time* 19, April: 19–20.

Federal Emergency Management Agency. 2004. *Federal Preparedness Circular 65.* Washington, D.C.

Geneva Conventions

Jordan, Amy. 2004. House rejects effort to curb Patriot Act. *American Libraries* 35, no. 7: 10.

Martin, Kate. 2004. Domestic intelligence and civil liberties. *SAIS Review* 24, no. 1: 7–21.

Perl, Raphael. 2005. Terrorism and national security: Issues and trends. *CRS issue brief for Congress.* Congressional Research Service. Library of Congress, Washington D.C: February 22: 8–13.

Polling Report. 2005a. War on terrorism 1. <http://www.pollingreport.com/terror.htm>.

———. 2005b. War on terrorism 2. <http://www.pollingreport.com/terror.htm>.

Rotunda, Ronald and Nowak, John. 2005. *Treatise on constitutional law-substance and procedure.*

U.S. Congress. 2001. *The USA Patriot Act.* H.R. 3162. 107th Cong., 1st sess. Government Printing Office, Washington, D.C.

———. 2005a. *Amendment to the USA Patriot Act.* H.R. 4647. 109th Cong., 1st sess. Government Printing Office, Washington, D.C.

———. 2005b. *H.R. 3199.* 109th Cong., 1st sess. Government Printing Office, Washington, D.C.

———. 2005c. *Legislative Day of June 15, 2005.* 109th Cong., 1st sess. Government Printing Office, Washington, D.C. <http://clerk.house.gov/floorsummary/floor.html?day=20050615>.

United States Department of Justice. 2004. *Report from the field: The USA PATRIOT Act at work.* Government Printing Office, Washington, D.C.: July.

———. 2005. The USA PATRIOT Act: Preserving life and liberty. <http://www.lifeandliberty.gov>.

United States District Court, Central District of California. 2004. *Humanitarian Law Project vs. Ashcroft.* Case No. CV 03–6107 ABC (MCx).

United States District Court, Eastern District of Virginia. 2006. *Omar Abu Ali vs. John Ashcroft.* Civil Action No. 04–1258 (JDB).

United States District Court, Southern District of New York. 2004. *ACLU, et. al vs. Ashcroft, et. al.* Case No. 04 Civ. 2614 (VM).

United States Supreme Court. 2003. *Hamdi vs. Rumsfeld.* Case No. 03–6696.

UN Declaration of Human Rights

Valsek, Tomas. 2003. New threats, new rules: Revising the law of war. *World Policy Journal* 20: 17–24.

Chapter Four
Information Intelligence

Table Top: Sharing Information in the Intelligence Community

Analysts at the NSA notice an unusually large amount of Internet traffic coming from a server located at a corporation in Iran. After intensive analysis, they determine that the corporation is collaborating with a U.S. counterpart to launch a denial of service attack against a popular on-line auction site. The analysts "hand-off" the assessment to their FBI liaison who notify the company under attack. Simultaneously, officers from the CIA and the Defense Intelligence Agency (DIA) detect increased "chatter" by known terrorist organizations in Eastern Europe. As these government intelligence agencies conduct their investigations, an explosion is reported along a commuter rail line outside Chicago. The FBI is called in to assess the situation.

Later that same day, FBI officials in Miami are notified of suspicious behavior outside Miami International Airport. While on their way to investigate, a loud explosion is heard near the airport. Witness reports of a commercial airplane taking off and being hit with a shoulder fired surface to air missile run rampant. Upon arriving on the scene, local police officers arrest two men who had arrived in the country a week earlier from Russia. As the arrest is being made, the CIA receives a report from an operative in Moscow that a group of Chechyan rebels has taken control of a short-range nuclear missile that has been launched and is targeted for Moscow. With Russia bracing for the detonation of a nuclear weapon, the president of the United States meets with the director of National Intelligence, the director of Central Intelligence, the secretary of Homeland Security, the secretary of Defense, and chairman of the Joint Chiefs of Staff to discuss the options of dealing with these tragic events as well as the existing intelligence that might point to future attacks.

Are these events related or are they isolated? What connections can be made? Could these events have been avoided? If so, how could these agencies have worked together in a more collaborative fashion?

Introduction

In this chapter, the reader will be introduced to the U.S. Intelligence Community and explore the challenges facing the nation following the end of the Cold War and the transition into the global War on Terror. As the terrorist threat has evolved, increased attention has been given to improving the nation's ability to gather, analyze, and act upon the abundance of information presented to the agencies, which make up what is known as the Intelligence Community. Information analysis and the use of *intelligence* is not only practiced in combating terrorism, but is also utilized in law enforcement; disaster planning and response; competitive analysis; and strategic planning. This chapter will focus on ways in which the public and private sectors are responding to the information analysis challenge and how this relates to the overall homeland security framework. Included in this analysis will be a discussion of intergovernmental relations and their political and policy implications.

Intelligence Analysis in the United States

From the American Revolutionary War to present day, effective intelligence analysis has played a critical role in preserving the overall security of the United States. Hollywood, television, and fictional authors have long used agents, spies, and analysts as heroic figures protecting national security. Whereas the individuals in these stories are often leading glamorous and dangerous lives, the actual daily life of an intelligence analyst involves much more routine data collection, analysis, and decision making. Without sound intelligence, the nation's homeland security efforts would be ineffective and the lives of military forces as well as civilians would be jeopardized. This chapter will explore how the U.S. Intelligence Community has grown and evolved, intelligence agencies and their specific roles, and how the Intelligence Community is responding to the ongoing war on terrorism and planning for natural disasters.

Intelligence analysis is a complex field, which currently encompasses fifteen U.S. government agencies and includes the practice of competitive analysis in the private sector. A practical definition of "intelligence" must first be established before studying the array of organizations and individuals engaged in the field. Intelligence can initially be defined as the process, which produces a product through a series of six steps (Richelson 1999, 8):

- Collection of data
- Processing this information
- Integration with other data
- Analysis of what has been assembled
- Evolution of the data
- Interpretation by the analyst(s)

In developing a definition of intelligence, key terms such as *attaché, espionage, counterintelligence,* and *reconnaissance* must be included. Along with the various types of data gathering processes and key terms, this definition is complete with the inclusion of the processes used to collect the data used by analysts to create intelligence (Krizen 1999, 11): Human Intelligence (HUMINT), Signals Intelligence (SIGINT), Imagery Intelligence (IMINT), Measurement and Signature Intelligence (MASINT), Open-Source Intelligence (OSINT), Geospatial Intelligence. Now that

---

Box 4.1   International Intelligence Agencies

1. MI5 (United Kingdom)
2. Canadian Security Intelligence Service (Canada)
3. Direction de la Surveillance du Territoire (France)
4. FSB (Russia)
5. Bundesnachrichtendienst (Germany)
6. International Liaison Department (China)
7. General Security Service (Israel)
8. Directorate of Inter-Services Intelligence (Pakistan)
9. Dairat al Mukhabarat (Jordan)

---

a definition for the intelligence analysis process has been developed, the history of the Intelligence Community in America will be outlined. With this historical perspective, a complete picture of the present day Intelligence Community model can be created. (See box 4.1 for a list of international intelligence agencies (Pike 2006).

History of Intelligence

Intelligence collection and analysis has been a cornerstone of American military action since the Revolutionary War. During the Revolution, General George Washington used a network of agents to collect information on British forces, communicated with other officers through the use of codes, launched sabotage and other clandestine missions, influenced the decisions of foreign governments through propaganda, and used decoys such as fake tents in New York causing British troops to stay while Washington diverted to Yorktown, Virginia, to defeat Cornwallis (Central Intelligence Agency 1999). Washington's effective use of intelligence and espionage led to the establishment of a "secret service fund," which was used by Presidents Jefferson and Madison to finance intelligence gathering activities abroad (Central Intelligence Agency 1999).

American intelligence continued to evolve and expand during the early history of the nation. Major advances in the intelligence process occurred during the Civil War, when both Union and Confederate forces extensively engaged in espionage and clandestine activities. Throughout this conflict, each side collected data through the use of agents and military scouts, captured documents, intercepted mail, decoded telegrams and newspapers, and interrogation of prisoners and deserters. Large volumes of information were gathered, analyzed, and incorporated into military strategy, but neither side had a formal military intelligence service. Throughout the war, the North was more effective at espionage and counterintelligence, whereas the South had more success at covert action including a few famous spies such as Belle Boyd.

Following the Civil War, intelligence activities continued to be refined and expanded. The Office of Naval Intelligence and the Army's Military Intelligence Division were established in the 1880s as the first formal permanent intelligence organizations (CIA) of the United States. They posted military attachés in several major European cities principally for open-source intelligence. When the Spanish-American War broke out in 1898, the attachés switched to espionage. They created informant rings and ran reconnaissance operations to learn about Spanish military intentions and capabilities.

When World War I started in 1914, the U.S. ability to collect foreign intelligence had shrunk drastically because of budget cuts and bureaucratic reorganizations. The State Department began small-scale intelligence analysis operations in 1916, but it was not until the United States declared war on Germany did Army and Navy intelligence organizations receive a budgetary increase. Without sufficient funding prior to the declaration of war, intelligence agencies lagged behind in preparing for war and were not staffed to handle the increased workload. The Justice Department's Bureau of Investigation (a precursor to the FBI) took on a counterintelligence role in 1916, and Congress passed the first federal espionage law in 1917.

Between World War I and II, American intelligence officers concentrated on codebreaking and counterintelligence operations against Germany and Japan. With this increased emphasis on intelligence gathering, by 1941 the United States had built a world-class signals intelligence capability. During the 1930s, the FBI launched an extremely effective counterintelligence attack on German and Japanese espionage and sabotage operations in the Western Hemisphere, infiltrating many networks and arresting dozens of foreign agents. The Bureau had less success against the successful Soviet efforts to penetrate U.S. governmental, scientific, and economic institutions following World War I.

As American entry into World War II drew closer in 1941, President Franklin Roosevelt created the country's first peacetime, civilian intelligence agency, the Office of the Coordinator of Information. This agency was established to organize the activities of several governmental intelligence agencies. Soon after, however, the United States suffered its most costly intelligence disaster in history when the Japanese bombed Pearl Harbor on December 7, 1941. This failure is attributable to analytical misconceptions, collection gaps, bureaucratic confusion, and careful Japanese denial and deception measures. In response to the attack on Pearl Harbor, the Office of Strategic Services was established as a larger and more diversified intelligence agency in 1942.

As a means of securing communications during World War II, the Marines used native speakers of the Navajo language as code talkers (Papich 2001, 38). Using the Navajo language, over 400 Native Americans were trained and served the nation by utilizing a language unfamiliar to the Japanese, who were tapping American military communication. The use of Navajo allowed for air support, battlefield maneuvers, and provided for almost instantaneous communication as against encrypted messages, which required time to be deciphered (39). As evidenced by the Navajo code talkers, language skills are critical elements in the intelligence arena for effective and reliable communication.

The CIA was created in 1947 with the signing of the National Security Act of 1947 by President Harry Truman. The act also created a Director of Central Intelligence (DCI) to serve as head of the U.S. Intelligence Community, act as the principal adviser to the president for intelligence matters related to national security, and serve as head of the CIA (U.S. Congress 1947). The National Security Act is one of the seminal pieces of legislation in the evolution of the Intelligence Community and has been at the center of continued reform within the intelligence field.

President Gerald Ford released Executive Order 11905 in 1976 to "improve the quality of intelligence needed for national security, to clarify the authority and responsibilities of the intelligence departments and agencies, and to establish effective oversight to assure compliance with law in the management and direction of intelligence agencies and departments of the national government" (Ford 1976).

The Intelligence Organization Act of 1992 was signed into law by President George H.W. Bush. Commonly referred to as the "Intelligence Organization Act of 1992," this legislation amends the 1947 National Security Act with respect to the organization of the Intelligence Community and the responsibilities and authorities of both the director of Central Intelligence and the secretary of Defense (Intelligence Authorization Act 1992). The title allows for further organizational changes, while establishing a legislative framework that accurately reflects the existing relationships between elements of the Intelligence Community.

Reforms within the intelligence arena often closely follow breakdowns in intelligence or the perceived need for increased intelligence activity. These reforms tend to require improved information sharing, access, and awareness between agencies and new training programs for intelligence analysts. In this vein, President Bill Clinton issued Presidential Decision Directive (PDD) 56 in 1997 in response to intelligence failures in Rwanda, Somalia, and Haiti. This executive order called for the National Security Council to work with the National Defense University, Army War College, Pentagon, State Department, CIA, and other agencies to develop and conduct multiagency training and planning focused on complex emergency issues. PDD 56 is just one of many such examples with the goal to increase communication between intelligence agencies.

Following the recommendations of the 9/11 Commission, the Intelligence Reform and Terrorism Prevention Act of 2004 was passed by Congress and signed into law by President George W. Bush. This legislation enacts the most dramatic reform of the nation's intelligence capabilities since President Harry Truman signed the National Security Act of 1947, which created the CIA. Under this law, the nation's vast intelligence enterprise became more unified, coordinated, and effective through the establishment of the Office of the Director of National Intelligence.

U.S. Intelligence Community

The Intelligence Community (IC) is a loose federation of executive branch agencies and organizations that work both separately and together to conduct intelligence activities. Ultimately, these activities include the conduct of foreign relations and the protection of the national security of the United States both at home and abroad (www.intelligence.gov). These activities include:

- Collection of information needed by the president, the National Security Council, the secretaries of State and Defense, and other Executive Branch officials for the performance of their duties and responsibilities;
- Production and dissemination of intelligence;
- Collection of information concerning, and the conduct of activities to protect against, intelligence activities directed against the United States, international

terrorist and international narcotics activities, and other hostile activities directed against the United States by foreign powers, organizations, persons, and their agents;

- Special activities;
- Administrative and support activities within the United States and abroad necessary for the performance of authorized activities; and
- Such other intelligence activities as the president may direct from time to time.

Each of the sixteen agencies that make up the IC is found in figure 4.1 and serve a unique function within the intelligence operations arena. The following is a discussion of only a handful of the members of the IC and includes the core functions of each agency and the distinct characteristics the agency serves. By studying and exploring the construction of intelligence agencies, policymakers will have a more complete picture of how to effectively operate within the complex world of the IC.

In studying the role of intelligence and reliance on the IC, one must recognize that under certain situations decision makers may not want intelligence in order to implement a policy. Desired end states for the government can be achieved without

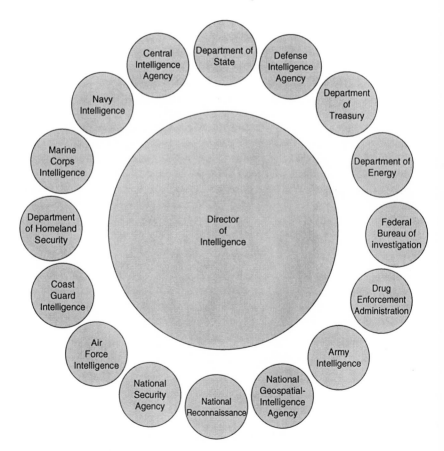

Figure 4.1 Members of the U.S. Intelligence Community.

input from the members of the IC. The role of intelligence analysis and production varies from scenario to scenario and the impact of using or not using intelligence must be considered by decision makers when faced with implementing government policy.

Before discussing specific agencies within the IC, a brief description of interagency operations is necessary. Performing analysis and preparing documents for decision makers are vital daily functions for members of the IC. Along with collecting and analyzing real-time data, a need for the forecasting of future events exists. The National Intelligence Council (NIC) serves as the IC's center for midterm and long-term strategic thinking. Its primary functions are as follows.

- Support the Director of National Intelligence (DNI) in his role as head of the IC.
- Provide a focal point for policymakers to task the IC to answer their questions.
- Reach out to nongovernment experts in academia and the private sector to broaden the IC perspective.
- Contribute to the IC effort to allocate its resources in response to policymakers' changing needs.
- Lead the IC effort to produce National Intelligence Estimates (NIEs) and other NIC products.

NIEs are the DNI's most authoritative written judgments concerning national security issues. They contain the coordinated judgments of the IC regarding the likely course of future events.

The NIC is staffed by twelve National Intelligence Officers' (NIOs), each with a specialized area of focus, whose primary functions are as follows.

- Advise the DNI.
- Interact regularly with senior intelligence consumers and support their current and longer-term needs.
- Produce top-quality estimative intelligence in a process that is efficient and responsive.
- Engage with outside experts to tap their knowledge and insights.
- Help assess the capabilities and needs of IC analytic producers.
- Promote collaboration among IC analytic producers on strategic warning, advanced analytic tools, and methodologies.
- Articulate priorities to guide intelligence collection, evaluation, and procurement.

One of the largest and best-known intelligence organizations is the CIA, whose mission is to be the eyes and ears of the nation. To accomplish this, the Agency historically collected intelligence; provided relevant, timely, and objective all-source analysis; conducted covert action at the direction of the president to preempt threats or achieve U.S. policy objectives (Central Intelligence Agency 1999). In order to accomplish its far-reaching mission, the CIA is organized into the following directorates <http://www.cia.gov/cia/information/info.html>.

- *The Directorate of Intelligence*, the analytical branch of the CIA, is responsible for the production and dissemination of all-source intelligence analysis on key foreign issues.

- *The National Clandestine Service* is responsible for the clandestine collection of foreign intelligence.
- *The Directorate of Science and Technology* creates and applies innovative technology in support of the intelligence collection mission.
- *The Directorate of Support* provides critical elements of the Agency's support foundation to the mission: people, security, information, property, and financial operations (fas.org lists this as the Directorate of Administration; <http://www.fas.org/irp/cia/ciaorg.htm>).
- *The Center for the Study of Intelligence* maintains the Agency's historical materials and promotes the study of intelligence as a legitimate and serious discipline.
- *The Office of General Counsel* advises the director of the CIA on all legal matters relating to his role and is the principal source of legal counsel for the CIA.
- *The Office of Public Affairs* advises the director of the CIA on all media, public policy, and employee communications issues relating to his/her role as CIA director and is the CIA's principal communications focal point for the media, the general public, and Agency employees.

In 2003, President George W. Bush established the Terrorist Threat Integration Center "to provide a comprehensive, all-source-based picture of potential terrorist threats to U.S. interests" (U.S. Congress 2004). The TTIC comprised elements of the DHS, the FBI's Counterterrorism Division, the DCI's Counterterrorist Center, the DoD, and other U.S. government agencies.

The TTIC was a short-lived organization and was replaced by the National Counterterrorism Center (NCTC), which works to "detect, prevent, disrupt, preempt, and mitigate the effects of transnational terrorist activities against the territory, people, and interests of the United States of America" (National Counterterrorism Center 2006). As expressed in numerous government reports and news stories, sharing information among the members of the IC has been a challenge given the overlapping missions and complexity of problems facing the security of the nation. Therefore, the NCTC has been tasked to serve as the interchange of terrorism information among agencies, facilitate the exchange of terrorism information between agencies and appropriate authorities of states and local governments, and protect the ability of agencies to acquire additional information.

A second well-recognized and referenced member of the IC is the FBI. Like the CIA, the FBI serves to accomplish a broad mission, which includes elements of law enforcement and intelligence analysis. Though the FBI plays a critical role in national security through its work in law enforcement, this chapter focuses on the Bureau's increasing responsibilities in the IC. Through its *Directorate of Intelligence*, the FBI's intelligence program is to optimally position the FBI to meet current and emerging national security and criminal threats by:

- Aiming core investigative work proactively against threats to U.S. interests
- Building and sustaining IC-wide intelligence policies and capabilities
- Providing useful, appropriate, and timely information and analysis to the national security, homeland security, and law enforcement communities (Federal Bureau of Investigation 2006)

Along with the CIA and FBI, the DIA operates under the mission to provide timely, objective, and cogent military intelligence to warfighters, defense planners, and defense and national security policymakers (Defense Intelligence Agency 2006). The DIA's primary role is to serve as a combat support agency and is administered through the DoD. With over 7,500 military and civilian employees worldwide, the DIA is a major producer and manager of foreign military intelligence. Contrary to the CIA and FBI, the DIA is dedicated solely to providing tactical, operational, and strategic intelligence in direct support of military activity. The DIA is not affiliated with any one branch of the military and supports all DoD functions—it is DoD's J2. Each military branch is equipped with its own intelligence agency, which supports branch-specific functions. It is important to distinguish the broad approach that the DIA uses to gather, analyze, and communicate data.

The final member of the IC this chapter will address is the NSA, which serves as America's cryptologic organization and is best known for its use of SIGINT to gather data. It coordinates, directs, and performs highly specialized activities to protect U.S. information systems and produce foreign intelligence information. A high-tech organization, NSA operates on the frontiers of communications and data processing. It is also one of the most important centers of foreign-language analysis and research within the government.

Each of the fifteen agencies that comprise the IC perform a unique and necessary function within the national security arena. The discussion above is only a selection of agencies from the IC; each agency is integral to the function of the entire intelligence enterprise. Whereas their individual missions are important, collaboration and information sharing among agencies is critical to insure the integrity of information and to develop strong and thorough intelligence documents for decision makers. The DNI is a key component to ensure the sharing of information between government agencies and to build strong and accurate intelligence reports.

Collection, Analysis, Action: Overview of Information Analysis

The intelligence cycle is the process of developing raw information into finished intelligence for policymakers to use in decision making and action. There are five steps that constitute the intelligence cycle (see figure 4.2).

Planning and Direction

Management of the entire effort, from identifying the need for data to delivering an intelligence product to the consumer, namely a policy or decision maker, is the beginning and the end of the cycle of intelligence gathering, analysis, and production. The intelligence cycle starts with drawing up specific collection requirements and it ends with finished intelligence, which supports policy decisions and generates new requirements.

The entire process depends on guidance from public officials. Policymakers, including the president, his/her aides, the National Security Council, and other major departments and administrative agencies of government all initiate requests for intelligence.

Figure 4.2 The Intelligence Cycle.

Collection

Collection is the gathering of the raw data needed to produce finished intelligence. There are many sources of information, including open sources such as foreign broadcasts, newspapers, periodicals, and books. Open source reporting is integral to the IC's analytical capabilities. There are also secret sources of information. Operations officers collect such information from agents abroad and from defectors who provide information obtainable in no other way.

Technical collection, which utilizes electronic devices and satellite photography, plays an indispensable role in modern intelligence, such as monitoring arms control agreements and providing direct support to military forces.

Processing

Processing involves converting the vast amount of information collected to a form usable by analysts. This is done through a variety of methods including decryption, language translations, and data reduction. In the expanding Information Age, an increased amount of reliance is placed on the use of computers to manage and process data. Advancements in IT have been both a help and hindrance to analysts in the processing phase. With a greater amount of information available, the time spent on processing has increased.

All-Source Analysis and Production

This step in the process includes the conversion of basic information into finished intelligence. It includes integrating, evaluating, and analyzing all available data and preparing intelligence products. Analysts, who are subject-matter specialists, consider the information's reliability, validity, and relevance. They integrate data into a coherent whole, put the evaluated information in context, and produce finished intelligence that includes assessments of events and judgments about the implications of the information for the United States.

The IC devotes the bulk of its resources to providing strategic intelligence to policymakers. It performs this important function by monitoring events, warning decision makers about threats to the United States, and forecasting developments. The subject of specific intelligence reports may concern different regions, problems, or personalities in various contexts such as political, geographic, economic, military, scientific, or biographic. Current events, capabilities, and future trends are examined and options are presented for the impacts of policy decisions.

A typical intelligence analyst or team of analysts will produce numerous written reports, which may be brief (one page or less) or more detailed and lengthy studies. They may involve current intelligence, which is of immediate importance, or long-range forecasting assessments. Once a written report is prepared, some finished intelligence is presented in the form of oral briefings. Members of the IC also participate in the drafting and production of NIEs, which reflect the collective judgment of the IC.

Dissemination

The last step, which logically feeds into the first, is the distribution of the finished intelligence to the consumers, the same policymakers whose needs initiated the intelligence requirements. Finished intelligence is provided daily to the president and key national security advisers. The policymakers, the recipients of finished intelligence reports, then make decisions based on the information, and these decisions may lead to the levying of more requirements, thus perpetuating the intelligence cycle.

Whereas all intelligence reports are disseminated to the appropriate policymaker, certain key intelligence reports are known throughout the IC and recognized by media sources. Well-recognized reports produced by intelligence agencies include:

- *Presidential Daily Briefing* (PDB). An extremely sensitive and closely held document produced each morning by the DNI for the president of the United States. For years, the PDB had been the sole province of the DCI and the latter tightly controlled who could see it. The document was almost never shared nor vetted with IC counterparts. A sample PDB is provided in box 4.2.
- *Patterns of Global Terrorism*. A report published each year by the United States Department of State. The report provides detailed assessments about each foreign country in where acts of international terrorism occurred; the extent to which foreign countries are cooperating with the United States in the apprehension, conviction, and punishment of terrorists; the extent to which foreign countries are cooperating with the United States in the prevention of further acts of terrorism; and activities of any terrorist group known to be responsible for the kidnapping or death of an American citizen.

With an understanding of the history of American intelligence efforts and the current structure of the IC presented earlier in this chapter, working in the intelligence field requires a knowledge of the classification and security clearance system. Following 9/11, greater emphasis has been placed on protecting the government's information, which in turn places an increased burden on the classification and clearance process.

Ensuring the integrity of intelligence, agencies must manage the access provided to analysts and the level of security placed on information processed by the agency.

To achieve the necessary security, a system of security clearance has been established for individuals practicing the art of intelligence and for the protection of intelligence documents. The U.S. government classification systems weres established under Executive Order 13292, the most recent in a series of executive orders on the topic of classification, issued by President George W. Bush in 2003. Executive Order 13292 lays out the system of classification, declassification, and handling of national security information generated by the U.S. government, its employees and contractors, as well as information received from other governments.

A security clearance generally specifies a level of access given to certain information and is a status granted to individuals, typically members of the military and employees of governments and their contractors. The term "security clearance" is also occasionally used in the private sector where a formal process is used to vet employees for access to sensitive information. A clearance by itself is normally not sufficient to gain access; the organization must determine that the cleared individual has a "need to know" sensitive information. Clearances are not generally awarded solely based on rank or position.

In the U.S. government there are three primary levels: confidential, secret, and top secret. These levels are hierarchical, therefore someone holding a secret clearance could access confidential information, but not top secret information. The vetting process for a security clearance is usually undertaken only when someone is hired or transferred into a position that requires access to classified information.

With an increased amount of material becoming classified, the clearance process has grown more complicated and requires an individual to wait a longer amount of time while going through the approval process. A threat is emerging from the time lag in the clearance process as agencies must wait longer for analysts to be given the appropriate levels of clearance before beginning their assignments. This causes a backlog of work and the potential for critical data to be missed, which may have prevented a future terrorist attack. Elected officials and policymakers must address the duration of the process while ensuring that only eligible candidates are awarded security clearances.

The level of clearance usually determines the level of scrutiny applied during the clearance process. A satisfactory background check may suffice for a confidential clearance. The full range of checks are applied for clearance to the most sensitive information. In order to obtain a high-level clearance the process can be lengthy, sometimes taking a year or more. This process can includes several steps, depending on the level of clearance required:

1. The first step requires a potential employee to fill out a detailed life history form, which becomes a starting point for investigation into the candidates suitability.
2. A background check includes a "national agency check" of government databases and sometimes commercial databases such as credit histories.
3. The third step in the process, a full field investigation, involves agents contacting employers, coworkers, and other individuals. Standard investigations include checks of employment, education, organization affiliations, and local agencies where the subject has lived, worked, or gone to school. Interviews are typically

conducted with persons who know the individual seeking to obtain a clearance. The investigation usually goes back five years.

4. Following a field investigation, a special background investigation (SBI) may be conducted. This process extends coverage of the person's background to provide a greater depth of knowledge than a standard background investigation. An SBI may include a national agency check on the applicant's spouse or cohabitant and any immediate family members who are U.S. citizens other than by birth or who are not U.S. citizens. The scope of an SBI can extend back fifteen years.

5. A polygraph test of the candidate. A polygraph test is not required for all security accesses. It is determined on an agency by agency basis and also varies based upon the level of security clearance required.

6. The final step in the process is adjudication, which is a review of all materials from the prior steps, and a conclusion is reached where the individual is either given or denied the requested level of clearance.

Levels of Classification

1. *Unclassified.* This is not technically a "classification," but is the default applied to government documents. Unclassified refers to information that can be released to individuals without a clearance. Information that is unclassified is sometimes "restricted" in its dissemination.

2. *Confidential.* This is the lowest classification level. It is defined as information that would "damage" national security if disclosed.

3. *Secret.* The second highest classification. Information is classified secret when its release would cause "serious damage" to national security. Most information that is classified is held at the secret sensitivity level.

4. *Top Secret.* This is the highest security level, and is defined as information that would cause "exceptionally grave damage" to national security if disclosed to the public. Despite public mystique, relatively little information is classified as Top Secret (when compared to the other levels of classification). Only that which is exceptionally sensitive (weapon design, presidential security information, nuclear-related projects, clandestine personnel and operatives, various intelligence information) is classified as Top Secret.

Role of Information Analysis in Homeland Security

Homeland security remains a relatively new term within the public sector; however, the concept of protecting the nation's interests run deep in American security policy. It is the transition of blending traditional military duties with civilian responsibilities that creates the new face of homeland security. As previously discussed, the U.S. IC is an intricate and complex organization comprising agencies with similar yet distinct missions. The DHS is actively engaged in the collection, analysis, and dissemination of intelligence as a means of providing the necessary defense of key assets. Without timely and accurate information, DHS functions cannot be completed.

Given the necessity of accurate and timely intelligence, a tightly knit relationship and understanding of a common language between all members of the IC is vital.

Future of Information Analysis

The American IC has been an integral component of the nation's security since the Revolutionary War. With a new and evolving terrorist threat, the IC is once again responding to meet the needs of the nation.

Following the tragic events of 9/11, the Madrid Train Bombings of 2004, and the London Train Bombings of 2005, a great deal of attention was given to the lack of information sharing between intelligence agencies. The creation of the DHS, the reorganization of the IC, and the establishment of the DNI will aid in the flow of information between government agencies; however, the problem of sharing information persists. As these initiatives grow and mature, the challenge of communicating between agencies will experience positive and negative events. The future success of information analysis and preparation of intelligence hinges on the ability of agencies to cooperate and share pertinent information to protect the nation's interests.

One emerging issue in the IC is the rising need for analysts as the existing workforce approaches retirement age. As within other sectors of government the workforce is aging and in danger of losing a great deal of expertise and experience to retirement. According to current estimates, 20,000–25,000 analyst positions in the IC will be available. New analysts with the requisite skills are needed to fill these positions. Institutions of higher education are offering courses and programs of study to help meet the need in the public sector created by the retirement of current employees. The homeland security challenge needs to be met by a new generation of information analysts who will gather, analyze, and disseminate critical intelligence.

A second vital issue shaping the future of the IC is the need for increased translators of foreign languages. During the Cold War, the primary language skills needed were in Russian- and Slavic-based languages. However, expertise is now needed in languages such as Arabic, Farsi, Urdu, and, Mandarin. A major obstacle facing intelligence agencies in hiring new language experts is the ability to provide security clearances to native speakers of the languages in need.

Conclusion

The next impasse of disaster response, whether natural or manmade, that policy makers and practitioners alike must address is intelligence failures. Many catastrophes share a common "weak" link, the ineffectiveness of vital intelligence communicated to all levels of the response structure. A recent example of this shortcoming was the intelligence failures contributing to the poor local, state, and federal response to Hurricane Katrina in September 2005. Though news of the severity of the impending hurricane saturated national media, specific data regarding the path, intensity, and dangerous nature of the storm failed to reach upper-level decision makers or lower-level responders. As a direct result of this intelligence failure, local first responders were not charged with the urgency of evacuating the population quickly enough. First responders immediately understood that Hurricane Katrina was a major natural disaster, but the depth of the threat and damage was not adequately communicated to them.

Another example of an intelligence failure in disaster response was the response effort during 9/11. First responders were not given vital information from military and IC agencies regarding the scope of the attack: information such as whether or not there were more planes that were suspect. Had first responders possessed this information, they would not have ordered civilians in the second World Trade Center Tower to remain in their offices.

It is very easy to look back on disasters and identify where failures occurred. It is much more difficult to remedy the causes of these failures. The core problem of intelligence failures stems from a lack of organizational communication, where it is common for the "middle layer" of analysts and experts to possess critical information but, due to bureaucratic or internal restrictions, are limited in what channels can be used to communicate that information. Prior to landfall of Hurricane Katrina, personnel at the National Weather Service knew how catastrophic the storm would be for New Orleans, but upper-level officials either were not available or were not listening. After the earthquake that caused the tsunami that ravaged South East Asia in 2004, mid-level analysts around the Pacific Rim knew the tsunami was coming, and how severe it was, but had no vehicle to communicate this information to the public. The thick buffer that is above and below the analyst level serves as an obstacle that policymakers must whittle down to mitigate future intelligence failures in disaster response.

Intelligence failures is a weak link in homeland security in general. As we have seen, intelligence failures can serve as the "weak" link in disaster response, but also in other areas such as in the IC, critical infrastructure protection, border and transportation security and information security among many. Through many of the challenges and strengths of these various components of homeland security, a failure for one layer of the organization to adequately communicate intelligence (information) to another layer can dismantle the entire effort. As with analyzing the shortcomings in disaster response, it is very easy for the student, citizen, analyst, or policymaker to acknowledge the threat of intelligence failures. The 9/11 Commission did exactly this, but the process for refining these issues out of the organizational structures is difficult at best because of the slow moving, bureaucratic nature of government. Years after the 9/11 Commission publicly addressed intelligence and communications failures as the leading causes of the 9/11 attacks, little has been done to remedy the problem. Perhaps the next generation of analysts and leadership will be able to recognize this shortcoming, and be able to change the culture in their field to be more accommodating of inter-layer communication.

This chapter has explored the agencies that constitute the American IC and has discussed the processes that dictate the behavior of those engaged in the practice of intelligence. As with many other areas of homeland security the intelligence arena must respond to the new and emerging challenges posed by the terrorist threat. Emerging concerns the IC faces in intraagency communication, an aging workforce, expanding availability of technological tools to the mass public, and foreign-language expertise must be addressed to meet the future of the intelligence profession.

Case Study: The Intelligence Failure that Led to 9/11

One of the most widely cited examples in recent history of an intelligence failure is the September 11, 2001 bombing of the World Trade Center and Pentagon. It transpired because of a lack of coordination and communication between agencies within the IC and because key details relating to the plans of the terrorists were not discovered and acted upon. The example of the 9/11 terrorist attacks provides a snapshot of operations within the IC and how policymakers are asked to react to an ever-evolving threat. This case study examines these events through the document prepared for the president by the IC in the form of the PDB (see box 4.2). The PDB comprises

---

Box 4.2 Sample Presidential Daily Briefing, August 6, 2001 (Central Intelligence Agency, 1998)

Declassified and Approved for Release, April 10, 2004

Bin Ladin Determined to Strike the United States

Clandestine, foreign government and media reports indicate that Bin Ladin, since 1997, has wanted to conduct foreign terrorist attacks on the United States. Bin Ladin implied in U.S. television interviews in 1997 and 1998 that his followers would follow the example of World Trade Center bomber Ramzi Yousef and "bring the fighting to America."

After U.S. missile strikes on his base in Afghanistan in 1998, Bin Ladin told followers he wanted to retaliate in Washington, according to a [deleted] service.

An Egyptian Islamic Jihad (EIJ) operative told an [deleted] service at the same that Bin Ladin was planning to exploit the operative's access to the United States to mount a terrorist strike. The millennium plotting in Canada in 1999 may have been part of Bin Ladin's first serious attempt to implement a terrorist strike in the United States. Convicted plotter Ahmed Ressam has told FBI that he himself conceived the idea to attack Los Angeles International Airport, but that Bin Ladin's lieutenant Abu Zubaydah encouraged him and helped facilitate the operation. Ressam also said that in 1998 Abu Zubaydah was planning his own U.S. attack.

Ressam says Bin Ladin was aware of the Los Angeles operation. Although Bin Ladin has not succeeded, his attacks against the U.S. embassies in Kenya and Tanzania in 1998 demonstrate that he prepares operations years in advance and is not deterred by setbacks. Bin Ladin associates had our embassies in Nairobi and Dar es Salaam under surveillance as early as 1993, and some members of the Nairobi cell planning the bombings were arrested and deported in 1997.

Al-Qaeda members—including some who are U.S. citizens—have resided in or traveled to the United States for years, and the group apparently maintains a support structure that could aid attacks. Two al-Qaeda members found guilty in the conspiracy to bomb our embassies in East Africa were U.S. citizens, and a senior member lived in California in the mid-1990s. A clandestine source said in 1998 that a Bin Ladin cell in New York was recruiting Muslim-American youth for attacks.

We have not been able to corroborate some of the more sensational threat reporting, such as that from a [deleted] service in 1998 saying that Bin Ladin wanted to hijack a U.S. aircraft to gain the release of "Blind Shaykh" Umar 'Abd al-Rahman and other U.S.-held extremists.

Nevertheless, FBI information since that time indicates patterns of suspicious activity in this country consistent with preparations for hijackings or other types of attacks, including recent surveillance of federal buildings in New York.

The FBI is conducting approximately seventy full field investigations throughout the United States that it considers Bin Ladin-related. The CIA and the FBI are investigating a call to our embassy in the UAE in May saying that a group of Bin Ladin supporters was in the United States planning attacks with explosives.

For the President Only
August 6, 2001

---

materials gathered through all source intelligence and used at the highest levels of the executive branch.

Many questions have been raised by the media and addressed in the 9/11 Commission Report in relation to the August 6, 2001, PDB, following the declassification of this document in April 2004. By reorganizing the IC into the structure discussed earlier in this chapter, the federal government has attempted to prevent similar failures from happening in the future.

Discussion Questions

1. How might information sharing between intelligence agencies be improved to prevent future intelligence failures?
2. The PDB is a key intelligence report. What other actions can be taken by the IC to alert policymakers of potential terrorist activities?
3. Once the president is briefed and made fully aware of the threat, who else should be notified and in what order?
4. Is the new structure of the American IC better equipped to prevent such intelligence failures? Why or why not?
5. Did policymakers react appropriately to this PDB at the time? If yes, why? If no, how should the federal government have responded given the structure of government pre-9/11 (that is, without the DHS)?

Key Terms and Definitions

all source analysis. Conversion of basic information into finished intelligence.

attaché. A military expert with diplomatic mission.

counterintelligence. The act of seeking and identifying espionage activities.

geospatial intelligence. This is the analysis and visual representation of security-related activities on the earth. It is produced through an integration of imagery, imagery intelligence, and geospatial information.

Espionage. Practice of obtaining secrets from rivals or enemies for military, political, or economic advantage.

Human Intelligence (HUMINT). Collection includes clandestine acquisition of photography, documents, and other material; overt collection by personnel in diplomatic and consular posts; debriefing of foreign nationals and U.S. citizens who travel abroad; and official contacts with foreign governments. Many citizens connect HUMINT with espionage and clandestine activities, yet, in reality, most HUMINT collection is performed by overt collectors such as diplomats and military attachés. HUMINT is the oldest method for collecting information, and up to the middle to late twentieth century it was the primary source of intelligence. (Goldman 2002)

Imagery Intelligence (IMINT). Includes representations of objects reproduced electronically or by optical means on film, electronic display devices, or other media. Imagery can be derived from visual photography, radar sensors, infrared sensors, lasers, and electro-optics. (Goldman 2002)

Intelligence. The product resulting from the collection, processing, integration, analysis, evaluation, and interpretation, of available information concerning foreign countries or areas.

Measurement and Signature Intelligence (MASINT). Technically derived intelligence data other than imagery and SIGINT. The data results in intelligence that locates, identifies, or describes distinctive characteristics of targets. It employs a broad group of disciplines including nuclear, optical, radio frequency, acoustics, seismic, and materials sciences. Examples of this might be the distinctive radar signatures of specific aircraft systems or the chemical composition of air and water samples. (Goldman 2002)

national intelligence estimates. An assessment of a situation in the foreign environment that is relevant to the formulation of foreign economic and national security policy, and which projects probable future courses of action and developments; it may be structured to illustrate differences of view.

Open-Source Intelligence (OSINT). Publicly available information appearing in print or electronic form including radio, television, newspapers, journals, the Internet, commercial databases, and videos, graphics, and drawings. Open-source collection responsibilities are broadly distributed through the IC; the major collectors are the Foreign Broadcast Information Service (FBIS) and the National Air and Space Intelligence Center (NASIC). (Goldman 2002)

Reconnaissance. Military term for active gathering of information about an enemy or other conditions, by physical observation. It is part of combat intelligence.

Signals Intelligence (SIGINT). Signals intelligence is derived from signal intercepts—however transmitted—either individually or in combination:

- All Communications Intelligence (COMINT)
- Electronic Intelligence (ELINT)
- Foreign Instrumentation Signals Intelligence (FISINT)

Additional Resources

The following organizations and articles provide additional information related to the field of information analysis.

- U.S. Intelligence Community: www.intelligence.gov
- Director National Intelligence: www.dni.gov
- International Association for Intelligence Education: www.iafie.og
- U.S. Department of State: www.state.gov
- Congressional Research Service: http://fpc.state.gov/c4763.htm

References

Central Intelligence Agency. 1998. *Intelligence in the war of independence.* Public Affairs, Washington, D.C.
———. 1999. *Factbook on intelligence.* Central Intelligence Agency, Washington, D.C.

———. 2001. Presidential Daily Briefing. August 6, 2001. <http://news.findlaw.com/hdocs/docs/terrorism/80601pdb.html>.

Defense Intelligence Agency. 2006. Defense Intelligence Agency: Committed to excellence in defense of the nation. <http://www.dia.mil>.

Federal Bureau of Investigation. 2006. <http://www.fbi.gov>.

Ford, Gerald. 1976. Executive Order 11905: United States foreign intelligence activities. *Weekly Compilation of Presidential Documents* 12, no. 8.

Goldman, Jan. 2002. *Intelligence warning terminology*. Joint Military Intelligence College, Washington, D.C.

Krizen, Lisa. 1999. *Intelligence essentials for everyone*. Joint Military Intelligence College, Washington, D.C.

National Counterterrorism Center. 2006. National Counterterrorism Center: United to protect. <http://www.nctc.gov>.

Papich, William. 2001. Declassified heroes: Honoring the Navajo codetalkers. *Native People* 14: 38–40.

Pike, John. 2006. World Intelligence and Security Agencies. Federation of American Scientists. <http://www.fas.org/irp/world/index.html>.

Richelson, Jeffrey. 1999. *The U.S. intelligence community*. Westview Press, Boulder, Colo.

U.S. Congress. 1947. *The National Security Act of 1947*. 80th Cong., 1st sess. Government Printing Office, Washington, D.C.

———. 1992. *The Intelligence Authorization Act, FY 1992: The Intelligence Organization Act*. 102nd Cong., 1st sess. Government Printing Office, Washington, D.C.

———. 2004. *The Intelligence Reform and Terrorism Prevention Act of 2004*. 108th Cong., 2d. Government Printing Office, Washington, D.C.

CHAPTER FIVE

CRITICAL INFRASTRUCTURE PROTECTION AND INFORMATION SECURITY

Table Top: Examining Complexity with Critical Infrastructure Systems

One morning on a brisk fall day in early November, technicians at the Springfield Nuclear Power Plant notice a malfunctioning steam release valve on Cooling Tank One. A mechanical problem was discovered in a leaky seal that had been recently patched. No one thought to check the plant's supervisory control and data acquisition (SCADA) system, which controls the cooling function for the plant. Technicians quickly recognized the leaky seal and corrected the problem without any impact on the plant's overall operation. Shortly after the repair a similar situation is discovered in Cooling Tanks Two and Three. This time the technicians did not discover any mechanical failures and did not recognize the significance in reoccurring events. It is not until an examination of the SCADA system that the problem is diagnosed; the automated software has given the command to close the valves in Cooling Tanks Two and Three when hot air should have been vented. How did this occur? Only authorized plant employees have access to the software, which is password protected.

IT professionals quickly begin an investigation into the SCADA system failures and discover an intrusion occurred from a remote computer in Eastern Europe. A hacker gained access to the critical systems of the Springfield Power Plant through an unsecured access port outside of the plant's firewall. One unprotected component of the network has enabled a technologically savvy hacker to cause a potentially catastrophic failure of the entire system.

As Cooling Tanks Two and Three are rapidly overheating, the possibility of a major meltdown is now facing plant managers and local decision makers. Upon notifying the Nuclear Regulatory Commission and DHS, plant managers are instructed to attempt to correct the problem while elected officials are instructed to coordinate with Emergency Services to begin evacuation of the highest risk areas. How much information and what type of information should be released to the media and citizens? What is the appropriate course of action for federal government?

Introduction

Critical infrastructure protection and information security are major components of homeland security efforts. This chapter will explore infrastructure systems, how they are interconnected, and the overlap between physical and cyber networks. Civilian infrastructures, which support financial, health, and other vital operations, are susceptible to natural disasters, human error, and are the direct target of malicious activities including terrorism and sabotage. They are an important area of focus of homeland security efforts. Included in this discussion will be an examination of the cyber, physical, and human aspects of critical infrastructure systems. Critical infrastructure systems include not just hardware and software, but the people and institutions responsible for their existence and operation.

Defining Critical Infrastructure Protection

Critical infrastructure systems have become increasingly complex and reliant on computer-based automated systems to provide the continuous operation of our critical systems. In this chapter, we will address technological and policy issues that affect both cyber and physical infrastructures.

As defined in the USA PATRIOT Act and the National Infrastructure Protection Plan (NIPP), critical infrastructures are "systems and assets, whether physical or virtual, so vital to the United States that the incapacity or destruction of such systems and assets would have a debilitating impact on security, national economic security, national public health or safety, or any combination of those matters" (USA PATRIOT Act 2001). A list of the critical infrastructure sectors, as identified in the NIPP, can be found in box 5.1. The NIPP goes on to define key assets as, "individual targets whose destruction could cause large-scale injury, death, or destruction of property, and/or profoundly damage our national prestige and confidence" (Department of Homeland Security 2005a).

Box 5.1 Critical Infrastructure Sectors as Defined in the National Infrastructure Protection Plan

- Agriculture and Food
- Public Health
- Water
- Energy
- Banking and Finance
- National Monuments and Icons
- Defense Industrial Base
- Information Technology
- Telecommunications
- Chemical
- Transportation Systems
- Emergency Services
- Postal and Shipping
- Dams
- Government Facilities
- Commercial Facilities
- Nuclear Reactors, Materials, and Waste

These broadly defined infrastructure sectors all have one characteristic in common: they rely on technology to support and protect the systems that provide the goods and services we need to survive as individuals and as a society. As the foundation for the function of our nation, these infrastructure sectors require attention from the policy community to ensure their continuity of operation. The federal government has issued several national strategies to introduce its policy agenda in securing the nation's infrastructure. Many of the suggestions found in these documents point to continued research and development in the science and technology community. National laboratories, private industry, and institutions of higher education all have vital roles in developing the means to improve the reliability and resiliency of infrastructure systems. Technology alone will not be able to solve infrastructure assurance problems, but when paired with policy and law it will help to ensure the nation's infrastructures are secure and operating properly.

One area not specifically addressed in the list of critical infrastructure sectors is the concept of humans as a critical infrastructure. Without the human component, the physical systems comprising critical infrastructure will not function. Thus infrastructure assurance must include protection of the people necessary for construction, management, operation, and maintenance of critical systems.

The criticality of the human infrastructure component was dramatically illustrated by recent natural disasters such as Hurricane Katrina in 2005. Evacuation planning and response hinged on the effective management of the population, including communication and leadership. Lack of planning, uncertainty of responsibilities, and poor trans-event management/coordination of the human response at all levels of government greatly exacerbated the disaster's consequences. A complete approach to infrastructure assurance must include the human factor.

Science and technology have long been key components to defending the nation and its citizens from its enemies and in increasing the resilience of infrastructure systems from natural disasters. In the post-9/11 environment, threats to the homeland increasingly include nonmilitary, transnational organizations. Along with sound public policy and law, technological innovations will factor heavily into solutions created for the DHS.

History of Critical Infrastructure Protection Policy in the United States

Historically, the United States has been shielded geographically from physical threats to the nation's infrastructures. With friendly neighbors to the north and south and vast oceans to the east and west, America was somewhat isolated from attacks by external enemies. In the early 1950s, technological developments in the nuclear field allowed for the creation of improved weapons, including intercontinental ballistic missiles (ICBM; The White House 1997, 7). Both military installations and civilian infrastructures were at risk of attack from these long-range weapons. The threat posed by the former Soviet Union and its nuclear ICBM capabilities was unique in American history. An enemy had never before threatened the United States from such a great distance. Technological advances in physical destruction capabilities put American soil in danger of attack.

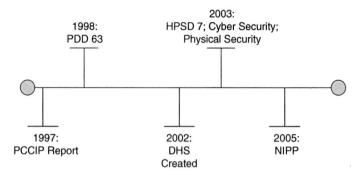

Figure 5.1 Timeline of Key National Policy Initiatives.

More recently, advances in information technology (IT) have led to increased vulnerability. Reliance upon computer-based systems is not a new phenomenon but with the increased propagation of worms, viruses, and malicious software code, added attention must be placed on the computer networks that operate many of our critical infrastructure systems. National-level efforts focused on improving cyber security received increased attention following the President's Commission on Critical Infrastructure Protection Report (PCCIP) in 1997 and in preparation for the Y2K bug. The National Cyber Security Summit, sponsored by the DHS, was held in December 2003. This important meeting brought together leaders from across the nation to make recommendations for solutions to the challenges posed in the *President's National Strategy to Secure Cyberspace*. (Figure 5.1 Timeline of Key National Polity Initiatives.)

Prior to the late 1990s, federal policy addressing infrastructure protection was scarce. Not until the PCCIP published its final report, *Critical Foundations: Protecting America's Infrastructures* in 1997, did a national-level policy initiative exist. This report was the guiding force in establishing future efforts with critical infrastructure protection. Major findings from this report include (The White House, 1997):

- Information sharing is the most immediate need.
- Responsibility is shared among owners/operators and the government.
- Infrastructure protection requires integrated capabilities of diverse federal agencies, and special means for coordinating federal response to ensure these capabilities are melded together effectively.
- The challenge is one of adapting to a changing culture.
- The federal government has important roles in the new infrastructure protection alliance with industry and state and local governments.
- The existing legal framework is imperfectly attuned to deal with cyber threats.
- Research and development are not presently adequate to support infrastructure protection.

Critical Foundations emphasized the emerging and expanding threats to infrastructure systems from cyber attacks and increased attention was given by this report to the reliance of physical systems on cyber networks. Through the report, the President's Commission argued for increased sharing of information between government and industry as a means of improving the overall resiliency of critical systems. The recommendations made by this Presidential Commission helped to shape the future path of infrastructure protection as many of the concepts introduced in *Critical Foundations* continue to be advocated in current policies and initiatives.

In response to the PCCIP report, President Clinton released the PDD 63 in 1998, which became the seminal document guiding U.S. policy in the arena of critical infrastructure protection. In PDD 63, the Clinton administration stated that the, "United States will take all necessary measures to swiftly eliminate any significant vulnerability to both physical and cyber attacks on our critical infrastructures, including especially our cyber systems" (The White House 1998). As noted in the plan, "No later than the year 2000, the United States shall have achieved an initial operating capability and no later than five years from the day the president signed Presidential Decision Directive 63 the United States shall have achieved and shall maintain the ability to protect our nation's critical infrastructures from intentional acts that would significantly diminish the abilities of:

- the Federal Government to perform essential national security missions and to ensure the general public health and safety;
- state and local governments to maintain order and to deliver minimum essential public services;
- the private sector to ensure the orderly functioning of the economy and the delivery of essential telecommunications, energy, financial and transportation services." (The White House 1998)

A major goal of PDD 63 was to establish robust public–private partnerships to ensure the sharing of information between government and the private sector through the establishment of Information Sharing and Analysis Centers. The presidential directive stated, "Since the targets of attacks on the nation's critical infrastructure would likely include both facilities in the economy and those in the government, the elimination of our potential vulnerability requires a closely coordinated effort of both the public and the private sector" (The White House 1998). It was estimated that 80–90 percent (The White House 1997) of the nation's critical infrastructures are owned and operated by the private sector. PDD 63 sought to "eliminate the vulnerabilities of our critical infrastructure," and recommended that "the U.S. government should, to the extent feasible, seek to avoid outcomes that increase government regulation or expand unfunded government mandates to the private sector" (The White House 1998). Individuals from the public and private sectors were asked to work together to develop a National Infrastructure Assurance Plan by:

- assessing the vulnerabilities of the sector to cyber or physical attacks;
- recommending a plan to eliminate significant vulnerabilities;
- proposing a system for identifying and preventing attempted major attacks;
- developing a plan for alerting, containing, and rebuffing an attack in progress and then, in coordination with FEMA as appropriate, rapidly reconstituting minimum essential capabilities in the aftermath of an attack. (The White House 1998)

Since 9/11, the federal government has released four national strategy documents that outline the federal government's agenda for infrastructure assurance. These publications address homeland security, both physical and cyber security, and explicitly mention the role that science and technology and public policy communities can play in finding solutions to combat threats to infrastructure systems. Recommended national strategy technology focus areas included:

- *Homeland Security.* Develop chemical, biological, radiological, and nuclear countermeasures; develop systems for detecting hostile intent; apply biometric technology to identification devices; improve technical capabilities of first responders; coordinate research and development of the homeland security apparatus; establish a national laboratory of homeland security; solicit independent and private analysis for science and technology research; establish a mechanism for rapidly producing prototypes; conduct demonstrations and pilot deployments; set standards for homeland security technology; and establish a system for high risk, high payoff homeland security research (Office of Homeland Security 2002, 68–69).
- *Securing Cyberspace.* Review and exercise IT continuity plans; DHS will lead in the development and will conduct a national threat assessment, including red teaming, blue teaming and other methods to identify the impact of possible attacks; adoption of improved security protocols; development of more secure router technology; adoption of a "code of good conduct"; develop best practices and new technology to increase security of SCADA that will determine the most critical SCADA-related sites; encourage the software industry to consider more secure "out-of-the-box" installation and implementation of their products; research and development in areas of intrusion detection, Internet infrastructure security, application security, denial of service, communications security, high assurance systems, and secure system composition (The White House 2003a, 53–60).
- *Physical Protection.* Advance modeling, simulation, and analysis capabilities and include an effort to enhance data collection and standardization; enhance detection and testing capabilities with agriculture and food networks; assess transportation and security risks; improve monitoring of the water sector; enhance surveillance and communications capabilities; develop redundant communications systems for emergency response agencies; expand infrastructure diverse routing capability in the telecommunications sector; develop a national system for measures to reconstitute capabilities of individual facilities and systems within the energy sector; increase cargo screening capabilities for the transportation sector; enhance exchange of security-related information in the finance sector.
- *National Infrastructure Protection Plan.* Protect critical infrastructure and key resources against plausible and specific threats; long-term reduction of critical infrastructure and key resources vulnerabilities in a comprehensive and integrated manner; maximize efficient use of resources for infrastructure protection; build partnerships among federal, state, local, tribal, international, and private sector stakeholders to implement critical infrastructure protection programs; continuously track and improve national protection.

Interdependencies among Critical Infrastructure Systems

We must first examine the scope in which critical infrastructures rely on technology before exploring ways in which public policy can be developed to address the security needs within critical infrastructure and information assurance. The most commonly used and farthest-reaching technology is the IT infrastructure. Without computers and networks, our economic and infrastructure systems would not function as we have become accustomed. A network of networks now directly supports operations within all sectors of the nation's economy: energy (electricity, oil, gas), transportation (rail, air), finance and banking, telecommunications, public health, emergency services, water, chemical, defense, food, agriculture, and postal (The White House 2003a, 6). A graphical representation of these interconnected systems can be found in figure 5.2. Physical infrastructures such as electrical transformers, trains, pipeline pumps, chemical vats, and radars are also dependent on computer networks (The White House 2003a, 6).

These networks are vulnerable to many types of cyber threats (including terrorist attacks, economic espionage, and random failures) and present new challenges to owners and operators of the nation's infrastructures. The high degree of automation and interconnectivity of computer networks, however, subjects them to potentially crippling and catastrophic attacks or failures.

Hazards and Threats to Critical Infrastructure Systems

The list of hazards and threats that exist to both physical and cyber components of our infrastructure is quite long. Major hazard categories include natural disasters,

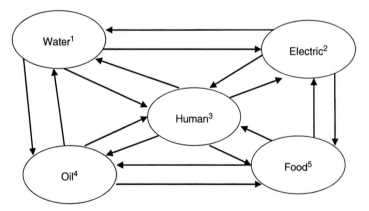

Figure 5.2 Critical Infrastructure Interdependencies.

1 = **Water infrastructure** supplies water for cooling, emissions reductions, production, and drinking for other infrastructures. It receives power for pumps and control stations, and human support and maintenance.
2 = **Electrical infrastructure** supplies energy to other infrastructures operations it receives fuel, cooling material, and human support and maintenance.
3 = **Human infrastructure** supplies intellectual operation of other infrastructures, innovation for increased efficiency, security, and organizational environment. It receives end product services from all other infrastructures.
4 = **Oil infrastructure** supplies fuel for other infrastructures. It receives cooling material, energy for pumps and operation, and human support and maintenance.
5 = **Food infrastructure** supplies food to human infrastructure to sustain its function, and supplies raw materials for alternative fuels. It receives energy, water for irrigation, fuel for equipment, and human support and maintenance.
* Adapted from Rinaldi, Peerenboom, and Kelly, 2001

Source: Barnes and Newbold 2005.

terrorist activities, human error, WMDs, and mechanical failure. Solutions that combine technology with multidisciplinary research provide the most complete answers to infrastructure assurance problems.

In the past decade, attacks against physical infrastructures have been executed successfully by exploiting technology. For instance, in the 1993 attack on the World Trade Center, a truck bomb was used. In 1995, a disgruntled citizen using simple technologies and common products detonated a truck bomb at the Murrah Federal office building in Oklahoma City. Moreover, the tragic events of 9/11 opened a new mode of threats to the nation's infrastructure—the use of civilian transportation systems as weapons. Based on these precedents, we need to be on guard to anticipate and prevent terrorist use of common commercial systems and technology that is readily available within our borders. Cyber threats to infrastructure systems are dissimilar to physical threats. The cyber threat spectrum to networks includes:

- isolated hacker attacks that spread nuisance viruses;
- major coordinated, multipronged terrorist or state-sponsored attacks that sever connections between networks or shut down networks (e.g., via distributed denial of service attacks), modify, delete, or destroy critical information residing on those networks; and
- major coordinated, multipronged attacks that physically destroy the hardware and software components comprising the networks.

A primary concern is the threat of organized cyber attacks that can debilitate our nation's critical infrastructure, economy, or national security (The White House 2003a). Computer networks can be attacked with little or no warning and cascade rapidly such that victims may not have time to respond. Even with warnings, victims may not have access to the proper tools and technologies to defend themselves. Efforts are underway worldwide to create models to simulate and visualize infrastructure networks. Figures 5.3 and 5.4 highlight two software tools being developed at James Madison University, with funding through the Critical Infrastructure Protection Project, which address specific infrastructure sectors, but are also able to model multiple infrastructure interdependencies.

In the past, geography played a large role in securing American infrastructure. Today, geography has become irrelevant as a defense against cyber attacks since these can be launched from anywhere in the world. Cyber attacks pose a unique set of legal questions as traditional boundaries and laws often differ from nation to nation. The Critical Infrastructure Protection Project at George Mason University has taken on the challenge of these complex legal issues and currently serves as the coordinating agency for the Information Sharing and Analysis Centers instituted in PDD 63. In addition to technical solutions, the development of legal means to prosecute cyber crimes across political boundaries is an extremely important part of the solution.

In addition to serving as a weapon and conduit for attacks, the IT infrastructure is, itself, an enticing target for attackers. Most other critical infrastructures rely on the IT infrastructure for data transmission and system control functions. A successful strike on critical IT networks could seriously impact the flow of necessary goods and services (food, water, electricity) and could also cause the loss of revenue and intellectual property, or, in the worst case, loss of life (The White House 2003a, 31).

107

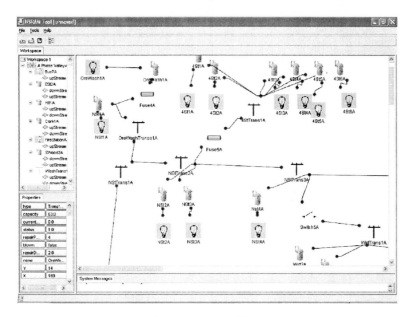

Figure 5.3 Network Security Risk Assessment Modeling Tool.
Source: Baker 2004.

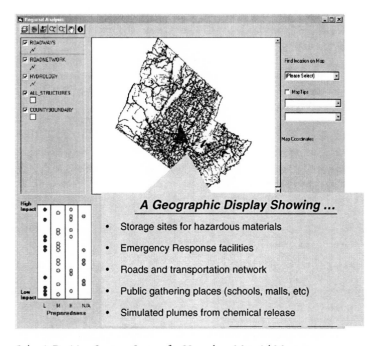

Figure 5.4 A Decision Support System for Hazardous Material Management.
Source: Deaton 2004.

An attack on the IT infrastructure can occur in three different modes. First, the action can come through the wires (i.e., virus, denial of service). Second, it can include the physical destruction of an IT element such as a communications center. And third, an attack can rely on the compromising of a trusted insider, for example, someone who may provide passwords to unauthorized personnel to gain entry (The White House 2003a, 42).

Cyber attacks are not the only threat to computers and networks supporting our infrastructures. Routine failures, poor software development, and human error should also be considered as vulnerabilities. Strong information security policy is of utmost importance; the physical security and building design are also critical. The location of computers and servers must be well planned to prevent damage from hazards such as flooding, fire, explosion, and intrusion. Fiber optic cable must be protected as well to prevent accidental damage from digging and malicious cutting of wires. Co-location of wires and cables introduces common, serious single-point failure vulnerabilities to be avoided in protection design. Consequences of cable co-location were evidenced by the Baltimore train fire of 2001. This accident occurred in a tunnel with co-located fiber optic cables whose failure interrupted telecommunications and Internet connectivity along the Washington–New York corridor.

In an increasingly complex and interconnected global community, the reliance on computers to store, transmit, and process data has grown exponentially. Wireless technology applications continue to increase society's dependence on the cyber infrastructure for communication and business processes. Private sector businesses, governments, and individuals have all become more reliant on IT to perform routine tasks. "Information security" has become extremely important and involves securing and ensuring the integrity of this data through technical savvy, strong policies, and ethical behavior in cyberspace.

Given the ubiquitous nature of computer networks and the reliance on cyber systems within everyday life, all segments of society play a role in securing cyberspace. The *National Strategy to Secure Cyberspace* released by the DHS in 2003 recommends five priorities to improve the security of cyber networks:

1. A National Cyber security Response System
2. A National Cyber security Threat and Vulnerability Reduction Program
3. A National Cyber security Awareness and Training Program
4. Securing Government's Cyberspace
5. National Security and International Cyberspace Security Cooperation

In order to accomplish the goals and objectives expressed in the National Strategy to Secure Cyberspace, individuals and organizations must be empowered through (The White House 2003a):

- *Awareness and Information.* Users and owners of cyberspace must be educated and trained on the risks and vulnerabilities of computer systems and means available to mitigate these risks.
- *Technology and Tools.* New and more secure technologies must be produced and implemented quickly.

- *Training and Education.* A large and well-trained cyber security workforce must be developed to meet the needs of government and industry.
- *Roles and Partnerships.* Responsibility must be fostered through the use of market forces, education and volunteer efforts, public–private partnerships, and, as a last resort, regulation and legislation.
- *Federal Leadership.* Improve federal cyber security to make it a model for other sectors in implementing, practicing, and assessing cyber security methods.
- *Coordination and Crisis Management.* Early warning and efficient information sharing systems between the public and private sectors to detect and respond to cyber attacks.

The Role of the DHS

Critical infrastructure protection and cyber security initiatives are major components of the efforts of the DHS. Figure 5.5 illustrates the organizational structure of the infrastructure and information assurance leadership within the leadership of DHS. The assistant secretary for Cyber Security and Telecommunications is responsible for identifying and assessing the vulnerability of critical telecommunications infrastructure and assets; providing timely, actionable, and valuable threat information; and leading the national response to cyber and telecommunications attacks. There is also an assistant secretary for Infrastructure Protection who is charged with cataloging the nation's critical infrastructure and key resources and coordinating risk-based strategies and protective measures to secure them from terrorist attack.

As the cognizant agency for coordinating federal activities within the area of infrastructure protection and information assurance, the DHS has established programs that address policy and action necessary for the continued operation of the nation's critical systems. It is through these programs that preparedness and response activities are developed and implemented.

Critical Infrastructure Protection and Response

One major DHS initiative is the Protected Critical Infrastructure Information Program (PCII), which is designed to encourage private industry and others with knowledge about our critical infrastructure to share sensitive and proprietary business

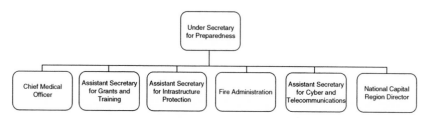

Figure 5.5 Organization of the Department of Homeland Security (Infrastructure/Information Protection).

Source: Department of Homeland Security 2005b.

information with the government. This program is used in pursuit of a more secure homeland, focusing primarily on analyzing and securing critical infrastructure and protected systems, developing risk and vulnerability assessments assisting with recovery (Department of Homeland Security 2006).

The PCII was established in accordance with the Critical Infrastructure Information Act of 2002. It creates a new framework that enables members of the private sector to voluntarily submit sensitive information regarding the nation's critical infrastructure to the DHS with the assurance that the information, if it satisfies the requirements of the Critical Infrastructure Information Act, will be protected from public disclosure. This program is managed by the PCII Office, which receives, validates, disseminates, and safeguards sensitive critical infrastructure information.

Knowledge gathered through this program may be used for many purposes, focusing primarily on analyzing and securing critical infrastructure and protected systems, risk and vulnerabilities assessments, and assisting with recovery as appropriate. The Preparedness Directorate plays a critical role in securing the homeland by identifying and assessing threats and mapping those threats against vulnerabilities such as critical infrastructure.

HSOC

A second key initiative is the establishment of the HSOC, which serves as the nation's center for information sharing and domestic incident management. One of the goals of this effort is to dramatically increase the coordination among federal, state, territorial, tribal, local, and private sector partners who provide constant watch for the safety of our nation (www.dhs.gov). The center includes partners from over thirty-five agencies and receives hundreds of calls, in its effort to collect and fuse information from a variety of sources everyday to help deter, detect, and prevent terrorist acts; they address about twenty incidents or cases per day. The HSOC is in constant communication with the White House, serving as a conduit of information for the White House Situation Room by providing the intelligence needed to make decisions and define courses of action. The information gathered and analyzed by the HSOC provides real-time situational awareness in monitoring the homeland. This program also coordinates incident and response activities, and issues advisories and bulletins concerning threats, as well as specific protective measures. Information on domestic incident management is shared with Emergency Operations Centers at all levels through the Homeland Security Information Network (HSIN).

Information is shared and fused on a daily basis by the two halves of the HSOC that are referred to as the "Intelligence Side" and the "Law Enforcement Side." Each half is identical and functions in conjunction with the other but requires a different level of clearance to access information. The "Intelligence Side" focuses on pieces of highly classified information and how specific details contribute to the current threat for any given area. The "Law Enforcement Side" is dedicated to tracking the different enforcement activities across the country that may have a terrorist nexus (www.dhs.gov). These efforts highlight the relationships and coordination between all levels of government: federal, state, and local. Without the cooperation between law enforcement agencies at all levels, the HSOC would not be effective in its efforts to thwart terrorist activities.

The HSOC communicates in real-time to its partners through the HSIN's Internet-based counterterrorism communications tool. This tool supplies information to all fifty states, Washington, D.C., and more than fifty major urban areas. Threat information is exchanged with state and local partners at the Sensitive-but-Unclassified level. Future plans for this program include linking additional cities and counties, communication capabilities at the classified secret level, and increasing the involvement and integration of the private sector. Participants in the HSIN include governors, mayors, state Homeland Security Advisors, state National Guard offices, Emergency Operations Centers, First Responders and Public Safety departments, and other key homeland security partners (Department of Homeland Security 2006).

Through this network, DHS has the capacity to send alerts and notifications to the private sector at a rate of (Department of Homeland Security 2006):

- 10,000 simultaneous outbound voice calls per minute
- 30,000 inbound simultaneous calls (hot line scenario)
- 3,000 outbound simultaneous faxes
- 5,000 outbound simultaneous Internet e-mails
- Immediate Internet website content changes made

The HSOC regularly disseminates domestic terrorism-related information generated by the IAIP. Information released by the HSOC comes in two forms:

1. *Homeland Security Threat Advisories.* These are the result of information analysis and contain actionable information about an incident involving, or a threat targeting, critical national networks, infrastructures, or key assets. They often relay newly developed procedures that, when implemented, significantly improve security and protection. Advisories also often suggest a change in readiness posture, protective actions, or response.

2. *Homeland Security Information Bulletins.* These are protection products that communicate information of interest to the nation's critical infrastructures that do not meet the timeliness, specificity, or significance thresholds of warning messages. Such information may include statistical reports, periodic summaries, incident response or reporting guidelines, common vulnerabilities and patches, and configuration standards or tools.

In March 2002, President Bush unveiled the HSAS as a tool to improve coordination and communication among all levels of government, the private sector, and the American public in the fight against terrorism. The Advisory System not only identifies the "Threat Condition," but also outlines protective measures that can be taken by partner agencies. The federal government, states, and the private sector each have a set of plans and protective measures that are implemented as the "Threat Condition" is raised or lowered, thus flexibly mitigating our vulnerability to attack. The HSOC is the distributor of the recommended security measures to our state and local partners when the threat level is raised or lowered.

The HSOC monitors vulnerabilities and compares them against threats and pertinent intelligence, providing a centralized, real-time flow of information between homeland security partners. This data collected from across the country is then compiled into a master template, which allows the HSOC to provide a visual picture of the nation's current threat status (www.dhs.gov). The HSOC has the capability to:

- Perform an initial assessment of the information to gauge the terrorist nexus
- Track operational actions taking place across the country in response to the intelligence information
- Disseminate notifications and alerts about the information and any decisions made

As information is shared across agencies, HSOC staff can utilize visualization tools by cross-referencing human intelligence against geospatial data that can isolate an area of interest on the Earth's surface. Satellite technology is then able to transmit pictures of the site in question directly into the HSOC. This type of geographic data can be stored to create a library of images that can be mapped against future threats and shared with our state and local partners.

The Interagency Incident Management Group (IIMG)is based in Washington, D.C., and comprises senior representatives from DHS, other federal departments and agencies, and nongovernmental organizations (NGOs). The IIMG provides strategic situational awareness, synthesizes key intelligence and operational information, frames courses of action and policy recommendations, anticipates evolving requirements, and provides decision support to the secretary of Homeland Security and other national authorities during periods of elevated alert and national domestic incidents.

During incidents such as Hurricanes Isabel (2003), Katrina (2005), Rita (2005), and Wilma (2005); the December 2003 Orange Alert; and the Northeast blackout, the IIMG was activated in less than ninety minutes and hosted assistant secretary–level members of federal agencies to provide strategic leadership (Department of Homeland Security 2006).

Along with the critical infrastructure initiatives discussed above, the DHS is also focused on improving cyber security efforts. As discussed earlier in this chapter, the consequences of an attack on our cyber infrastructure can cascade across many sectors, causing widespread disruption of essential services, damaging our economy, and imperiling public safety. (Box 5.2 shows Infrastructure and information assurance initiatives within the DHS.)

The speed and maliciousness of cyber attacks have increased dramatically in recent years. Accordingly, the Preparedness Directorate places an especially high priority on protecting our cyber infrastructure from terrorist attack by unifying and focusing the key cyber security activities. The Directorate augments the capabilities of the federal government with the response functions of the National Cyber Security Division of the United States Computer Emergency Response Team (US-CERT). Due to the interconnected nature of information and telecommunications sectors, the DHS will also assume the functions and assets of the National Communications System within the DoD, which coordinates emergency preparedness for the telecommunications sector.

Box 5.2 Infrastructure and Information Assurance Initiatives Within the DHS (Department of Homeland Security 2005).

- Protected Critical Infrastructure Information (PCII) Program
- Homeland Security Operations Center (HSOC)
- Homeland Security Information Network (HSIN)
- Homeland Security Advisory System (HSAS)
- Interagency Incident Management Group (IIMG)
- United States Computer Emergency Response Team (US-CERT)
- National Communications System

Providing indications and warning advisories is a major function of the DHS's efforts within cyber security. In advance of real-time crisis or attack, Preparedness will provide:

- threat warnings and advisories against the homeland including physical and cyber events;
- processes to develop and issue national and sector-specific threat advisories through the HSAS;
- terrorist threat information for release to the public, private industry, or state and local government.

Given the distributed nature of the nation's infrastructure systems, the sharing of information between the public and private sectors and across the critical infrastructure sectors is imperative. As discussed above, the DHS places a priority on initiatives that emphasize and facilitate the flow of information crucial to preventing or responding to a disaster. Though the DHS has focused on the area of information sharing, greater efforts need to be taken to engage the appropriate participants. Without coordinated activities at the federal level, policymakers may be missing crucial information in a time of crisis. Data gathered by the DHS must be verified and trustworthy before details are released to localities and the communication of threats needs to be articulated clearly in order for appropriate measures to be taken. Other chapters in this book address the issues of information integrity and communication. It is key to remember that coordination of efforts in the areas of infrastructure protection and information assurance relies on accurate and well-communicated details.

Prior to the creation of the DHS, the responsibility for the nation's efforts to secure cyberspace and protect critical infrastructure was distributed within a number of federal agencies. Today, the DHS is the primary organization for all cyber and physical security initiatives. The programs highlighted above address the key areas of focus for the DHS as the organization addresses an ever-evolving and growing number of threats. All levels of government are important stakeholders in securing critical assets; however, only with cooperation from the private sector and individual citizens will the efforts of the DHS be effective.

Case Study: 2003 Blackout

We can learn much from major infrastructure system failures of the past. This case study examines a recent widespread outage of the Northeast electric power grid.

On August 14, 2003, a series of events unfolded, which caused a loss of power for residents of Ontario, Canada, and the northeastern United States. This was the largest blackout in North American history. Approximately forty million Americans and ten million Canadians lost power and experienced the adverse effects of the resulting cascading failures of water distribution, telecommunications, transportation, and power generation infrastructures. Outage related costs are estimated at $6 billion across eight affected states within the United States.

Before examining the specific details of the 2003 Blackout, an understanding of electric power distribution is necessary. Since electricity cannot easily be stored over extended periods of time, the demand load on any power grid must be matched by the supply generation and the ability to transmit that power. Any great overload of a power line or underload or overload of a generator can cause difficult-to-repair and costly damage. Monitoring systems are in place to disconnect the power grid if a serious imbalance is detected somewhere within the grid. Power-level changes from a line going out of service can cause cascading failures in adjoining areas as other parts of the system recognize the fluctuations. These fluctuations are normally controlled by delays built into the shutdown processes and by robust power networks with many alternative paths for power to take, which have the effect of reducing the size of the ripples.

The operators of electric power distribution facilities are responsible for ensuring that they balance the supply of power with the demand and the capacity of transmission lines, so that their system is in a state where no single fault can cause the entire system to fail. After a system failure, operators are required, within thirty minutes, to obtain more power from generators or other regions, or to offload demand by cutting power to some areas within their network. Remedial measures are pursued until operators are confident that the worst remaining possible failure anywhere in the system won't cause a system collapse. In an emergency situation, power suppliers are expected to immediately shed load as required to stabilize the system.

Operators are assisted by computer systems, with backups, that issue alarms when there are faults in the transmission or generation system. Power flow modeling tools exist, which allow operators to analyze what is currently happening across their network; they predict whether any parts of the grid may be overloaded or imbalanced so a change in power generation levels can be made if necessary. If computer systems and backups fail, operators are required to analyze the data manually. Backing up the local operators are regional coordinating centers that bring together information from adjacent areas and perform larger-scale checks on the system, looking for possible failures and alerting operators in different systems to any system imbalance.

Timeline of Events: August 14, 2003

- 2 p.m. FirstEnergy's Eastlake Unit 5, a 680-megawatt coal generation plant in Eastlake, Ohio, trips off. A giant puff of ash from the plant rains down on neighbors. On a hot summer afternoon, this "wasn't a unique event in and of itself," says Ralph DiNicola, spokesman for Akron, Ohio-based FirstEnergy. "We had some transmission lines out of service and the Eastlake system tripped out of service, but we didn't have any outages related to those events."

- 3:06 p.m. FirstEnergy's Chamberlin–Harding power transmission line, a 345-kilovolt power line in northeastern Ohio, trips. The company hasn't reported a cause, but the outage put extra strain on FirstEnergy's Hanna–Juniper line, the next to go dark.
- 3:32 p.m. Extra power coursing through FirstEnergy's Hanna–Juniper 345-kilovolt line heats the wires, causing them to sag into a tree and trip.
- 3:41 p.m. An overload on First Energy's Star–South Canton 345-kilovolt line trips a breaker at the Star switching station, where FirstEnergy's grid interconnects with a neighboring grid owned by the American Electric Power Co. AEP's Star station is also in northeastern Ohio.
- 3:46 p.m. AEP's 345-kilovolt Tidd–Canton Control transmission line also trips where it interconnects with FirstEnergy's grid, at AEP's connection station in Canton, Ohio.
- 4:06 p.m. FirstEnergy's Sammis–Star 345-kilovolt line, also in northeast Ohio, trips, then reconnects.
- 4:08 p.m. Utilities in Canada and the eastern United States see wild power swings. "It was a hopscotch event, not a big cascading domino effect," says Sean O'Leary, chief executive of Genscape, a company that monitors electric transmissions.
- 4:09 p.m. The already lowered voltage coursing to customers of Cleveland Public Power, inside the city of Cleveland, plummets to zero. "It was like taking a light switch and turning it off," says Jim Majer, commissioner of Cleveland Public Power. "It was like a heart attack. It went straight down from 300 megawatts to zero."
- 4:10 p.m. The Campbell No. 3 coal-fired power plant near Grand Haven, Michigan, trips off.
- 4:10 p.m. A 345-kilovolt line known as Hampton–Thetford, in Michigan, trips.
- 4:10 p.m. A 345-kilovolt line known as Oneida–Majestic, also in Michigan, trips.
- 4:11 p.m. Orion Avon Lake Unit 9, a coal-fired power plant in Avon Lake, Ohio, trips.
- 4:11 p.m. A transmission line running along the Lake Erie shore to the Davis–Besse nuclear plant near Toledo, Ohio, trips.
- 4:11 p.m. A transmission line in northwest Ohio connecting Midway, Lemoyne, and Foster substations trips.
- 4:11 p.m. The Perry Unit 1 nuclear reactor in Perry, Ohio, shuts down automatically after losing power.
- 4:11 p.m. The FitzPatrick nuclear reactor in Oswego, New York, shuts down automatically after losing power.
- 4:12 p.m. The Bruce Nuclear station in Ontario, Canada, shuts down automatically after losing power.
- 4:12 p.m. Rochester Gas & Electric's Ginna nuclear plant near Rochester, New York, shuts down automatically after losing power.
- 4:12 p.m. Nine Mile Point nuclear reactor near Oswego, New York, shuts down automatically after losing power.
- 4:15 p.m. FirstEnergy's Sammis–Star 345-kilovolt line, in northeast Ohio, trips and reconnects a second time.
- 4:16 p.m. Oyster Creek nuclear plant in Forked River, New Jersey, shuts down automatically because of power fluctuations on the grid.

- 4:17 p.m. The Enrico Fermi Nuclear plant near Detroit shuts down automatically after losing power.
- 4:17–4:21 p.m. Numerous power transmission lines in Michigan trip.
- 4:25 p.m. Indian Point nuclear power plants 2 and 3 in Buchanan, New York, shut down automatically after losing power.

On November 19, 2003, the U.S.-Canada Power System Outage Task Force released a report placing the cause of the blackout on FirstEnergy Corporation's failure to trim trees in part of its Ohio service area. Despite claims by terrorist groups such as al-Qaeda, this report finds the blackout to be caused by a technological failure and lack of proper monitoring by systems in place to prevent such a cascading event. The report said that a generating plant in the Cleveland, Ohio, area went off-line amid high electrical demand; strained high-voltage power lines later went out of service when they came in contact with "overgrown trees." It also found that FirstEnergy did not take remedial action or warn other control centers until it was too late because of a bug in computer-based monitoring systems that prevented alarms from showing on FirstEnergy's control system. Adequate staff was not available to detect and correct the software bug. The cascading effect that resulted ultimately forced the shutdown of more than 100 power plants across the United States and Canada.

The example of the 2003 Northeast Blackout provides unique insight into the deeply interconnected nature of our infrastructure networks and the reliance physical systems have on computer systems. By examining this failure, it is evident that the nation's infrastructure comprises a complex network that is reliable yet can be fragile and fail with even a minor insult such as a tree branch falling in Ohio (U.S.–Canada Power Systems Outage Task Force 2004, 31–45).

Discussion Questions

1. What could have been done to prevent such as widespread power outage?
2. Technological solutions are not the only options available to address critical infrastructure failures, what can be done through policy to improve the resiliency of these systems?
3. What policy changes could be made to prevent a similar widespread failure of the energy, telecommunications or other critical infrastructures?

Key Terms and Definitions

Blue Team. Used in wargaming and simulations, a blue team is the defending force in a simulated military conflict.

cascading failure. Failure in a system of interconnected parts, where the service provided depends on the operation of a preceding part, and the failure of a preceding part can trigger the failure of successive parts.

critical infrastructure. Systems and assets, whether physical or virtual, so vital to the United States that the incapacity or destruction of such systems and assets would have a debilitating impact on security, national economic security, national public health or safety, or any combination of these matters.

distributed denial of service. Attack in which a multitude of compromised systems attack a single target, thereby causing denial of service for users of the targeted system. The flood of incoming messages to the target system essentially forces it to shut down, thereby denying service to the system to legitimate users.

key assets. Individual targets whose destruction could cause large-scale injury, death, or destruction of property, and/or profoundly damage our national prestige and confidence.

malicious software code. Programming or files developed for the purpose of doing harm.

Red Team. Used in wargaming and simulations, a red team is the opposing force in a simulated military conflict.

risk assessment. Produced from the combination of threat and vulnerability assessments. Characterized by analyzing the probability of destruction or incapacitation resulting from a threat's exploitation of a critical infrastructure's vulnerabilities.

viruses. A program or piece of code that is loaded onto a computer without the knowledge of the user and runs against the user's wishes.

vulnerability assessment. Systematic examination of a critical infrastructure, the interconnected systems on which it relies, its information, or product to determine the adequacy of security measures, identity security deficiencies, evaluate security alternatives, and verify the adequacy of such measures after implementation.

Worms. A worm is a special type of virus that can replicate itself and use memory, but cannot attach itself to other programs.

Additional Resources

The following organizations and articles provide additional information related to the field of critical infrastructure protection and information security.

- DHS Daily Open Source Infrastructure Report: <www.dhs.gov/dhspublic/display?content=4689>
- National Infrastructure Advisory Council: <www.dhs.gov/dhspublic/display?theme=9&content=4278>
- United States Computer Emergency Response Team (US-CERT): <www.us-cert.gov>
- Federal Bureau of Investigations Infragard Program:
- North American Electric Reliability Council (NERC): <http://www.nerc.com/>
- Institute for Infrastructure and Information Assurance: <http://www.jmu.edu/iiia>
- Critical Infrastructure Protection Program: <http://cipp.gmu.edu/>
- Institute for Information Infrastructure Protection: <http://www.thei3p.org/>

References

Baker, George. 2004. *Critical infrastructure protection program workshop I working papers.* George Mason University Press.

Barnes, Joshua and Newbold, Kenneth. 2005. *Humans as a critical infrastructure.* IEEE Critical Infrastructure Protection Conference.

Deaton, Michael. 2004. *Critical infrastructure protection program workshop I working papers.* George Mason University Press.

Department of Homeland Security. 2005a. *Interim National Infrastructure Protection Plan.* Washington, D.C.

———. 2005b. Strategic plan. <http://www.dhs.gov/interweb/assetlibrary/DHS_StratPlan_FINAL_spread.pdf>.

———. 2006. <www.dhs.gov>.

Office of Homeland Security. 2002. *National strategy for homeland security.* Washington, D.C.

U.S.-Canada Power System Outage Task Force. 2004. Final report on the August 14, 2003 blackout in the United States and Canada: Causes and recommendations.

USA PATRIOT Act. 2001. 42 USC 5195c(e).

The White House. 1997. *Critical foundations: Protecting America's infrastructures.* Washington, D.C.

———. 1998. *Presidential Decision Directive 63.* Washington, D.C.

———. 2003a. *National strategy to secure cyberspace.* Washington, D.C.

———. 2003b. *National Strategy for physical protection of critical infrastructures and key assets.* Washington, D.C.

CHAPTER SIX

RISK COMMUNICATION,
PSYCHOLOGICAL MANAGEMENT, AND
DISASTER PREPAREDNESS

Table Top: DC Sniper Attacks

The DC sniper attacks by John Allen Muhammad and Lee Boyd Malvo terrorized the Baltimore/Washington, D.C., area for three weeks in October 2002. Armed with a Bushmaster XM-15 semiautomatic .223 caliber rifle, the pair claimed ten victims with an additional three injured. Muhammad and Malvo used a specially outfitted Chevrolet Caprice to carry out the attacks and elude the authorities. The car was modified so that a person could shoot from the trunk without the trunk door ever being open. In 2004, a jury handed down a death sentence to Muhammad and multiple life imprisonment sentences without the possibility of parole for Malvo's role in the shootings. Law enforcement officials have been praised for their identification and arrest of the DC snipers, but investigations have shown numerous areas where better communication practices could have ended the shooting spree sooner.

The most common tip the police received identified a white van at the scene of many of the shootings. This was a result of the "Be a Good Witness" fact sheet (see figure 6.1) distributed to Baltimore/Washington, D.C., residents to pay attention to the physical surroundings if they should be in the vicinity of an attack. With the focus on a white van, police dismissed numerous reports about a blue Chevrolet Caprice exiting some of the shooting locations. Furthermore, the license plate number of the Caprice had been written down numerous times during the investigation near the crime scenes.

In addition to the confusion caused by the focus on the wrong getaway vehicle, an acquaintance of Muhammad and Malvo, Harjeet Singh, alerted the FBI that the duo were likely to perform sniper attacks with the intent to kill. The FBI were unable to question Muhammad or Malvo before they were apprehended.

Setting aside ideology or prophetic motivations, one could argue the attacks were carried out for money. Notes were left at the crime scenes demanding $10,000,000 deposited into a bank account. The account was linked to a stolen credit card and closed six months earlier. A possible, but unconventional course of action might have been to reactivate the account and transfer the money. The crime scene notes specifically mentioned the use of an ATM card. If that were the case, law enforcement officers might have

How to be a Good Witness

The mantgomery County Police Department issued these suggestions yesterday:

❶ Remember personal safety comes first. If you hear a gunshot, get down and seek cover.

❷ Look in the direction of the sound, and make a note of people or vehicles in that area.

❸ Remember that some descriptive characteristics are permanent and some can be altered. Some elements can be changed more easily than others.

Some examples:

	Permanent	Temporary
People	Height / weight / build Complexion	Clothing / color Hairstyle or color, facial hair (beard or mustache)
Vehicles	Make Model	Color Tag number Denters / primer Lights on / off, broken / burned out

❹ Commit what you saw to memory. Keep a pen available; if paper is not available, write what you saw on your hand.

❺ Remain on the scene, in a safe place, untill police arrive.

❻ Do not allow another witness or media to contaminate your memory. Do not compare or discuss what you saw with another witness.

▪ TIP LINE
Police urge anyone with information related to the sniper attacks to call 1-888-324-9800.

Figure 6.1 How to Be a Good Witness Fact Sheet.

Source: Montgomery County Police Department

had the opportunity to track the withdrawals of Muhammad and Malvo, aiding in an earlier capture. How could better communication amongst the investigating authorities have eliminated the misguided pursuit of a white van? How can law enforcement agencies avoid jurisdictional boundaries to prevent the loss of valuable information? With the War on Terror reaching the continental United States through the sniper attacks was $10,000,000 an acceptable amount to risk for a possible arrest? (CNN, MSNBC, and *Washington Post* coverage)

Introduction

One of the leading post-9/11 concerns regarding homeland security is a trustworthy level of communication between the government and U.S. citizens. Major changes in intelligence gathering have been implemented since the devastating attacks. Thousands working for the government, private firms, and academia have researched and formed numerous emergency response plans, evacuation plans, disaster preparedness presentations, guidebooks and kits in order to better inform the public of the necessary changes vital for the security of the nation. Disseminating this information to the mass public engages a field known as risk communication. Risk communication addresses the current security beliefs in Washington, D.C., that the best way to keep American citizens informed is through a well-planned distribution system of preparedness materials and local planning. Municipal governments, civic organizations, and academic institutions can provide the medium to link terrorist, natural disaster, and technological disaster response plans to communities across the United States.

History of Risk Communication

The public interest in risk communication parallels the environmental movement of the 1970s. With various environmental and regulatory agencies established at the time, it appeared as though rapid progress on the environmental front had finally arrived. However, by 1979, two major incidents—the nuclear accident at Three Mile Island, PA and the chemical waste site at Love Canal, NY—changed the public's view of government with regard to environmental disasters, and ushered in the age of risk communication.

Four Stages of Risk Communication

The field of risk communication focuses on communicating risk and preparedness strategies with all stakeholders involved *before* an event occurs. It should not be confused with crisis communication, actions taken either *during* or *after* a catastrophic event occurs. Over the past twenty-five years there have been four distinct stages of risk communication as defined by risk communication expert Peter Sandman:

1. *Ignoring the Public.* The "government officials" deemed the public useless and ignorant. The government used a three-tier approach to diffuse the environmental issues of the day (nuclear power and toxic waste disposal): first, ignore the public's attempt to access the truth; second, mislead the public in various directions; and third, if one can get away with it, lie. Fortunately for the mass citizenry, this stage came to an end in the mid-1980s.

2. *Explaining Risk Data Better.* For the first time, risk communicators had a genuine desire to address public outcry and skepticism. The breakthrough in this stage was motivation. The more the public was motivated, the more they gained access to information. Standards were set governing the dissemination of risk communication materials at a sixth to ninth grade comprehension level, so that a maximum number of people could benefit. The motivation factor played a key role in helping the public focus on what risks were the most threatening. Until then, the public often over-analyzed dreadful risks that had small probabilities of ever occurring.

3. *Hazard and Outrage.* By the late 1980s, the United States reached the third stage of risk communication. Instead of handing out pamphlets with instructions to the public, risk communicators sought to open up a dialogue within communities about risk prevention. Peter Sandman coined the equation: Risk = Hazard + Outrage. This equation means that a person's perception of a Risk is determined by the Hazard, the statistics measuring the probabilities of a risk, combined with Outrage, the factors that cause a person to fear a risk. Also during this time, the Environmental Protection Agency, with the assistance of Vincent T. Covello,

published the *Seven Cardinal Rules of Risk Communication*. This publication describes how a risk communicator can effectively manage the many facets of a public response. The third stage's inclusion of hazard and outrage changed the focus of risk communication, "This new, expanded concept of 'risk' also pointed to the need for real dialogue among all the interested parties. It led to the then revolutionary idea that the essence of risk communication is not just explaining risk numbers—it is also reducing (or increasing) outrage" (Covello and Sandman 2004, 10).

4. *Treating the Public as a Full Partner*. The final stage of risk communication, engaging the public as an equal, is extremely difficult to implement and currently operates in a small percentage of public and private communication methodologies. One of the problems lies in the basic foundation of risk communication. It has always relied on the scientific method and expertise from the science and technology communities. Bringing nonexperts to the table as full partners may limit the science-based approach of the technical experts. The only way to fully shift into the fourth stage is for deliberate and noticeable changes within the government and private organizations that communicate with the public on risk issues (Covello and Sandman 2004, 10).

The Seven Cardinal Rules and
Seventy-Seven Questions

One of the first major publications to come out of the risk communication movement was the 1988 guide, *Seven Cardinal Rules of Risk Communication*, published by the Environmental Protection Agency based on the work of Vincent T. Covello and Frederick H. Allen. The guide lists seven basic rules about how to message the public, concerns of honesty and truthfulness, coordination efforts, dealing with the media, planning, and evaluating (see box 6.1).

Box 6.1 Seven Cardinal Rules of Risk Communication

Rule 1: Accept and involve the public as a legitimate partner. Disaster managers must realize in advance that the public is going to want to be involved and will find a way to be involved. It makes sense to openly include them early on.

Rule 2: Listen to the audience. An effective dialogue will occur only after the communicators find out what is important to the public. In some cases it may be trust, caring, and courtesy, whereas other communities will value quantitative statistics or a combination.

Rule 3: Be honest, frank, and open. The two greatest attributes in a risk communicator's arsenal are trust and credibility. These are judgments made early on and are highly resistant to change. If answers are unknown one should say, "We do not have the answer at this time, but are working on it." Lies and misleading statements will destroy any trust already gained.

Rule 4: Coordinate and collaborate with other credible sources. One of the best ways to ensure inter-organizational and intra-organizational lines of communication is to set up specific tasks early on. Agencies should know whom to contact outside of their team for information and have lines of communication already established. Once communication to the public takes place it will look much more credible coming from many highly trained sources.

Rule 5: Meet the needs of the media. Know what the media is interested in. "The media are generally more interested in politics than in risk; more interested in simplicity than in complexity; and more interested in wrongdoing, blame and danger than in safety" (Covello and Sandman 2004, 13). The overall goal with the media should be the same with the public—"establish long-term relationships of trust."

Rule 6: Speak clearly and with compassion. Overly technical speech damages risk communication more than it helps. Describe technical aspects only when necessary. The public is more concerned with empathy and caring over numbers.

Rule 7: Plan carefully and evaluate performance. This essentially reiterates what risk communication is—planning. Start early on with clear objectives. Properly train staff to deal with stakeholders, the public, and other technical workers.

Source: Covello and Sandman 2004.

Another useful guide is Covello's, *The Seventy-Seven Questions Commonly Asked by Journalists during a Crisis*, as a media-specific communication guide. Covello uses the five "w's"and one "h": who, what, when, where, why, and how combined with: what happened, what caused it to happen, and what does it mean to formulate the seventy-seven questions public relations and press representatives will most likely encounter from the media (Covello 2003).

Risk Communication Terminology

In the last ten years, certain aspects of risk communication have grown by leaps and bounds requiring subcategories. One of these facets is risk perception, a person's recognition of risk based on at least fifteen risk perception factors (see box 6.2). Examples of these factors include: (1) how familiar a person is with a risk; (2) the amount of dread that a particular risk evokes; (3) how personal a risk is to the stakeholder, which will determine "levels of concern, worry, anger, anxiety, fear, hostility, and outrage, which, in turn, can significantly change attitudes and behavior" (Covello et al. 2001, 6).

Understanding a person's risk perception is absolutely essential to communication goals. Unfortunately, this understanding is most notably utilized by terrorists. Terrorist attacks do not need to be large-scale strikes on national or international symbols to achieve their intended outcomes. Even small, relatively inexpensive attacks that claim few lives can cause an exorbitant amount of psychological damage to the public. This can cause losses in the millions of dollars through the economic impact of people feeling frightened, as exhibited by reduced activity and consumption. As discussed in chapter one, the psychology of terrorism is complex and driven by a variety of motivating factors. This chapter examines the psychological impact of terrorist activity and the means of limiting long-term effects. The goal of terrorists is not to kill or destroy, but to upset, frighten, create a sense of vulnerability, confusion, and ultimately a state of panic. As presented by Paul Slovic, "The power of terrorism lies precisely in its pervasive ambiguity, in its invasion of our minds" (Slovic 2003, 10). Reinforcing this idea is the work of the Harvard Center for Risk Analysis (2005). On the Center's website is a list of the average American's chance of dying in a particular

---

Box 6.2 Risk Perception Factors

1. *Voluntariness.* Risks perceived to be involuntary or imposed are less readily accepted and perceived to be greater than risks perceived to be voluntary.
2. *Controllability.* Risks perceived to be under the control of others are less readily accepted and perceived to be greater than risks perceived to be under the control of the individual.
3. *Familiarity.* Risks perceived to be unfamiliar are less readily accepted and perceived to be greater than risks perceived to be familiar.
4. *Equity.* Risks perceived as unevenly and inequitably distributed are less readily accepted than risks perceived as equitably shared.
5. *Benefits.* Risks perceived to have unclear or questionable benefits are less readily accepted and perceived to be greater than risks perceived to have clear benefits.
6. *Understanding.* Risks perceived to be poorly understood are less readily accepted and perceived to be greater than risks from activities perceived to be well understood or self-explanatory.
7. *Uncertainty.* Risks perceived as relatively unknown or having highly uncertain dimensions are less readily accepted than risks that are relatively known to science.
8. *Dread.* Risks that evoke fear, terror, or anxiety are less readily accepted and perceived to be greater than risks that do not arouse such feelings or emotions.
9. *Trust in institutions.* Risks associated with institutions or organizations lacking in trust and credibility are less readily accepted and perceived to be greater that risks associated with trustworthy and credible institutions and organizations.
10. *Reversibility.* Risks perceived to have potentially irreversible adverse effects are less readily accepted and perceived to be greater than risks perceived to have reversible adverse effects.
11. *Personal stake.* Risks perceived by people to place them personally and directly at risk are less readily accepted and perceived to be greater than risks that pose no direct or personal threat.
12. *Ethical/moral nature.* Risks perceived to be ethically objectionable or morally wrong are less readily accepted and perceived to be greater than risks perceived not to be ethically objectionable or morally wrong.
13. *Human versus natural origin.* Risks perceived to be generated by human action are less readily accepted and perceived to be greater than risks perceived to be caused by nature or "Acts of God."
14. *Victim identity.* Risks that produce identifiable victims are less readily accepted and perceived to be greater than risks that produce statistical victims.
15. *Catastrophic potential.* Risks that produce fatalities, injuries, and illness grouped spatially and temporally are less readily accepted and perceived to be greater than risks that have random, scattered effects.

---

way for the year 2000. Some of these include: heart disease (1 in 397), stroke (1 in 1699), fire (1 in 82,977), and bio-terrorism (1 in 56,424,800). Despite bio-terrorism measuring as an extremely low risk, people perceive it to be more threatening than eating fast food or checking their fire detectors, when in reality, there is a much greater chance of dying from heart disease or in a fire.

A second subcategory of risk communication is risk assessment, the identification of a risk through a four-step scientific process involving: hazard identification, hazard characterization, exposure assessment, and risk of characterization. From the counterterrorism perspective, it is the difference between suicide bombings and cyber terrorism. Once risk assessment has taken place, the risk management process begins. Risk management consists of "weighing policy alternatives in light of the results of risk assessment and, if required, of selecting and implementing appropriate control options, including regulatory measures" (Comprehensive Risk Analysis and Management Network 2000–2004, Risk Definitions). The bulk of risk communication work is in the field of risk management. This leads to one final fact checking process—risk analysis.

Risk analysis occurs after risk assessment, risk management, and risk communication have all been completed. Technically, risk analysis does not have a measurable ending point, because risks are always evolving, along with the tools to conduct proper risk communication. Risk analysis monitors how the communication process has developed for a specific risk at a particular point in time. Its primary function is to analyze what has been accomplished and what yet needs to be accomplished to improve risk communication (Comprehensive Risk Analysis and Management Network 2000–2004).

The Psychology of Bio-Terrorism and Avoiding Panic

The History of Bio-Defense

Since the anthrax attacks on Capitol Hill, the last four years have seen biological weapons assume a major role in the risk debate. The U.S. bio-defense industry has responded with massive growth. The modern roots of bio-defense can be traced to the Executive branch during former president Bill Clinton's time in office. In a high-level meeting on April 10, 1998, senior White House advisors notified Clinton, "that the nation was dangerously underprepared for a biological attack and needed to develop and stockpile vaccines, antibiotics, and other therapies, and to train first responders to cope with epidemics" (Wright 2004, 2). As a result, Clinton introduced a new bio-defense strategy in the beginning of 1999. The four areas of concern included (2):

1. Training first responders to cope with a bio-weapons attack.
2. Nationwide surveillance of disease.
3. Establishing a national stockpile of vaccines and therapeutic agents for emergency use.
4. Launching a program to develop new vaccines and therapeutic agents for civilian use.

Through his predecessor's recommendations and the 9/11 attacks, President George W. Bush laid the framework for the expansion of bio-defense. Immediately following the discovery of the anthrax letters, President Bush went to Congress asking for emergency funds to counter bio-terrorism. The request was in excess of $1.5 billion. Congress appropriated $2.5 billion to start the revamp of the bio-defense industry. Currently, this budget has grown to $7.45 billion for the FY 2005. DHS also expanded their role in bio-defense with a focus on these (Wright 2004, 3):

- Expansion of the Strategic National Stockpile, which includes smallpox vaccines for every American.
- Project BioShield: $5.6 billion vaccine program that targets suspected bio-agents (first received public attention after the 2002 State of the Union).
- BioWatch: a surveillance system set up in major U.S. cities to detect a biological attack.
- National Biodefense Analysis and Countermeasures Center (NBACC): composed of four separate centers, the NBACC is to be the cornerstone of bio-defense practices.

The substantial investment of $23 billion already committed to bio-defense since 2001 has caused policymakers to question the value of the investment. Congress allocated much of the money for new labs that will enable scientists to study and manipulate deadly viruses, pathogens, and bacteria. The current mind-set is that the United States must be prepared for any type of pathogen, which means developing the weaponized strains first and learning how to protect the populace from an outbreak. This reasoning has been around since at least 1958, when General William Creasy, commander of the U.S. Army Chemical Corps articulated to Congress, "A defensive [chemical and biowarfare] program not supported by an offensive program can well be worthless. You cannot know how to defend against something unless you can visualize various methods which can be used against you, so you can be living in a fool's paradise if you do not have a vigorous munitions and dissemination type program" (Choffnes 2002, 1).

Those who criticize this thinking cite that more labs and research on deadly pathogens might serve as a breeding ground for terrorists. *The Bulletin of the Atomic Scientists* examined the possible scenario:

> At biosafety level-4 labs, the most dangerous of all pathogens—for which there are no known treatments or cures—are studied. These laboratories might become a pathogen-modification training academy or biowarfare agent "superstore." The physical tools and technology of bioterror are relatively cheap—it's the knowledge and experience of working with pathogens that's priceless. Currently, there are no requirements for rigorous background or security clearance checks for those who work in such facilities. Oversight is focused on containment and limiting exposure to the pathogens; making sure those who work with them are psychologically fit to do so is not a priority." (Choffnes 2002, 4)

These criticisms are not without practical proposals to prepare for a secure future. Three proposals include maintaining an advanced medical surveillance system, funding for universal health care, and implementing domestic and international policies that keep bio-weapon production in check around the globe. Approximately, forty-five million Americans are without health insurance. Should a biological attack occur, the lack of immediate healthcare and proper medical attention could turn any one of the forty-five million uninsured into a walking biological time bomb (Wright 2004, 7).

Bio-Terrorism, Disaster, and Panic

A major goal of terrorism is to incite fear among a mass public. One of the ways to instill this fear is to engage in bio-terrorism. What makes this an effective tool for terrorists is that the mere mention of bio-terrorism frightens people. It is the terrorists' intention to use bio-terrorism as a catalyst for outbreaks of panic in the general public, rather than to obtain a high kill count.

Before addressing panic in terms of terrorism—where, if any place in our society, does panic currently fit? Panic is defined as dysfunctional behavior that occurs when a crisis takes place. It is a misleading definition, and one that might be better suited to describe events in fictional settings, such as literature and film.

Over the last 100 years, the United States has seen numerous crises, catastrophes, terrorist attacks, and natural disasters. However, the specter of panic rarely, if ever, occurs. The theme of panic revolves around flight behavior. When faced with extreme danger, human beings will do absolutely anything to escape. As described by E.L. Quarantelli, the Director of the Disaster Research Center, ". . . the essence of panic is the overt behavior that is marked by the setting aside of everyday social norms, even the strongest, such as parents abandoning their young children trying to save themselves in a life threatening crisis" (2001, 5). This type of behavior is seldom reported.

During these major catastrophic events people did not succumb to panic: Three Mile Island in 1979, Oklahoma City in 1995, and at the World Trade Center in 2001. At many times during these crises people were confused, scared, and worried; all common emotions in dangerous situations. However, these emotions did not progress into panic because members of the groups involved did not put others at risk to save their own lives.

One type of real event that is historically highlighted by panic is fire in a crowded building. The most recent situations are theatre productions or rock concerts in older buildings with questionable electric wiring and few exits. Norris Johnson examined this phenomenon using the Beverly Hills Supper Club fire. The fire occurred outside of Cincinnati in 1977, and claimed the lives of 171 people. With such a high death toll, one would assume a breakdown of the social order during the evacuation. However, Johnson's findings showed, "The great majority of involved persons did not engage in animal like behavior, contrary to what many early writers on panic suggest occurs. Instead of ruthless competition, the social order did not breakdown with cooperative rather than selfish behavior predominating" (Quarantelli 2001, 8). Findings such as this further demonstrate the false concept of panic applied to real events.

As previously stated, panic rarely occurs and is preventable when dealing with an informed citizenry. The idea of panic still creates a growing fear as a central psychological role in a terrorist's arsenal. The 1993 and 9/11 attacks on the World Trade Center illustrate why social norms, not panic, ruled the day.

The 1993 bombing: The calm and orderly evacuation of the towers was aided by the fact that people in the buildings knew each other from working together and sharing the same office floor. Because of these social ties and the perception that exits and stairways were accessible, groups of office workers cooperated in vacating the building calmly and efficiently.

The 9/11 attack: Initial reports about the evacuation of the World Trade Center during the attack that occurred on September 11, 2001, suggest that people's responses were equally clearheaded and cooperative. Panic does not occur in disaster situations because people tend to respond in accordance with their customary norms and roles (e.g., the able-bodied assist the impaired, supervisors assume responsibility for the safety of those they supervise, and friends look out for friends). (Glass and Schoch-Spana 2002, 219)

Engaging the Public in Disaster Planning

Once emergency communicators address the concept of panic, it is their responsibility to provide communities with resources to stave off panic-like behavior, even if the probability of said behavior is low. The objective is to adequately educate the public on the most dreadful of dreaded events, so they can employ an active role in lowering their risks. Bio-terrorism specialists Thomas A. Glass and Monica Schoch-Spana of the Johns Hopkins University Bloomberg School of Public Health have highlighted five guidelines to integrate the public in bio-terrorism response planning (Glass and Schoch-Spana 2002, 218).

1. *Recognize that panic is rare and preventable.*
   - Create a positive, constructive role for the general public.
   - Release timely, accurate public information, including instruction in personal protective measures.
2. *Enlist the public as a capable partner.*
   - Use civic organizations to assist with information dissemination, outbreak monitoring, and medication distribution.
3. *Think beyond the hospital for mass-casualty care.*
   - Develop plans for home-based patient care and infection control as part of plans for a community-wide response to deal with mass casualties.
   - Involve lay and alternative care providers.
   - Use family, neighbors, and community groups to identify patients, disseminate information and therapies, and assist affected individuals in obtaining treatment.
4. *Provide information, which is as important as providing medicine.*
   - Plan a health communication strategy that empowers the general public.
   - Produce multilingual and culturally relevant health information.
   - Educate the educators; make use of local spokespersons to disseminate information.
   - Be timely and forthcoming with information about the limits of what is known.
5. *Assume that the public will not take the pill if it does not trust the doctor.*
   - Educate the public, before an attack, about what is being done to prepare and respond.
   - Ensure open flows of information during an attack through mass media outlets and interpersonal exchanges.
   - Build nonadversarial relations with the press and respond to media requests for information.
   - Create participatory decision-making processes by including the public, especially in discussions about how to allocate scarce resources and institute epidemic controls that compromise civil liberties.

The utilization of the public as a resource is a theme that will be revisited more and more often as risk communication takes centerstage in disaster preparedness. A disaster creates a situation where available resources are exhausted, overworked, and insufficient. During this time the general public has the ability to participate usefully during a crisis. Additionally, Glass and Schoch-Spana draw attention to a seldom discussed detail about the "general public," quite bluntly there is no such thing as a "general" public.

There is an ". . . interconnected matrix of networks and subnetworks organized around social institutions and relationships" (219). Many of these networks already contain existing hierarchies and communication systems that can greatly aid information distribution. For example, Bible study groups could distribute medications, service organizations like the Rotary could start a phone tree, or shopping centers could serve as a center for base of operations. A principle concern of the health industry is the lack of hospital beds in case of an emergency. Many medical centers are already at or near capacity without a catastrophic event landing on their doorstep. Research shows that family members and other nonprofessionals constitute 70–90 percent of total daily health care. Israel used community information centers during the Persian Gulf War to sustain their health system.

Another topic at the forefront of risk communication is efficient information dissemination. If disaster occurs, people will need immediate reassurances about what the situation is and how it is being remedied. Table 6.1 shows the right and wrong ways of timely risk communication.

During the West Nile Virus outbreak in New York City, emergency officials used a variety of risk communication tools including: "daily press conferences, regular media releases, a telephone hotline, Web-site updates, multilingual brochures and fliers, and personal contact at the epicenter of the outbreak" (Glass and Schoch-Spana 2002, 221). This was a huge human resource undertaking and will certainly be dwarfed by the extent of communication necessary if a biological attack occurred.

Table 6.1 Risk Communication Dos and Do nots

Task	Do	Do not	Explanation
Finding an honest, trusted member of the community to speak candidly during a disaster.	Seek out a trusted community member to contribute to the disaster planning process.	Wait until an emergency to contact someone and expect them to help calm anxiety and fears.	It is important to have contacts, but establish them well in advance of an emergency to ensure cooperation.
Releasing emergency guides, brochures, and manuals on disaster planning to the public in a timely manner.	Distribute updated information regularly throughout the year, detailing preparedness strategies.	Wait until an emergency to distribute information on how to protect against said event.	The public deserves information updated often and requires ample time to implement plans.
First communication with the public at the beginning of an event or disaster once an assessment is made.	Prepare statements that can be understood at no greater than a middle school comprehension level.	Use industry jargon or excessively technical and scientific terms to describe events or actions taken.	First impressions are essential opportunities to establish trust and credibility, and only happen once.

Box 6.3   CDC's Principles of Communication

CDC will make available timely and accurate information—through proactive news releases or in response to specific requests—so that the public, Congress, and the news media may assess and understand its scientifically based health information and programs.

1. Final reports, information, and recommendations will be made fully and readily available.
2. Communication will be open, honest, and based on sound science, conveying accurate information.
3. Information will not be withheld solely to protect CDC or the government from criticism or embarrassment.
4. Information will be released consistent with the Freedom of Information Act (FOIA).
5. Prevention messages will be based on supportable scientific data and sound behavioral and communication research principles. At all times, health messages will remain scientifically valid and accurate. CDC will honor embargo agreements with standards or peer-reviewed periodicals in the scientific and medical communities.
6. Targeted health messages will be sensitive to language and cultural differences and community norms.

One way to ease the implementation of the abovementioned risk communication tools is to recognize what the media wants before a crisis occurs. The media can be simple to please if a few guidelines are followed. Among these guidelines are: "equal access to information, honest answers, the timely release of information, rumors squashed quickly, commitment to a schedule for media updates, and subject matter experts to explain official views" (Reynolds 2002, 25). The Centers for Disease Control and Prevention provide a set of rules for the public and media on how they will communicate during disasters (see box 6.3 for an example).

Public officials need to establish a positive relationship with the media before an attack occurs in order to accurately describe events, responses, and justify decision making. The media can easily manipulate an official's response in any way they deem necessary to uphold their journalistic integrity or bottom line. Ascertain trust with the media first, and the public's trust will follow.

Shelter-in-Place and Evacuation

Now that the philosophies and concepts of risk communication have been described, the next step is identifying important tools in community risk communication, such as shelter-in-place and emergency evacuation. Natural disasters and terrorist attacks may compromise the safety of the outside air. In the event of an emergency, it may be safer to shelter in a school, vehicle, office building, or residence and wait for the atmosphere to clear the toxic material, than to use the traditional means of escaping danger through evacuation. The decision will depend on weather conditions and characteristics of the chemicals, organisms, or particulate matter suspended in the air. Since shelter-in-place is a relatively new feature in risk communication, the focus is on its use in conjunction with the community shielding concept, which will be explained later in this chapter. As stated by the National Institute for Chemical Studies, shelter-in-place ". . . uses a structure and its indoor atmosphere to temporarily separate people from a hazardous outdoor atmosphere" (2001, 2).

The Call to Shelter-in-Place

Before a call for shelter-in-place is given, it must be determined that evacuation poses a threat to the population. Also, evacuation will only work if transportation lines are open and shelters exist.

The chemical industry has researched the question of whether to shelter-in-place or evacuate for the past four decades in search of a suitable methodology. (For the purposes of this chapter, shelter-in-place will refer to a protection plan against a chemical attack, spill, or natural release.) The general answer lies in the specifics of the problem. Local emergency planners need a sufficient amount of knowledge on what events could trigger either a call for evacuation or shelter-in-place. Only then can the proper decision-making paradigm be implemented.

The first step in deciding if shelter-in-place is the appropriate course of action is an analysis of the agent involved. In addition, the thickness of the toxic material plume and the speed with which it is traveling will provide those with decision-making responsibility a clear picture of the situation. Also, the amount of toxin released and whether or not more will be released are important figures that must be obtained immediately.

Shelter-in-place works best for a short period of time. If the release stays in the atmosphere for an extended time period the situation could deteriorate for those sheltering. The outside environment must clear relatively quickly, that is, within hours for sheltering to be effective. Emergency officials will need access to the meteorological conditions of the day to guide the procedures. The wind speed and direction will assist an official with advising segments of the population farther away from the plume. During the planning process, organizers will need to gather and disseminate information on the efficiency of buildings in the community as shelters (Shumpert et al. 2002).

The older the building, the less reliable its ability as a shelter-in-place structure becomes. This is determined by the air exchange rate of the building in question. Before 1965, energy conservation standards did not exist. This means that houses built forty years ago or more were constructed with less emphasis on weatherization methods such as seals. Structures built after 1965 can have an air exchange rate as low as 0.1 acph (air changes per hour). This does not mean that it takes ten hours for the outside air to completely replace the air inside the structure. Some of the air moving into the house will filter back out while the exchange process is happening. On average, the outside air will replace 95 percent of the air in a house with 0.5 acph in about 6 hours. This is under ideal conditions, which means low to no winds and little to no temperature differential between the outside and inside air. Most homes range from 0.7 to 0.8 acph (2002).

Even more reliable than homes are office buildings. Studies have placed the average acph in a high-rise structure at 0.66, whereas an industrial building registers at 0.31 acph. A nonmoving vehicle has a wide range of acph values depending on the wind: 0.5 acph with 1 mph winds compared to 9 acph with 10 mph winds. Vehicles in motion offer the least protection; a car traveling 35 mph can expect 15 acph. These numbers show that in a compromised environment remaining at home or in an office building are the safest choices (2002).

Types of Shelter-in-Place

There are four degrees of shelter-in-place:

1. *Normal sheltering.* All windows and doors are closed in the structure and any ventilation units (air conditioners) are shut off.
2. *Expedient sheltering.* Using plastic sheeting and duct tape to seal windows, doors, and other areas of the house where outside air can penetrate the house.
3. *Enhanced sheltering.* Using weatherization methods to further reduce air infiltration into the structure. This includes caulking cracks, replacing windows, and upgrading the insulation.
4. *Pressurized sheltering.* This is the most protection a building can receive. A ventilation unit blocks the outside air from coming in, and then creates a pressurized environment indoors.

Normal and expedient sheltering are the most commonly used and most efficient. Enhanced and pressurized require major planning and investment on the part of the home or building owner (National Institute for Chemical Studies 2001).

The North Atlantic Treaty Organization (NATO) is credited as the first to suggest the use of the expedient level of shelter-in-place describing it as an "ad-hoc shelter." Its primary purpose was ". . . to protect civilian populations from chemical warfare agent exposure" (Sorensen and Vogt 2001, 1). The Israeli Civil Defense also stressed the need for an expedient level of shelter during the mid-1980s after their invasion of Lebanon and conflict with the Palestinian Liberation Organization (PLO). The Oak Ridge National Laboratory (ORNL) has declared the implementation of duct tape and plastic sheeting as necessary tools for the most accessible level of quality shelter-in-place–expedient.

Duct Tape and Plastic Sheeting

As a means of equipping the public to shelter-in-place, tests on duct tape began in 1993 to measure its resistance to certain chemicals. DIMP (Di-isopropyl methyl phosphonate) was used to simulate Sarin (GB), DMMP (Dimethyl methyl phosphonate) to simulate VX, MAL (an organophosphorus pesticide), and DBS (Dibutyl sulfide) a mustard stimulant. The duct tape showed the most resistance to MAL and DBS, compared to DIMP and DMMP (Sorensen and Vogt 2001).

Similar tests were performed at ORNL on plastic sheeting of various thicknesses; 2.5, 4, 10, and 20 millimeter plastic sheeting underwent tests against a live Hydrogen-based chemical agent and VX. At 10 millimeters and above the plastic sheeting performed effectively against the agents. The Hydrogen chemical breached the shelter after 2 hours at the 10-millimeter level, whereas the VX needed 30 hours at the same thickness (Sorensen and Vogt 2001).

Research performed by the National Institute for Chemical Studies has mirrored that of the ORNL experiments. In their average model, a structure will have one-tenth the dose of a chemical whose plume takes 10 minutes to pass when properly sheltered.

There are case studies of chemical releases that provide good evidence of the success of shelter-in-place when properly executed. One of the best examples is a chemical spill in West Helena, Arkansas, on May 8, 1997. In this instance, an agricultural chemical called azinophos-methyl caught fire, causing an explosion at a chemical repackaging plant. Three firemen died from the ensuing incendiary event. The surrounding population was advised to both evacuate and shelter-in-place, depending on their distance from the plant (National Institute for Chemical Studies 2001). Both forms of disaster preparedness worked as no subsequent deaths were reported.

Now that statistical evidence has been presented on the ability of duct tape to protect citizens from a toxic release, why was there so much criticism when the former secretary of DHS, Tom Ridge, advised Americans to buy plastic sheeting and duct tape after 9/11? The reason duct tape and plastic sheeting were ridiculed has little to do with the physical materials, and everything to do with how the communication was presented. Duct tape is not the solution to bio-terrorism, and DHS never alluded to it being so. However, there should have been more emphasis on duct tape and plastic sheeting as parts of a comprehensive shelter-in-place plan.

The White House and DHS did not anticipate that recommending duct tape and plastic sheeting to thwart a terrorist attack might be met with skepticism. Ridge should have acknowledged the possibility of skepticism and given the public a way to deal with their fears; specifically, that the government is placing the fate of the masses into the hands of a popular household item. As soon as the recommendation to purchase duct tape and plastic sheeting was delivered, DHS should have listed sources where more information on the previously mentioned experiments involving duct tape could be found. In addition, it was a prime opportunity to develop some graphics for distribution in press circles. The media would have found it difficult to criticize the genuine efforts of DHS and the Bush administration while introducing statistical research.

Community Shielding

Expanding upon the concept of shelter-in-place is community shielding, which involves the vast network of an entire community to address transportation, communication, food and medical supply delivery. It has a much longer quarantine period compared to shelter-in-place as explained by Gregory Saathoff, the executive director of the Critical Incident Analysis Group (CIAG) at the University of Virginia, "Depending on the disease released in the attack, the community shielding period could last from seven to, at the very longest, 28 days" (Marshall 2002, 2). Community shielding lowers the risk associated with biological terrorism. Exemplified by the doomsday scenarios in the popular films *The Stand* and *Outbreak*, a disease can move from one coast to another by the flight of a single person. Community shielding initiates the quarantine process for first responders to prevent an outbreak.

One of the beneficial aspects of community shielding is that transportation routes remain decongested allowing emergency officials through. It also raises the bar in community planning, as numerous services must be coordinated within hours of a community shielding event. Saathoff further describes the advantages of the process: "Voluntary programs help build trust in the government's response . . . Our society is better set up to incorporate shielding than it has ever been in the past" (Marshall 2002, 2).

The chairman of CIAG, Ambassador W. Nathaniel Howell, presents a few guidelines for the community shielding process. He starts out by recognizing the broad number of institutions within communities across the United States, "Homeowner or community associations, neighborhood watch, or local chapters of civic organizations . . . can offer a framework for development of disaster response plans" (Howell 2005, 6). If these organizations do not exist, or do not wish to be participants, it is the job of community activists to develop new institutions for community readiness.

Once this has been accomplished the community must organize. Contact lists should be made that include all emergency agencies in the area. Each community member who wishes to participate should be given an active role. It is his/her job to ensure that all necessary tasks are accomplished to the fullest. It is likely assignments will require the cooperation of more than one person. Teams must be established to care for the elderly and the disabled.

Communities are constantly evolving, shrinking, growing, and changing. A plan developed five years ago cannot be expected to have the necessary preparations to reflect changes within a town or city. Here are some steps to ensure emergency plans are up-to-date:

1. Establish meetings for the discussion of emergency procedures several times a year.
2. Run drills, both planned and unplanned, within different sectors of the community.
3. Allow for feedback after natural disasters such as snow storms or an earthquake (Howell 2005).
4. Run table-top scenario exercises.

Placing community preparedness at the forefront of a town or city's agenda keeps disaster plans current, and provides community members with the best possible protection.

Evacuation and the Shadow-Effect

If the call to evacuate is made there are numerous factors that must be assessed beforehand. Evacuation is the mobilization of a population from a dangerous environment due to a threat or an event. It is difficult as it requires coordination with multiple agencies and political jurisdictions. Evacuation routes should be established in advance of an event. Emergency officials should be in place on the ground keeping the flow of evacuation steady. One of the benefits of evacuation is the high compliance rate. When a call to evacuate is given in an emergency with little to no warning, evacuation rates often rest in the 90 percent range and higher. This makes the planning for an evacuation all the more necessary to assure the population has unobstructed access to evacuation routes, and the necessary materials waiting for them at emergency shelters or wherever their final destination may be. The decision to evacuate rests on two questions: Will the evacuation be completed before the plume reaches the target population? Will the shelters or areas of relocation provide adequate protection from the plume? (Shumpert and Vogt 2002).

The phenomenon where a large group of people evacuate as a result of doing what is in their own best interests is known as the evacuation shadow effect. Three Michigan State University geographers coined the term after the near meltdown at the Three Mile Island nuclear power plant in Pennsylvania (Erikson 1994). Three Mile Island evacuees traveled a median distance of 85 miles in one study and 100 miles in a third (Johnson and Zeigler 1983). In another example, in 1961, Hurricane Carla pushed evacuees a median distance of 80 miles from the Texas coast.

As Hurricane Carla shows, Three Mile Island was not the first time the evacuation shadow effect had happened, but it occurred at an unprecedented magnitude. Concerned with what they perceived to be half-truths and lies coming from plant officials, Harrisburg, Pa., residents did what they thought to be in the own best interests. Those living under the governor's conditions for evacuation within a five mile radius of the plant numbered 3,500. The actual number who evacuated was 144,000. Over forty times the advised amount of people left the area. They accounted for 39 percent of the population in a 15-mile radius (Johnson 1985).

Researchers have concluded that the reason for this phenomenon lies in the public perception of nuclear energy. The worst case scenario for a nuclear accident is much greater than the average human being can handle. There is also a clear difference between a natural disaster and a technological accident. "They [technological accidents] provoke outrage rather than acceptance or resignation" (Erikson 1994, 143). Also, a nuclear accident can create an uninhabitable environment in a massive area for thousands of years. Radiation is virtually impossible to detect. It has no odor, is invisible, and tasteless, despite the fact that it has the potential to kill millions and cause widespread harmful health effects (Erikson 1994). These characteristics contribute to the fear.

School Safety and Risk Communication

An important sector of society that should not be overlooked when discussing risk communication is the education system. With respect to terrorism from abroad, the U.S. school system has avoided direct attack by foreign terrorist entities. However, America's schools witnessed numerous domestic violent events in the last thirty years, such as Columbine, Colo., and Jonesboro, Arkansas. Currently, there are approximately 60 million children in more then 119,000 schools. School safety is a primary concern for lawmakers and citizens to protect these students. In America today, schools are thought of as a "safe haven" for children; few parents worry about a child's safety while in the custody of school educators and administration. In order to ensure schools remain a safe place, certain steps should be considered to bring the physical protection of schools into the twenty-first century.

Targeted School Violence

The Safe School Initiative, a joint undertaking conducted by the U.S. Secret Service, now a part of DHS and the U.S. Department of Education, seeks to minimize the threat to schools from targeted school violence. Targeted violence is defined as, ". . . any incident of violence where a known or knowable attacker selects a particular target prior to their violent attack" (Fein et al. 2002, 4). The Secret Service's National Threat Assessment Center conducted much of the research on the thirty-seven school-based attacks committed from 1974 to 2000. It was a task well-suited for the Secret Service, given their exceptional experience providing security to thousands of "protectees" from hundreds of thousands of threats. The data collected was organized into five primary areas of concern (19):

1. *Characterizing the attacker.* One of the main duties of the Secret Service is creating a profile for would-be attackers. In a school setting, however, the Secret Service found that the forty-one perpetrators of school violence did not fit any specific profile. Less than one-third of the attackers had a documented history of violence.
2. *Conceptualizing the attack.* The findings show school violence is a planned event, not an impulsive act. In addition, an act of revenge was given as a motive in over half the attacks.
3. *Signaling the attack.* Another person knew of the planned event in more than 80 percent of the cases. The person with prior knowledge was rarely the target, and perpetrators rarely made direct threats.
4. *Advancing the attack.* Over half the attackers had access and/or experience with firearms.
5. *Resolving the attack.* Law enforcement officials were the intervening party in only one-quarter of the cases. School officials, students, or the attackers stopping by their own means were the most common ends to the crises.

Threat Assessment

The information collected from these categories is used to develop two types of threat assessments. School officials can conduct either a threat assessment inquiry or threat assessment investigation based on available information. An inquiry is initiated under the direct supervision of school officials with law enforcement monitoring when requested. The investigation is the same as the inquiry, but with law enforcement taking the leadership role (Fein et al. 2002, 44).

One of the most troubling aspects of cases of school violence is the high percentage of individuals possessing information prior to an act of violence. School officials can lower this occurrence by mitigating the unwritten rule of secrecy among school-aged children. There are too many barriers stopping children from divulging valuable information. A possible remedy is to make anonymous reporting of at-risk behaviors more accessible to students. Once this happens, school officials can make a decision on whether or not to move forward, typically based upon, "When information about a student's behavior and communications passes an agreed-upon threshold of concern, school officials should initiate a threat assessment inquiry" (48). School conducted inquiries seek information that falls into five specific categories:

- The facts that drew attention to the student, the situation, and possibly the targets.
- Information about the student.

- Information about "attack-related" behaviors.
- Motives.
- Target selection.

The most common sources of material for the assessment include school information, collateral school interviews, parent/guardian interviews, interviews with the student of concern, and target interviews.

When a situation is deemed threatening, time is of the utmost importance. School officials must immediately contact law enforcement officials to thwart any possibility of an attack. Known targets must be taken out of harm's way and psychological support initiated immediately to both the would-be attacker(s) and target(s). Schools should be prepared to enact two threat management plans, one for the short term and one for the long term. The short-term plan refers to the time the threat is deemed credible until initial prevention intervention is made. The long-term plan addresses the future welfare of the student, and how to learn from the specific event in order to deter future violence (63).

Analysis of Boyertown Area School District's All Hazards Plan

Boyertown Area School District, located forty-five miles northwest of Philadelphia, has one of the top school emergency plans in the country, entitled the *All Hazards Plan*. The district's proximity to both a nuclear power plant in Limerick, Pa., and a rare metals plant in Boyertown provided unique challenges for the district at the time of the All Hazards Plan's inception in 1999. After assembling a team consisting of private firms, school personnel and administration, emergency agencies, and fire and police, a plan was developed outlining procedures in the event of bomb threats, evacuation, explosion, fire, hazardous materials, natural disaster, radiological exposure, security situations, terrorism, casualties, and crisis intervention. With the initial framework defined, each individual school principal modified the plan to fit their building and student's needs (Office of Safe and Drug Free Schools 2003, 6–15).

The physical makeup of the plan is one of its defining characteristics. Unlike some guides that use a spiral bound notebook design, Boyertown uses a three-ring binder. This makes modifications to the plan as easy as removing an expired section and replacing it with the updated procedure(s). In addition, the entire plan is color-coded. Each category of risk (radiological, terrorism, evacuation, and so forth) is assigned a colored folder. Every staff member, teacher, and administrator receives a copy of each folder defining their role, specific to the incident. If the threat is credible and action must be taken, principles can alert staff using the color system, thereby preventing fear and panic among the student body.

Furthermore, Boyertown has a threat assessment policy in place, enabling the district's Safety Office to make quick decisions. Depending on the level of threat, Boyertown will alert the proper authorities to mitigate the situation as quickly as possible. A collective/shared decision-making process has been established with the surrounding emergency responders and police (John Stoudt, personal communication, October 17, 2005).

Conclusion

With the recent natural disasters and constant threat of terrorist attack, emergency planning has reached a new level of importance both in the U.S. government and private sector. For every time a Hurricane Katrina or terrorist hoax in the New York City subway system, government officials should be analyzing the event and updating their emergency procedures and means of alerting the public. Risk communicators have the technical know-how to amend evacuation routes, relocate shelters, and organize community response plans while keeping public hysteria at a minimum. As outlined in the chapter, there are numerous mediums transmitting risk communication and emergency preparedness information. Websites and journals are a good place to start, but should not overshadow the benefits of local planning. Unified, community involvement is the best way to prepare for a disaster. It would be a mistake to declare a town "disaster-proof" as disasters and emergencies will happen. However, the response to a disaster should be outlined well in advance through coordination with local, state and federal officials, community members and emergency planners.

Case Study: 2001 Anthrax Attacks

On September 18, 2001, one week after the 9/11 attacks, a new terrorist threat emerged in the U.S.—biological terrorism. Four letters containing the anthrax bacterium arrived in the mailrooms of ABC News, CBS News, NBC news, and the *New York Post* in New York City. A fifth letter arrived at American Media, Inc. in Boca Raton, Fla. The letters shared a Trenton, N.J., postmark. Two more additional letters carrying a weaponized form of anthrax postmarked October 9, also from Trenton, N.J., traveled to the offices of Senator Tom Daschle, a Democrat from South Dakota and Senator Patrick Leahy, a Democrat from Vermont (Lake). When a device, naturally occurring agent, or other material is weaponized it is manipulated to function as a weapon or with the potential to act as one.

As a result of the mailings, the anthrax bacterium infected twenty-two U.S. citizens killing five. Here is a timeline of the Anthrax Attacks:

Timeline of Major Events

- September 22–October 1: Nine people contract anthrax, but are not diagnosed.
- October 5: Robert Stevens, 63, dies; the first known death from inhalation of anthrax in the United States since 1976.
- October 17: Thirty-one Capitol workers (five Capitol police officers, three Russ Feingold staffers, twenty-three Tom Daschle staffers) test positive for the presence of anthrax (presumably via nasal swabs, etc.)
- October 22: Federal officials announce that two D.C. area United States Postal workers have died from what appeared to be pulmonary anthrax contracted from handling mail.
- October 23: It is confirmed that the two postal handlers died of pulmonary anthrax. The men are Joseph P. Curseen, 47, and Thomas L. Morris Jr., 55.

- October 31: Kathy Nguyen, a New York City hospital worker dies of inhalation of anthrax.
- November 21: Ottilie Lundgren, 94, is the fifth and final person to die as a result of the mailings.
- December 5: The Leahy letter is opened at the American bio-facility, the United States Army Medical Research Institute of Infectious Diseases (USAMRIID), Fort Detrick, Maryland.
- December 16: DNA testing of the anthrax matches the Ames strain at USAMRIID (CCR 2002).

Fast-forward four years after the attacks and investigators are still seeking their first arrest. The FBI and postal inspectors have tracked leads on four continents and interviewed over 8,000 people. All the while, the $2.5 million reward for any information leading to an arrest has not been incentive enough for a break in the case.

According to the *Washington Post* article, "Little progress in FBI probe of anthrax cases," the FBI declared Steven J. Hatfill as a "person of interest," in August of 2002. Hatfill, a physician and bio-terrorism expert was once employed at the USAMRIID in Fort Detrick, Md., from 1997 to 1999. To this day, Hatfill maintains his innocence and has not been charged with a crime (Lengel 2005).

The case is now referred to as Amerithrax, and is still a top priority for both the FBI and the United States Postal Service. FBI agents brief Director Robert S. Mueller III every Friday on the status of the case, as noted in Scott Shane's *New York Times* article: "In 4-year anthrax hunt, FBI finds itself stymied and sued" (2005). In addition to the ongoing official investigation, many amateur detectives labeled as "armchair sleuths" have been investigating the crime. One of the most well-known is State University of New York at Purchase professor Dr. Barbara Hatch-Rosenberg. Her research led her to profile a possible suspect whom she believed worked with the CIA and had a level of expertise in bio-warfare. This information came from defense insiders and eventually guided her profile to Hatfill, sparking the highly publicized investigation.

A forensic linguist at Vassar College, Donald Foster, is doing his part to solve the case. Foster has worked with the FBI on other cases and claims two former workers at USAM-RIID as possible suspects. However, Foster has never revealed the names of his suspects.

In a *Wall Street Journal* article entitled, "Armchair sleuths track anthrax without a badge," Antonio Regalado accounts the efforts made by amateur investigator, Richard M. Smith, a computer expert. His investigation revealed an interesting piece of evidence. The two letters sent to Senators Daschle and Leahy, respectively, had nine-digit zip codes in the address. Smith was able to locate two websites that carried both addresses with the nine-digit zip codes. He then contacted Dr. Juan Cabanela, an assistant professor at Haverford College who maintained one of the two sites. Cabanela researched the records at the site and found three computer servers that accessed both addresses. He notified the FBI's Philadelphia field office, but never received word if any evidence had been collected (2002). To this day the perpetrator(s) of this crime have not been brought to justice.

Discussion Questions

1. What strategy would you implement to combat bio-terrorism: Funding for bio-defense labs and germ warfare programs or funding to eliminate bio-weapons production and improvements in health monitoring systems? Cite examples from at least two sources.

2. Imagine a similar bio-terrorist event occurring in the United States. Write at least a one-page press release communicating to the public what happened. Remember not to over-reassure, include what risk perception factors they might be suffering from, and suggest active roles for the public to assume. Use outside sources where necessary.

Risk Communication Emergency Guides, Organizations, and Publications

There is a wide variety of information available through the Internet and libraries on risk communication and disaster preparedness at the international, national, state, and local levels. Many guides address a wide variety of issues from risk communication policy to specific recommendations for shelter-in-place. Risk communication centers are found in both the public and private sectors and are often located in university settings. Weekly, monthly, and quarterly publications are available from many sites and can be easily accessed through an e-mail address. Here are three sections containing emergency guides, organizations, and publications.

Emergency Guides

The authoring party is listed below the emergency guide followed by a short description.

- *Public Preparedness: A National Imperative Symposium Report*
  - American Red Cross and George Washington University
  - Four primary objectives to improve the emergency preparedness capabilities of the public: (1) define public preparedness; (2) identify barriers to engaging the public in preparedness activities; (3) develop recommendations and ideas for helping the public become more prepared; (4) identify best practices that help the public become more prepared.
- *Introduction to NBC Terrorism: An Awareness Primer and Preparedness Guide for Emergency Responders*
  - Disaster Preparedness and Emergency Response Association
  - This is an introductory guide for first responders to a nuclear, biological, or chemical release. It includes basic information on the common weapons involved and how to safeguard oneself when arriving on the scene.
- *National Response Plan (December 2004)*
  - U.S. DHS
  - The National Response Plan (NRP) is an all-discipline, all-hazards plan that establishes a single, comprehensive framework for the management of domestic incidents. It provides the structure and mechanisms for the coordination of federal support to state, local, and tribal incident managers and for exercising direct federal authorities and responsibilities. The NRP assists in the important

homeland security mission of preventing terrorist attacks within the United States; reducing the vulnerability to all natural and manmade hazards; and minimizing the damage and assisting in the recovery from catastrophic events.

- *Emergency Preparedness Guide: Protecting Your Family and Your Home*
  - ○ Homeownership Alliance and the DHS
  - ○ This is a concise manual detailing ways to safeguard a residence. It includes emergency supply lists, planning tips, terrorist threats, and a communications plan.
- *The National Strategy for the Physical Protection of Critical Infrastructures and Key Assets*
  - ○ Office of the White House
  - ○ This report defines the current national security objectives as identified by President Bush. It is a thorough manual with an emphasis on numerous critical infrastructures. Information sharing, research and development, and use of simulations are some of the re-occurring themes.

Governmental Agencies, NGOs, and Educational Centers

The authoring party is listed below the agency, organization, or center followed by a short description from the group's website.

- *Comprehensive Risk Analysis and Management Network (CRN)*
  - ○ The Swiss Federal Institute of Technology
  - ○ The CRN works on the premise that national security can be achieved best through international cooperation. The CRN's goal is to provide and expand its international partner network in order to exchange knowledge on risks and risk analysis methodology, and to share and review national experiences in an open, nonhierarchical dialog.
- *Federal Emergency Management Agency (FEMA)*
  - ○ Department of Homeland Security Emergency Preparedness and Response
  - ○ FEMA: A former independent agency that became part of the new DHS in March 2003. It is tasked with responding to, planning for, recovering from, and mitigating against disasters. FEMA can trace its beginnings to the Congressional Act of 1803. This act, generally considered the first piece of disaster legislation, provided assistance to a New Hampshire town following an extensive fire. FEMA's mission is to lead America to prepare for, prevent, respond to, and recover from disasters with a vision of "A Nation Prepared."
- *American Red Cross*
  - ○ NGO
  - ○ The American Red Cross, a humanitarian organization led by volunteers, is guided by its Congressional charter and the Fundamental Principles of the International Red Cross Movement. It provides relief to victims of disasters and helps people prevent, prepare for, and respond to emergencies.
- *Center for Risk Communication*
  - ○ NGO

- The Center for Risk Communication is a pioneer in the development and use of advanced communication methods based on decades of university-level behavioral-science research and practice. Research and experience clearly prove that one of the most important keys to communication success is an organization's ability to establish, maintain, and increase trust and credibility with key stakeholders, including employees, regulatory agencies, citizen groups, the public, and the media.

- *Russian American Nuclear Security Advisory Council (RANSAC)*
  - NGO
  - RANSAC is an independent, nongovernmental research organization dedicated to increasing the security of WMDs and reducing proliferation risks. RANSAC's priority is supporting the cooperative threat reduction agenda between the United States, Russia, and the other former Soviet states and promoting its expansion to address global proliferation dangers. Founded in 1997, RANSAC's key issues are ensuring the security of WMD materials, warheads, and technologies; downsizing the Russian WMD complex and transitioning excess scientists and workers to peaceful careers; limiting the production and use of fissile material; and disposing of excess weapons and materials.

- *Peter Sandman Risk Communication Web Site*
  - NGO
  - Established in 2000, "The Peter Sandman Risk Communication Web Site" is devoted to risk communication professional and educator Peter Sandman's distinctive approach to risk communication. It is one of the most extensive and most used risk communication sites on the Web.

- *Center for Risk Perception and Communication*
  - Carnegie Mellon University
  - The main goals of the center are: (1) to bring together researchers interested in studying risk perception and risk communication; (2) to establish a common framework within which these researchers can communicate and collaborate; (3) to bring our collective expertise to a diverse set of risk-related projects.

- *Critical Incident Analysis Group*
  - University of Virginia's School of Medicine
  - The CIAG is an interdisciplinary consortium of academician, professionals, and experts in the University of Virginia's School of Medicine dedicated to improving the public's and the government's ability to understand and cope with critical incidents and the government's capacity to anticipate, prevent, and manage them effectively.

- *Critical Infrastructure Protection Program*
  - George Mason University School of Law
  - The Critical Infrastructure Protection Program (CIPP) seeks to fully integrate the disciplines of law, policy, and technology for enhancing the security of cyber networks, physical systems, and economic processes supporting the nation's critical infrastructure. The CIPP grant is used to fund basic and applied research as well as support information and outreach activities related to the key components of the national research agenda. Among the many topics explored, key areas of focus have been cyber security, physical security, information sharing between public and private sectors, regional, state, and local issues, and privacy concerns.

- *Environmental Risk Analysis Program*
  - Cornell University Department of Communication
  - The goals are: (1) Meet societal needs to better understand, evaluate, and communicate environmental risks; (2) Improve methods of environmental risk analysis and communication; (3) Facilitate the use of risk analysis by citizen leaders, educators, and policymakers as they tackle complex local and regional environmental issues; (4) Develop resources and training programs that will help citizens and policymakers.
- *Harvard Center for Risk Analysis (HCRA)*
  - Harvard University School of Public Health
  - Many public health activities focus on understanding and reducing one particular disease or hazard, such as AIDS, pollution, or poor nutrition. HCRA was launched in 1989 with the mission to promote public health by using decision sciences to take a broader view. By applying these analytic methods to a wide range of risk and health issues, and by comparing various risk management or health intervention strategies, HCRA hopes to empower informed public response to health, safety, and environmental challenges by identifying policies that will achieve the greatest benefits with the most efficient use of limited resources.
- *Homeland Security Policy Institute* (HSPI)
  - George Washington University
  - The HSPI draws on the expertise of The George Washington University and its partners from the academic, nonprofit, policy and private sectors for a common goal of better preparing the nation for the threat of terrorism. HSPI frames the debate, discusses policy implications and alternatives, and recommends solutions to issues facing America's homeland security policymakers. By linking academicians and scientists to decision makers at all levels of government, the private sector, and the communities we live in, HSPI is working to build a bridge between theory and practice in the homeland security arena. In its first year, HSPI has made major progress in fulfilling its multifaceted mission to pursue homeland security research, policy analysis, education, and training.
- *Institute for Infrastructure and Information Assurance*
  - James Madison University
  - The mission of the Institute is to facilitate development, coordination, integration, and funding of activities and capabilities of the James Madison University academic community to enhance information and critical infrastructure assurance at the federal, state, and local levels. The Institute is guided by an advisory board that includes a distinct group of individuals representing business, academia, and government.
- *Risk Sciences and Public Policy Institute*
  - Johns Hopkins University's Bloomberg School of Public Health
  - The Risk Sciences and Public Policy Institute of the Johns Hopkins Bloomberg School of Public Health is dedicated to the protection of health through education, service, and research in risk and policy. The Institute's activities are designed to provide practitioners, scientists, and decision makers with the tools necessary to ensure that environmental health policies lead to improved public health.

Publications

The authoring party is listed below the publication followed by a short description provided by the author.

- *Critical Infrastructure Protection (CIP) Report*
    - Critical Infrastructure Protection Program: George Mason University and James Madison University
    - The CIP Report is published once a month and can be accessed on-line. Each issue takes on a theme pertaining to critical infrastructure protection for industry, government, and academia.
- *Journal of Homeland Security and Emergency Management*
    - George Washington University
    - "Its intent is to provide quality content in the new realm of homeland security and to discuss the relationships between emergency management (for natural, technological and industrial, and terrorism events) as currently understood and conducted and the new field of homeland security." It is a quarterly publication.
- *Risk Analysis*
    - Society for Risk Analysis
    - Risk Analysis provides a focal point for new developments in risk analysis for scientists from a wide range of disciplines. It is designed to meet these needs of organization, integration, and communication. The bimonthly journal covers topics of great interest to regulators, researchers, and scientific administrators. It deals with health risks, engineering, mathematical, and theoretical aspects of risks, and social and psychological aspects of risk such as risk perception, acceptability, economics, and ethics.
- *Risk in Perspective*
    - Harvard University School of Public Health
    - Risk in Perspective is often devoted to a fuller explanation of the work of HCRA faculty that has already been published, in shorter form, in academic journals. The series gives the author an opportunity to express views and policy suggestions which can not be included in some peer-reviewed journals. It is a bimonthly.

Key Terms and Definitions

risk communication. An interactive process of exchange of information and opinion among individuals, groups, and institutions using a science-based approach for communicating effectively in high concern situations (Covello et al. 2001, 2–3).

crisis communication. Communication as a result of five primary factors:

1. A potentially hazardous situation.
2. Requiring immediate, rapid action.
3. Management has little control.
4. Unpredictable effects and consequences.
5. An interest from the public and media (Comprehensive Risk Analysis and Management Network (CRN), Risk Definitions).

risk perception. At least fifteen factors determine how a person views a risk: voluntariness, controllability, familiarity, equity, benefits, understanding, uncertainty, dread, trust in institutions, reversibility, personal stake, ethical/moral nature, human vs. natural origin, victim identity, catastrophic potential (detailed list found in box 6.2; Covello et al. 2001, 16).

risk assessment. A scientific process consisting of four steps:

1. Hazard identification
2. Hazard characterization
3. Exposure assessment
4. Risk of characterization (CRN, Risk Definitions)

risk management. Weighing policy alternatives in light of the results of risk assessment and, if required, of selecting and implementing appropriate control options, including regulatory measures (CRN, Risk Definitions).

risk analysis. A process that consists of risk assessment, risk management, and risk communication (CRN, Risk Definitions).

panic. Dysfunctional escape behavior generated by fortuitous, varied circumstances, but involving impending danger (Quarantelli 2001, 4).

shelter-in-place. Using a structure and its indoor atmosphere to temporarily separate people from a hazardous outdoor atmosphere (National Institute for Chemical Studies 2001).

community shielding. Combining individual and community responses in a broader form of shelter-in-place may be the best type of community protection. Remaining in homes or other community safe havens will contain a contagion after an attack with a dirty bomb or biological agent. Shielding limits unnecessary and dangerous evacuation attempts that can leave first responders overwhelmed (Critical Incident Analysis Group).

table-top exercise. Exercises usually conducted around a conference table—involve the discussion of issues and "what-if" situations, and the development of response options. Examples of topics include suspected outbreak of a contagious disease or response to a multicity bio-terrorist incident (Association of State and Territorial Health Officials 2002).

evacuation. The flight of persons from a dangerous location, when faced with a threat from an emergency event.

evacuation shadow effect. Shadow evacuation occurs when people evacuate as a result of receiving incorrect information or overreacting to a threat. Shadow evacuations are problematic because they may prevent truly threatened populations from leaving and can overly congest already limited transportation resources (Wolshon 2004).

targeted violence. Any incident of violence where a known or knowable attacker selects a particular target prior to their violent attack (Fein et al. 1995).

threat assessment inquiry. Initiated and under the direct supervision of school officials with law enforcement monitoring when requested (Fein 2002, 44.)

threat assessment investigation. The same as the inquiry, but with law enforcement taking the leadership role (Fein 2002, 44).

weaponize. To give a device, naturally occurring substance, or other material properties to allow it to function as a weapon or with the potential to do so.

References

Association of State and Territorial Health Officials. 2002. Guide to preparedness: Evaulation using drills and table top exercises. <http://www.naccho.org/toolbox/Guide%20to%20 Preparedness_Evaluation%20using%20Drills%20and%20Tabletop%20Exercises.pdf#sea rch='guide%20to%20preparedness%20evaluation%20using%20drills%20and%20table %20top%20exercises'>.

Center for Counterproliferation Research (CCR). 2002. Anthrax in America: A chronology and analysis of the fall 2001 attacks, November.

Choffnes, Eileen. 2002. Bioweapons: New labs, more terror? *Bulletin of the Atomic Scientists* 58, (5): 28–32.

Comprehensive Risk Analysis and Management Network (CRN). 2000–2004. Risk definitions. *Swiss Federal Institute of Technology*. <http://www.isn.ethz.ch/crn/risk_issues/risk_ definitions.cfm>.

Covello, Vincent T. 2003. Keeping your head in a crisis: Responding to communication challenges posed by bioterrorism and emerging infectious diseases. *Association of State and Territorial Health Officers (ASTHO)*. <http://www.dshs.state.tx.us/riskcomm/documents/ 77_Questions.pdf>.

Covello, Vincent T. and Allen, Frederick. 1998. *Seven Cardinal Rules of Risk Communication*. Environmental Protection Agency. Washington, D.C.

Covello, Vincent T. and Sandman, Peter. 2004. Risk communication: Evolution and revolu- tion. *Peter Sandman Website*, August. <http://www.petersandman.com>.

Covello, Vincent T., Peters, Richard G., Wojtecki, Joseph G., and Hyde, Richard C. 2001. Risk communication, the West Nile virus epidemic, and bioterrorism: Responding to the communication challenges posed by the intentional or unintentional release of a pathogen in an urban setting. *Journal of Urban Health: Bulletin of the New York Academy of Medicine* 78 (2): 382–391.

Critical Incident Analysis Group. What is community shielding? *University of Virginia*. <http://www.healthsystem.virginia.edu/internet/ciag/communityshieldinghome.cfm>.

Erikson, Kai. 1994. *A new species of trouble*. W.W. Norton and Company, New York.

Fein, R. A., Vossekuil, B., and Holden, G. 1995. Threat assessment: An approach to prevent targeted violence. *National Institute of Justice: Research in Action*. U.S. Department of Justice, Office of Justice Programs, National Institute of Justice, Washington, D.C.

Fein, Robert A., Vossekuil, Bryan, Pollack, William S., Borum, Randy, Modzeleski, William, and Reddy, Marisa. 2002. Threat assessment in schools: A guide to managing threatening situations and to creating safe school climates. *United States Secret Service and United States Department of Education*. Washington, D.C., May.

Harvard Center for Risk Analysis. 2005. Harvard School of Public Health. <http://www. hcra.harvard.edu/>.

Howell, W. Nathaniel. 2005. Circling the wagons: Community-based responses to bioterrorism. *University of Virginia Health System*. <http://www.healthsystem.virginia.edu/internet/ciag/ reports/circlingthewagons>.

Glass, Thomas A. and Schoch-Spana, Monica. 2002. Bioterrorism and the people: How to vaccinate a city against panic. Confronting biological weapons, *Clinical Infectuous Diseases: Confronting Biological Weapons* 34. The University of Chicago Press, Chicago.

Johnson, James H., Jr. 1985. A model of evacuation—Decision making in a Nuclear Reactor Emergency. *Geographical Review* 75 (4).

Johnson, James H., Jr. and Zeigler, Donald J. 1983. Distinguishing human responses to radiological emergencies. *Economic Geography* 59 (4).

Lake, Ed. 2005–2006. Analyzing the anthrax attacks. <http://www.anthraxinvestigation.com>.

Lengel, Allan. 2005. Little progress in FBI probe of anthrax attacks. *Washington Post*, September 16.

Marshall, M. 2002. What to do in a biological weapons attack. *University of Virginia Law.* http://www.law.virginia.edu/home2002/html/news/2002_fall/bioterror.htm>.

Montgomery County Police Department. 2002. How to be a good witness. <http://www.washingtonpost.com/wp-srv/metro/daily/graphics/sniper/sniper_witness.html>.

National Institute for Chemical Studies. 2001. Sheltering in place as a public protective action. Charleston, West Virginia.

Office of Safe and Drug Free Schools. 2003. Practical information on crisis planning: A guide for schools and communities. *United States Department of Education.*

Quarantelli E. L. 2001. The sociology of panic. *University of Delaware Disaster Research Center.*

Regalado, Antonio. 2002. Pentagon plans smallpox shots for up to 500,000. *Wall Street Journal*, October 14.

Reynolds, Barbara. 2002. Crisis and emergency risk communication: By leaders for leaders. *Centers for Disease Control.* Atlanta, Georgia.

Shane, Scott. 2005. In 4-year anthrax hunt, F.B.I. finds itself stymied, and sued. *New York Times*, September 17.

Sorensen, John H. and Vogt, Barbara M. 2001. Will Duct Tape and Plastic Really Work? Issues related to expedient shelter-in-place. *Oak Ridge National Laboratory*, August.

Shumpert, Barry, Sorensen, John H. and Vogt, Barbara. 2002. Planning protective action decision-making: Evacuate or shelter-in-place? *Oak Ridge National Laboratory*, June.

Slovic, Paul. 2003. A difficult balance: Risk communication in an age of terrorism. *Paper prepared for the Terrorism Task Force of the American College of Neuropsychopharmacology.*

Wolshon, Brian. 2004. A way out. *Transportation Management and Engineering.* <http://www.itsworld.com/tme/Index.cfm?powergrid=rfah=|cfap=&fuseaction=show Article&articleID=5048>.

Wright, Susan. 2004. Taking biodefense too far. *Bulletin of the Atomic Scientists*, November/December.

CHAPTER SEVEN

TRANSPORTATION AND BORDER SECURITY ISSUES

Table Top: Securing the Borders

At approximately 9:34 am one spring morning, a white van crashes into the lobby of the Bank of America Tower in Seattle, Wash. Immediately, the van erupts, decimating the first ten floors and doing extensive damage to the remaining ones. The loss of life is initially reported at 1,200 and growing. Later in the day, the FBI receives a tape from a known terrorist organization claiming responsibility for the attack. In it, the man states that this is just the first bombing in a series of attacks on American symbols of capitalism.

In the days following, the intelligence community is working in a panic to not only determine how the first attack occurred, but also what attacks will follow. Investigation shows that the elements used in the bomb are not widely common in the United States and must have been imported, most likely through the Port of Seattle. The U.S. Customs and Border Patrol cross-references all containers shipped to Seattle. The owner of one container in particular from Shanghai is Alexsandr Stranislov, a suspected terrorist on the Terrorist Screening Center's (TSC) database. After locating the container, Explosive Detection Systems found trace elements of explosive materials and evidence that the container was tampered with at some point.

Days later, Mikel Achmetin arrives at Boston Logan International Airport. The U.S. Customs screening proceeds routinely. However, upon finger print analysis as a part of his VISA check-in, agents quickly discover the man to be another suspected terrorist involved with the Seattle attack on the TSC's watch list. Interrogation leads nowhere. All the DHS knows is that this organization has found a way to infiltrate the country's borders and are successfully orchestrating these attacks.

How were these armed men capable of getting past so many checkpoints in the nation's highest security? What can be implemented to prohibit it?

Introduction

Thousands of miles outline the United States, over 12,000 miles of coastline, 5,525 miles along the U.S./Canadian border, and 1,933 miles between the U.S. and Mexico. Historically, U.S. Border Agents have been concerned with illegal immigration and drug trafficking. However, as a result of terrorists infiltrating the borders for the 9/11 attacks and boarding airlines, transforming them into missiles, a reexamination of the nation's transportation security is one of the highest priorities of the DHS.

This chapter will explore the various modes of transportation, their respective agencies, and the technologies and policies being implemented to improve transportation and border security. Since the attacks, the attention of the nation has been primarily on aviation; however, the government is addressing all means of travel and trade with great concern.

The goal of the DHS is to develop a fluid system that seamlessly works together. The complexities of transportation and border security require long-term, intricate solutions. Even several years after the 9/11 attacks, the DHS is still testing new policies in various sectors. This chapter analyzes steps being taken by the DHS to improve security, and illustrates how the terrorist attacks changed the government's perspective toward such security policies.

Transportation Security

Transportation security, by no means, is a new idea. The U.S. government has always been concerned with transportation security, dating back to the early days of the republic. Following the tragedy of 9/11, the government was faced with the immense task of overhauling domestic security policies. Years of Congressional debate about what steps were necessary halted, clearing the path for various forms of security acts to be signed into law. However, with this influx of new laws and agencies, the government's difficulty of streamlining these additions with our existing infrastructure became evident. As soon as the shock of the attacks wore off, the public began to again question the extensive security now in place. The overriding issue of balancing security with privacy is played out thousands of times each day in our nation's transportation facilities. Much of the public outcry has been toward aviation security, but all modes of transportation have experienced this dilemma. The 9/11 attacks forced the nation to accept two hard truths: first, terrorists were orchestrating these attacks against the U.S. Second, they were passing through the borders somehow. As a result, new legislation regarding border and immigration security like the Visa Entry Reform Act of 2002 passed into law.

Before discussing the emerging policies and technologies, it is necessary to have a clear understanding of the organization of various transportation security agencies. With the creation of the DHS, four directorates were established to govern emergent issues: Border and Transportation Security, Emergency Preparedness and Response, Science and Technology, and IAIP. Within the Border and Transportation Security directorate is the TSA, the Immigration and Naturalization Services (INS), the Coast Guard, and the United States Customs and Border Patrol. These agencies work in conjunction with the IAIP to examine information regarding potential terrorists. In addition, to consolidate intelligence gathered from the CIA, FBI, DIA, and the NSA, the TSC was created (Department of Homeland Security 2005a).

Whereas the majority of these agencies existed prior to the attacks, TSA and the TSC were created with specific focus on combating terrorism. A part of the Aviation and Transportation Security Act (ATSA), TSA was signed into law by President

George W. Bush on November 19, 2001, and was assigned to the Department of Transportation (DoT). However, because of interagency communication issues, TSA was relocated to the DHS in 2003. Much like the DHS, TSA is a consolidation effort to give the federal government more control over the agencies dealing with transportation security. The mission of the organization is to "protect the Nation's transportation systems to ensure freedom of movement for people and commerce" (Transportation Security Administration 2005a).

Initially, TSA's infrastructure and planning were chaotic. Hardly two months had passed since 9/11 when TSA took form. In many cases, programs and policies were being implemented as they were being debated. TSA has been criticized for several of its initiatives and for being too restrictive on civil liberties, primarily the aviation screening programs CAPPS II and Secure Flight, which will be discussed later in the chapter.

With so many different agencies screening people and cargo, a consolidated list of all possible terrorists was needed. By compiling the information from the various intelligence agencies, TSC was created to, as stated in the *Homeland Security Presidential Directive-6*, "consolidate the Government's approach to terrorism screening and provide for the appropriate and lawful use of Terrorist Information in screening processes" (The White House 2003). Since its inception on September 16, 2003, TSC has since experienced assimilation and operational shortcomings. The organization has continually dealt with a wide range of issues, such as fully executing its database with all participating agencies; many need substantial upgrades to operate such an evolving system. However, as the development of the system progresses, biometric data regarding those suspects will also be implemented to increase security (Helm 2005).

Established on October 21, 2001, the National Targeting Center (NTC) analyzes information regarding passengers and cargo entering the country to identify potential terrorists using several layers of technology. One is the Automated Targeting System (ATS). As a result of the Custom and Border Patrol's requirement for all exporters to the United States to declare cargo information ninety-six hours prior to the loading date at the foreign port, the NTC receives that information and analyzes it through the ATS. Once receiving the information, the system checks for any inconsistencies and questionable information; the same is done with passengers. Past history is brought up for passengers that raise red flags and provide evidence for investigations. With upcoming improvements, the ATS will also be able to analyze vehicles along with the passengers they carry (U.S. Customs and Border Patrol 2005b).

Because intercommunication with other federal agencies is mandatory to battle terrorism, NTC maintains daily communication with the FBI's Counterterrorism Watch unit (CT Watch). Much like NTC, CT Watch compiles daily reports on possible terrorist activity and shares it among law enforcement agencies, with any possible matches between agencies being handled through the Joint Terrorism Task Force (Mefford 2003).

Aviation Security, Border and Immigration Security, Port Security, Rail Security

Despite hijacking instances in recent decades, Congress had never passed sweeping legislation for transportation security to address hijacking and other aviation security threats. In the January 2, 2002, edition of the *Toronto Star*, Matthew Brzezinksi explains that in 1995, the intelligence community revealed a terrorist plot known as "Operation Bojinka," in which terrorists conspired to destroy eleven U.S. airliners in Asia and crash a plane into CIA headquarters; however this plan was thwarted weeks before launch. The government's ability to stop these attacks in time gave the country a sense of ease that its security measures were suitable effective. However, following 9/11, the government's attention, and consequently its funding, for transportation and border security increased dramatically.

The various areas of transportation and border security receive funding from multiple sources. The monetary allocations of the DHS illustrate the breakdown of finances. From the FY06 Department of Homeland Security Appropriations Bill, Congress allotted approximately $5.6 billion for aviation security, $19.1 billion for border, immigration, and port security ($14.9 billion for border and immigration security and $4.2 billion for port security), $2.6 billion for the Coast Guard, and $150 million for rail security (U.S. Congress 2005a). Many argue that this funding is not balanced: passenger rail systems are some of the most heavily traveled modes of transportation; yet, it receives significantly less funding compared to aviation and border security. According to the July 15, 2005, *New York Times* article, "Senators clash over where to spend for Homeland Security"; since 9/11, aviation security has received an estimate of $15 billion, opposed to the $250 million allocated for transit security. Furthermore, the majority of that rail security funding was received in 2005 when Congress granted $150 million as opposed to the $65 million and $50 million received in 2003 and 2004, respectively (Peterman 2005, 6). Further arguments will be discussed later in the chapter.

With increased funding and policy focus, significant improvements have been made in transportation and border security. Due to the fact the 9/11 attacks involved airplanes, immediate attention went toward improving aviation security, with attention to port, border, and rail security quickly following. Many people speculate on how the terrorist took control of the airplanes, but a more serious and fundamental concern should address how they were able to penetrate U.S. borders. Government action cannot change the past; but still, the government does have a duty to respond to obvious threats that have been exploited in the past.

Aviation and Airport Terminal Security

By 10:00 am, September 11, 2001, the aviation industry was masked with fear. Before the attacks, most people were apprehensive of flying due to mechanical or external factors. Though hijackings have occurred in the past, such precise and orchestrated sieges had never been seen. Not surprisingly, one of the first issues to pass through Congress was aviation security. Most experts agree that previous screening processes were outdated and security measures were too relaxed. In a GAO report issued nine days after 9/11, multiple concerns were cited regarding Federal Aviation Administration's (FAA) security measures. For instance, FAA had not secured airport computer systems, baggage- screening equipment produced serious weaknesses, and airport security officials are critically undertrained when compared to other nations (General Accounting Office 2001, 1). An immediate and extensive transformation of aviation security was due.

To perform such a renovation, Congress passed the Aviation and Transportation Security Act in 2002. In order to fund this task, in Title 49, Subtitle VII, Part C, Chapter 483 stated, "Congress authorizes the appropriate funding for aviation security. They are authorized to be appropriated for fiscal years 2002, 2003, 2004, and 2005 such sums as may be necessary to carry out chapter 440 and related aviation security activities under this title." For FY 2006, President Bush urged Congress to budget an increase of $156 million for TSA, bringing their budget to over $5.6 billion.

Curb to the Cockpit

The "Curb to the Cockpit" initiative describes the range of TSA's views toward aviation security. In the ATSA, many improvements were mandated. Whereas some concerns were unrealistic for immediate action, others were plausible and necessary, leading to the development of Phases I and II. Phase I addressed the urgent concerns, mainly improvements in cockpit doors and onboard cockpit regulations, and Phase II monitored the progression of more time consuming projects. By and large, the goals set forth by Phase I were successful. By April 9, 2003, FAA announced that all commercial aircrafts were outfitted with the modified, hardened cockpit doors. Designed with stronger steel bars and improved locking mechanisms, the doors are secure enough to repel forced entry. To coincide with these modifications, only designated flight officers were permitted in the cockpit during flight and cockpit doors are required to remain locked. Although the cockpit doors add a heightened level of security, the passengers still remain susceptible to the threat of potential terrorists (Federal Aviation Administration 2002).

A part of the Homeland Security Act, Title XIV required TSA to begin development for a plan to train flight officers to carry firearms, consequently creating the Federal Flight Deck Officer (FFDO) program. Not only do flight officers receive weapons training, but also defensive tactics, safety procedures, and legality issues surrounding appropriate uses of force. Initially, the program was narrowly limited to pilots of commercial passenger aircrafts. However, in December 2003, President Bush signed the Century of Aviation Reauthorization Act, which expanded the list of eligible officers to cargo pilots and specific other crewmembers. One flaw critics point to regarding the FFDO program is training locations. Only one site exists at Artesia, New Mexico, and with demanding flight schedules for pilots, it is difficult to attend. Nevertheless, in January 2006, a bill was proposed in the House of Representatives to improve training availability for interested pilots. Sponsored by Representative Dan Lungren, (R-CA), if passed the bill will keep eligible pilots alert on upcoming training dates and provide charter flights to training facilities (U.S. Congress 2005b).

In addition to the FFDO program, initiatives were taken to increase the number of air marshals deployed daily. Prior to 9/11, the Federal Air Marshal Program consisted of 33 marshals, who were commonly restricted to international flights (9/11 Commission). The heightened fear of terrorist attacks allowed for the air marshal service to be greatly expanded through the ATSA. For security purposes, the number of air marshals currently in service is classified, but it is reported that the number is near 4,000 (Savino 2003).

On December 7, 2005, the Federal Air Marshall Program faced its first hostile situation resulting in gunfire. A 44-year-old man, Rigoberto Alpizar, was shot and killed by air marshals at Miami International Airport after he became agitated and claimed he had a bomb. After leaving the plane, he started running down the airfield, at which point, the federal agents opened fire. Upon further investigation, Alpizar did not have any explosives, and his wife claimed he suffered from a bipolar disease. Even though he did not have any explosives in his baggage, the incident received mixed reviews among Congress and the security community. "This shows that the program has worked beyond our expectations," said Rep. John L. Mica, (R-FL), chairman of the House transportation subcommittee on aviation. "This should send a message to a terrorist or anyone else who is considering disrupting an aircraft with a threat." Others feel that though the air marshals are necessary and acted within protocol, they need expanded training. Jon Adler, national executive vice president of the Federal Law Enforcement Officers Association, claimed that air marshals need more training beyond accessing the severity of a situation and marksman skills (CNN 2005).

Aviation Defense Technology

In fall 2003, former secretary of state Colin Powell claimed that "no threat is more serious to aviation" than Man Portable Air Defense Systems (MANPADS). Simply put, MANPADS are shoulder-armed missile launchers. Approximately 500,000 MANPADS exist, thousands of which are dealt on the black market (U.S. Congress 2003a). It is a justified fear that in the near future, terrorists could begin using MANPADS against commercials airliners. On August 12, 2003, British-Indian Hemant Lakhani attempted to sell undercover FBI agents such a missile while in Newark, N.J. Lakhani's selling point of the missile was to shoot down commercial airliners. Following the initial sale of the missile, Lakhani promised an additional fifty missiles (Department of Justice 2003). The fifty-one anti-aircraft missiles that Lakhani planned to sell only accounts for .01 percent of the missiles existing in the black market today. Some weapons experts claim that MANPADS are not as serious a threat because of their poor accuracy, but it is a major concern that the federal government must address due to the number in circulation and the interest they draw to terrorists.

Aware of this threat, the DHS has begun researching technologies to counter such attacks. In October 2003, the Science and Technology directorate's Counter-MANPADS Office began using existing technologies developed by the military and commercial aviation industry. However, because of the limitation of the counter-MANPADS, they cannot seamlessly transition from military use to commercial use. One technology used is the Direct Infrared Countermeasure (DIRCM), a device that emits beams of light that interferes with the guidance system of a missile. Under their current design, DIRCM's only have 300 hours of use before needing refurbishing. While this is suitable for military use, the costs required to maintain such technology in the commercial industry would be crippling. However, the Science and Technology directorate is using the underlying plans for these devices to develop a commercial one for future use (Pike 2005). Although MANPADS are a necessary concern, more prevalent security questions exist.

One of the largest responsibilities for TSA has been the need for enhanced screening of baggage for airline travel. Prior to 9/11, only 5 percent of all baggage was screened. Upon realization of this statistic, the DHS made it a priority to greatly increase this number. This was simply not possible without major upgrades in baggage screening devices.

TSA began development on Explosive Detection Systems (EDS) in order to accomplish this goal. Initially, TSA attempted to meet the goal using larger devices, such as the CTX and L-3 machines. While the previous standard for EDS, many critics were skeptical of their use on a wide scale. Many airports experienced trouble housing such large devices in an already hectic environment. In addition, the CTX and L-3 are known for having a high false-positive alarm rate. Something more efficient would be needed to check all baggage on a routine basis. The answer was trace detection equipment.

Instead of using the previous technology that acted similar to a CAT scan, trace detections work by a security officer rubbing a cloth over baggage and running the cloth through a machine that checks for trace explosive materials. However, there is a trade-off between these two systems: the previous systems produced size issues, and the trace systems require more labor from the security officers (U.S. Congress 2003b).

As the need for more thorough inspection rises, new detection systems are making their way to airports and other border crossings. Varying systems exist to offer an array of services, such as the Explosive Detection Personnel Portal (EDPP). Much like the traditional metal detectors in design, EDPP collects particles off the subject by shooting blasts of air over the body, and any trace particles with bomb residue are then identified. Another is a vehicle detection system, which has recently been developed by the research corporation Sandia National Technology. The Trace Explosive Detection Vehicle Portal offers a new level of automotive inspection. Prior detections systems require passengers to exit the vehicle. This causes lengthier inspections and a less efficient system of inspection (Sandia National Labratories 2005). Similar to the Personnel Portal, it uses compressed shots of air to pick up any questionable particles. The benefits of this system are that inspection time is at roughly three minutes, it is a one-man operation, and it can be configured to search for illegal drugs as well as explosives. Handheld detection systems offer the ease and versatility that inspectors need. Used mainly for scanning personal items, the handheld devices are capable of detecting less than a fingerprint of explosive elements.

In the event that an item is highly suspected to contain explosive materials, it is necessary to have a method of inspection that does not endanger security staff. To enable this, Remote Explosive Detection systems are being introduced throughout the country, in which the inspector can control the portable detection system from a remote location. Being just as accurate as other methods, it acts as a perfect substitute in a high-risk situation (Sandia National Labratories 2005). Technology like this is essential for winning the war on terrorism, but older forms of explosive detection still have a significant role to play.

Over the years, canines have become an established fixture in law enforcement for purpose of detection. With an acute sense of smell, they can easily be trained to incorporate the investigation of terrorist attack. Like many post-9/11 changes, the preconception of using canines for drug detection changed to identifying bomb residue. In 2005, 364 teams existed at 82 airports, compared to the 289 teams at 64 airports in May 2003. The dogs go through an intense training camp, similar to any other field agents might experience. For eleven weeks, dogs are trained to detect explosive residue in simulated airports, planes, warehouses, and cars. In addition to the canine's training, handlers are also skilled in the managing of any possible explosive they encounter. Upon completion of instruction, the canines return to their assigned location and are evaluated on their ability to complete their tasks in a real-life environment (Transportation Security Administration 2005c).

CAPPS II/Secure Flight Controversy

During the 1990s, FAA realized the growing need for new ways to screen passengers to identify security risks. In 1994, they provided funding to develop a computerized system for such screening methods. Four years later, the Computer-Assisted Passenger Prescreening System (CAPPS) was implemented. The system worked by cross-referencing details about the passengers with their itinerary and biographical information, which then surveyed a federal watch list. Should an alert be present, the passenger was subject to further inspection (General Accounting Office 2004, 5–7). However, 9/11 exposed a serious flaw with the system. People who pose a threat to security were still boarding the planes.

In the Homeland Security Act of 2002, Congress mandated all passengers were subjected to a more intense system, resulting in the creation of CAPPS II. Based on the idea of its predecessor, CAPPS II was a screening process designed to be integrated with the reservation process to check all passengers. When a reservation is made, a Passenger Name Record (PNR), consisting of a person's full name, home address, home phone number, and date of birth, is created and sent to CAPPS II. There, the PNR is verified against personal information from commercial data providers. Once confirmed, the commercial data provider sends a confidential authentication score regarding the passenger so no personal information is transmitted. CAPPS II then uses the score to conduct risk assessments on the passenger based on classified government databases, which searches not only for suspected terrorists but also anyone associated with violent crimes. Once the assessment is completed, the passenger is given one of three risk levels: acceptable, unknown, or unacceptable. Upon check-in, the airline will use these risk levels to determine what level of scrutiny is required for the passenger. Those with an unacceptable risk level will be met with law enforcement agents (General Accounting Office 2004, 7). Figure 7.1 further illustrates this system.

Implementation of this system was continuously delayed due to concerns expressed by the public and Congress that TSA could not properly alleviate. Numerous privacy groups also protested because of the invasive nature of the system. Recognizing that CAPPS II utilized questionable and uncertain practices, a new plan was developed in 2004, Secure Flight. Designed as a less-intrusive version of CAPPS II, Secure Flight offers authorities a more secure way of screening passengers (figure 7.2). Instead of relying on commercial data providers, the PNRs are sent to the TSC, where they are cross-referenced against the Terrorist Screening Database (TSDB).

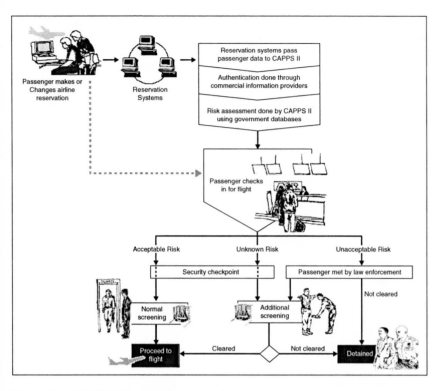

Figure 7.1 CAPPS II Passenger Prescreening Process.
Source: General Accounting Office 2004.

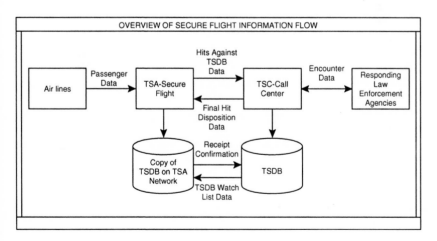

Figure 7.2 Secure Flight Chart.
Source: Office of Inspector General 2005.

Unlike the searches done with CAPPS II, this database will only relate to those suspected of terrorism, not other crimes (General Accounting Office 2005b). The TSA had hoped to have the plan operational by late 2005/early 2006; however, testing procedures continue to hinder the process. Due to the failed attempts of CAPPS II, TSA has felt the pressure to present a working system to the public. Consequently the rushed attempts have led to many of the same problems found with CAPPS II. In February 2006, TSA Assistant Secretary Kip Hawley testified before Congress that TSA would be "re-baselinging" the Secure Flight program. The rushed advancement of the Secure Flight program only caused a later projected release. Currently, TSA is hesitant about discussing any possible timeframe relating to Secure Flight's release (Airport Security Report 2006).

CAPPS II and Secure Flight are just two examples of instances where security and liberty clash. This dilemma is nothing new. For centuries, the pendulum has swung back and forth between the two. History has shown that whenever the country has withstood human-related catastrophe, the pendulum takes a drastic swing toward security. Unfortunately, this overreaction may lead to discriminatory actions. Following the Pearl Harbor attack, hundreds of Japanese Americans were forced in internment camps. Fear of Communism resulted in the McCarthy trials that boldly threatened freedom of speech. The 9/11 attacks are by no means immune to this paranoid phenomenon. The public's outcry against CAPPS II is evidence of this.

Border and Immigration Security

At the turn of the twentieth century, the United States was seen as the world's melting pot. "Give me your tired, your poor, your huddled masses yearning to breathe free," greeted hopeful immigrants at Ellis Island by the boatloads. However, the events of the later half of the century made the nation look at foreign countries with a more watchful eye. No longer was America the young, hopeful nation eager to rise among the world's elite; following World War II, it emerged as one of the world's superpowers. Since that time, immigration procedures have become more meticulous. It is the government's goal to develop a system that protects the nation from dangerous foreign intruders, but it should be a system that is fair to those seeking the necessary steps to enter the country.

The nation's heightened xenophobia caused by the 1920s sparked concern with the borders. In the interest of national security, immigration quotas were set for specific countries and certain ethnicities were turned away at the nation's previously open doors. In order to secure the nation's borders, Congress mandated the formation of the U.S. Border Patrol. Like any organization, the Border Patrol grew and changed with the times. Expanding from mainly 450 former Texas Rangers on horseback with six-shooters, the modern Border Patrol is a legion of over 9,500 officers patrolling twenty sectors along the country's borders (U.S.Customs and Border Patrol 2006).

Many believe that strengthening border control is a mandatory step toward homeland security. It is estimated that between eleven and twelve million illegal immigrants live in the United States, as of 2005 (General Accounting Office 2005a). Many simply migrate for hopes of a better future; however, the vast number of undocumented aliens creates a serious security problem. Following the 9/11 attacks, the Border Patrol's concern shifted from the issue of illegal immigrants and drug trafficking to terrorism. The organization is still concerned with the former issues, but the threat of future terrorist attacks has taken priority. Because the goals have changed, a new strategy needed to be developed to replace the successful 1994 model based on "prevention through deterrence." The following is the five-part list of national objectives set by the Border Patrol's 2004 National Border Patrol Strategy, in attempts to secure the United States from intruders:

National Border Patrol Strategy 2004

1. Establish substantial probability of apprehending terrorists and their weapons as they attempt to enter the United States illegally between the ports of entry.
2. Deter illegal entries through improved enforcement.
3. Apprehend and deter smugglers of humans, drugs, and other contraband.
4. Leverage "smart border" technology to multiply the effect of enforcement personnel.
5. Reduce crime in border communities and consequently improve quality of life and economic vitality of targeted areas.

Through this plan, the Border Patrol hopes to successfully find unique methods for securing the nation's distinctly different border regions, while maintaining a unifying set of guiding principles.

Secure Border Initiative

DHS Secretary Michael Chertoff stated in 2005, "This is a complex problem with a complex solution." The overall framework for the future of border security lies with the Secure Border Initiative. It is not merely based on adding new technology and agents to the borders; it is an overarching initiative consisting of a myriad of strategies to secure the borders. The DHS intends all aspects of border security, staffing, technology, and detection to work together seamlessly. The first step of this initiative is appropriating funding to ensure that all necessary steps can be taken. Since 9/11, the CBP has received a $2.8 billion increase in border security spending. Through legislation signed by President Bush, the number of border agents is 12,500 from 9,500, up 30 percent since the attacks (The White House 2005). In addition, the ICE received approximately $3.9 billion (Department of Homeland Security 2005c). With the added funding, the ICE will employ more criminal investigators to access problems areas.

While additional funding is expected for new technologies to better secure the borders, some border control policies are inefficient and outdated. For years, the policy of detection has been to detain and release illegal immigrants; basically, anyone that is caught is released back to the Mexican or Canadian border. This does little to solve the problem because the aliens generally simply try again. The DHS hopes to switch to a "catch and return" policy. Under this change, illegal immigrants will be detained and then returned to their native home. By doing so, the financial burden will inhibit them from returning to the border (Department of Homeland Security 2005b). To implement this change though, additional difficulties arise, and it will not be put into practice before fall 2006, according Chertoff. In order to return illegal aliens to nations other than Mexico, clearance must be granted from the foreign nations, which generally takes weeks or months.

The "catch and return policy" will improve border security, but measures also need to be taken to secure the nation from those who successfully enter the country. In 2004, President Bush proposed a new reform to America's immigration policy, the Fair and Secure Immigration Reform. Holding true to his priority to employ U.S. citizens first, President Bush's plan seeks to grant temporary worker status to immigrants when no citizen is willing to take the job. The program is available to foreign citizens, and it will allow undocumented illegal aliens to enlist in legal employment. By enlisting these previously illegal men and women, the program hopes to decrease exploitation of undocumented workers. Participants would be granted a three-year license with a one-time renewal, after which they would return to their native country. Just like all other immigrants, they may apply for citizenship; however, involvement with the program does not expedite the process (The White House 2004).

Even though the Bush administration hopes that this reform will curb the number of unregistered illegal aliens residing in the United States, others see it as a failure in the long term. Texas Senator Lamar Smith stated, "When you have people living here for six years who have brought their family, who have put down roots, it makes no sense to think they're going home." Greater opportunities and a better future are some of the reasons many immigrants flock to the United States. This reform does pose the threat of the same problem resurfacing when the temporary liscenses expire.

Stocking Up the Borders

In regard to technology, this initiative plans to integrate existing technology with new innovations to provide a compatible, comprehensive system. Some new technologies include critical infrastructure systems, high traffic areas, and Unmanned Aerial Vehicles (UAVs). In September 2005, the DHS approved a 14-mile infrastructure system for San Diego, Calif. This system will include added security such as stadium lighting, surveillance cameras, and more access roads for better mobility (Chertoff 2005). UAVs are critical because of the area they cover without needing a pilot to operate the aircraft. The DHS is cooperating with the DoD to further research on technologies that will advance security efficiency.

Ushering in a new era of immigration standards, the US-VISIT program is the cornerstone to the future of automated entry/exit procedures. Using biometric and biographical information, all foreign visitors will be cross-referenced against watch lists in government databases. Anyone entering the United States through a US-VISIT station will have to undergo a biometric finger scan along with a digital facial picture. Being able to accurately identify a visitor with these measurements will reduce secondary inspections. Currently, US-VISIT entry stations are at 115 airports, 15 seaports, and 50 of the busiest land ports of entry (U.S. Customs and Border Patrol 2005a).

The Future of Immigration and Border Security

As technology continues to improve and gain sophistication, issues pertaining to its implementation and related policies still weigh on Congress and the Hispanic community. In the early months of 2006, immigration debate escalated to rare heights, causing dissention among the Republican-dominated Congress and White House. Several House Resolutions passed in December 2005 prompted this controversy, most notably H.R. 4437, the Border Protection, Antiterrorism, and Illegal Immigration Control Act of 2005. In summary, the resolution would make all illegal immigrants felons and mandate all employers to supply documentation for all employees. In addition to penalizing illegal immigrants, the bill also makes aiding and abetting illegal immigrants a felony (U.S. Congress 2005a). Furthermore, a 700-mile fence between Mexico and the United States is also being proposed (Hendricks 2006).

As the House agreed on resolutions that would expel millions of illegal immigrants, the Senate discussed plans for amnesty. On March 27, 2006, the Senate Judiciary Committee passed a bill to the full Senate that would legalize approximately eleven million illegal immigrants, and allow 400,000 foreigners into the United States each year as part of a guest worker program (Swarns 2006).

This is not the first attempt at granting amnesty to those residing in the United States illegally. The Immigration Reform and Control Act of 1986 addressed both sides of the issue. First, the bill made it illegal for employers to knowingly hire undocumented workers. Second, the bill granted one-year amnesty to those that had been in the United States for at least five years. Over six million illegal immigrants were granted amnesty through the Act; however, the aftereffects have been felt since (General Accounting Office 2005b, 2). Even though the bill prohibits undocumented employees, only three citations were issued to companies nationwide in 2004, down from 417 in 1999, according to a GAO report. Also, since 1986, the number of illegal immigrants has escalated to between eleven and twelve million (6–7). Many social conservatives criticize the previous bill because families came to the United States to join those granted amnesty.

Many of the fundamental arguments in the debate are nothing new. Two opposing sides on the issue remain. Many social conservatives see illegal immigrants as a threat, not only a security threat, but a threat toward Americans vying for blue-collar jobs, such as construction and farming. Additionally, because illegal immigrants do not pay taxes, their children suffer the misfortune of being denied public education. On the other hand, others believe that these immigrants benefit our economy. Their willingness to work for low pay keeps costs down for services. Also, the speculated eleven million illegal immigrants in the United States still are consumers, which helps the economy. The future for illegal immigrants living in the country remains unresolved, but it will be an important issue to study with regard to border security.

Maritime and Port Security

Prior to the 9/11 attacks, maritime security was largely limited to navigational and environmental concerns. Although application to terrorism and port security did not seem relevant for the majority of Congress, several pieces of legislation was proposed shortly before the attacks. Former Senator Bob Graham (D-FL) was a proponent for such legislation. Reaching as far back as 1999, Graham advocated for the agreement of the Seaport Security Commission from the Clinton administration.

On July 20, 2001, Senator Graham and Senator Fritz Hollings (D-SC) introduced the Maritime and Port Security Act of 2001, a precursor to the Maritime Transportation

Security Act that was proposed after the attacks. The bill appropriated approximately $230 million for the Coast Guard and the Maritime Administration (MARAD) between FY 2003 and 2006 for screening technology and vulnerability assessments (Hollings 2001).

Securing the Seas

Since 9/11, maritime security has been subjected to the same reevaluation that aviation and border security has undergone; the previous threats of drug trafficking and alien smuggling no longer take precedence. Whereas it is has been a common fear that terrorists themselves will find a way through the nation's borders, the government must also be vigilant with those items being shipped into ports from foreign soil. So far, situations involving catastrophic weapons being shipped to terrorists already on U.S. soil have been limited to fictional novels and films; however, it is a possibility the United States must be prepared to defend against. In response to such threats, the DHS is drastically improving port security, utilizing new technologies and existing ones.

Like the ATSA, maritime security required a large overhaul of its security practices, started in the Maritime Transportation Security Act of 2002 (MTSA). From an economic point of view, the nation's ports are not only the most crucial, but also some of the most vulnerable trade hubs. Maritime transportation accounts for over 95 percent of U.S. international trade. With so many miles of open water and thousands of cargo containers entering ports daily, the Coast Guard and Customs face the daunting task of developing security policies that ensure safety in a plausible way.

Under the MTSA, the U.S. Coast Guard will:

- Conduct vulnerability assessments of all vessels and facilities that pose a high risk for security incidents
- Develop National and Regional Security Plans
- Develop regulations for secure areas in ports

Other policies to be implemented are:

- Ports, facilities, and vessels are required to develop comprehensive security and incident response plans
- Local port security committees are required to improve coordination with federal agencies
- A grant program is to be established to make equitable allocations to port authorities, waterfront facility operators, and state and local agencies
- Grant monies are to be specified for research and development and security training for federal, state, and private security personnel
- A collective maritime intelligence system is to be established to analyze information on vessels operating in U.S. waters
- A Coast Guard Marshall program is authorized and supplemented by Maritime Safety and Security Teams (MSSTs) to safeguard the public, vessels, harbors, ports, and waterways
- A Maritime Security Advisory Committee is required to report on National Maritime Security matters (U.S. Congress 2002)

However, the reach of the MTSA is far less than sufficient to properly secure the shipping industry. Within international waters, the country's jurisdiction becomes a large gray area, and the enforcement of regulations loses its bite. Fortunately, much of the world agreed with U.S. concerns regarding maritime security following the terrorist attacks. After a year of researching for ways to improve upon the 1974 Safety of Life At Sea Convention, the International Maritime Organization met in December 2002. What resulted from the convention was the International Ship and Port Facility Security Code (ISPS Code).

In many ways, the ISPS Code mirrors the MTSA. The underlying theme of the ISPS Code is improving security by reducing vulnerability. Each participating country is to conduct risk assessments of their ports, through which they will develop appropriate security plans. All importing ships will undergo a risk assessment and suitable measures will be taken regarding how the ships and the port security assessments align (International Maritime Organization 2002).

What's Coming in, When It's Coming in

In addition to these policies, several programs and technologies are being implemented to further the success of port security. One of the most notable is ACE, Automated Commercial Environment. First proposed ten years ago to replace the Automated Commercial System, ACE has found difficulty receiving funding for development. ACE was not designed to function as a security measure, but more as a system to revolutionize trade information (see figure 7.3). As stated in the GAO Report on ACE, its purpose is to (1) promote more efficient movement of legitimate trade and more effective enforcement of trade laws; (2) strengthen border security

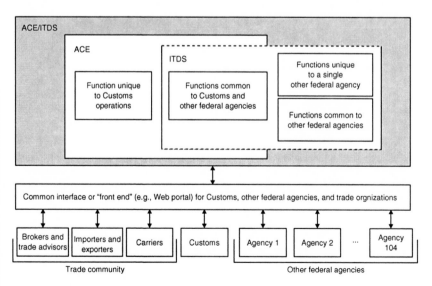

Figure 7.3 Flow Chart of ACE Operations.
Source: General Accounting Office 2003.

operations; (3) include a single system interface between the trade community and the federal government, known as the International Trade Data System, which is to reduce the data-reporting burden placed on the trade community and facilitate the collection and dissemination of trade data for agencies with trade-related missions (General Accounting Office 2003, 9).

Despite its ability to change the infrastructure of global trade, Congress did not believe it was entirely necessary to fund the project. However, with the 9/11 attacks, Customs was given more attention from Congress and the funding for the project was provided with the expectation that ACE would also function as a security measure. Even though a similar project, Customs-Trade Partnership Against Terrorism (C-TPAT), was designed entirely for trade security, ACE's automated data collection will make it easier for Customs to screen cargo.

Before 9/11, U.S. ports were the country's first and last lines of defense when it came to containerized shipping. As 90 percent of the nation's imports arrive in containers, it is one of the nation's most vulnerable points. As a result, in January 2002, the CBP announced the establishment of the Container Security Initiative. The goal was to establish Custom Agents at foreign ports to inspect containers before their arrival at U.S. ports. Similar to the concepts behind Secure Flight, containers will be prescreened for security risks using new detection technologies. Also, improved tamper-evident containers will alert agents of any wrongdoing (U.S. Customs and Border Patrol 2006). Initially, the program was implemented at twenty foreign ports. However, the CBP hopes to increase the number of ports from forty-two to fifty by the end of 2006 (Trade Facilitation Alliance 2006). The CSI is also beneficial to participating countries. In a reciprocal manner, countries in the program are permitted to deploy agents to U.S. ports for similar inspection.

Along with seeking to improve container security, the CBP is taking its initiative a step further. The C-TPAT is a voluntary initiative to strengthen relationships and communication between the United States and foreign businesses that are responsible for the supply chain of imports to the United States. C-TPAT hopes to encourage foreign consolidators, manufactures, and related businesses to take a higher responsible in their security measures and streamline them with those of the CBP. Once these companies have established a low-risk level, the CBP can focus its attention on other unknown companies (U.S. Customs and Border Patrol 2005c).

Whether companies are applying for the program because of willingness or force is still to be determined. The program is voluntary, but retailers such as JC Penny and Target require their vendors to participate to ensure security in their supply chains. In order to maintain business, thousands of companies are attempting to join C-TPAT, causing an excess of applications with the review board. To review an entire application can take up to a year (Gooley 2004). Regardless of its difficulties, C-TPAT will improve trade by ensuring a company's entire supply chain is secure.

Another project to improve port security is Operation Safe Commerce. Enacted by TSA with the CBP, the project is a pilot program to give port authorities inclusive information regarding containers throughout all stages of shipment. To further this program, "smart containers" are being developed and tested. With a "smart container," the CBP will have access to real-time information about the container's location and tampering notification. Full deployment of "smart containers" could exponentially increase port security; however, finding an inexpensive method of production that is both sustainable in ocean environments and precise regarding tampering notification is still a complex issue (Transportation Security Administration 2003).

Because there are so many ports with varying needs, the 2005 Port Security Grant Program was designed to fund sustainable risk-based efforts for maritime port protection from terrorism, explosives, and other nonconventional threats leading to significant loss of infrastructure and possibly life. The ports highest at risk will have access to the program's $140 million budget to fund programs developing IED and other technologies. To establish a port's appropriate risk level, the ODP, the U.S. Coast Guard, and the IAIP Directorate created a formula to gauge all elements that would affect a port during an attack. As stated in the ODP's FY 2005 Port Security Grant Program:

$$Risk = Consequence \times Vulnerability \times Threat$$

The elements of each risk factor include (Department of Homeland Security 2004):

- consequence: people, economic, national security, port specific special considerations (hazardous materials, oil);
- vulnerability: distance from open water, number of port calls, presence of tankers; and
- threat: credible threats and incidents (intelligence community, USCG, IA), less credible threats and incidents (operational indicators), vessels of interest.

Tension in port security escalated again in February 2006 when Dubai Ports World, a company of the United Arab Emirates, announced their plans to purchase six U.S. ports. After reviewing the proposal, President Bush stated he believed the deal was sound, creating an upheaval throughout Washington, D.C. Republicans and Democrats alike announced their dissatisfaction. After incessant pressure from Congress, Dubai declared its plans to abandon the deal and sell off its remaining U.S. operations to a U.S.-based firm (CNN 2006).

Such events further illustrate the continued apprehension surrounding transportation security. As this new age of security progresses, the nation must remain sensitive when dealing with bold actions affecting travel and trade.

Rail Security

Early one summer morning, Americans woke up and began their daily routine. Settling down at their desks, or sipping a cup of coffee, they turned on the television only to find startling reports. All over CNN were shots of hysteria, people running everywhere, ambulances blaring, and news anchors trying to make sense of the situation. However, this was 2005, not 2001.

On July 7, 2005, strategically placed explosives detonated on three London subway trains and one bus. The reports were eerily familiar; terrorists had infiltrated a mass transit system and succeeded in creating terror. Unfortunately, this was not the first time such an event occurred in a subway system. On March 11, 2004, in Madrid, Spain, four trains were attacked during rush hour, taking the lives of 191 people and wounding 1,460 others. Evidently, passenger rail attacks is not just a speculated fear, but an experienced reality, especially in Europe.

Making Ends Meet

Even though the most recent publicized terrorist attacks in a Western nation have been against rail systems, it only received $150 million in 2005 compared to the $15 billion appropriated to airline security. Part of the problem is public interest. The 9/11 attacks were so shocking, in part, because flying is an established fear for many. Even though transportation bills aiding aviation and border funding are passed with relative ease, those concerning rail systems are viewed as expendable. In 2004, the Rail Security Act was introduced in the Senate. If passed, the bill would have appropriated $1 billion to fund rail security in addition to conducting risk assessments on all commuter and freight systems. The bill succeeded in the Senate in October 2004, but never became a law. However, a new bill, the Rail Security Act of 2005, was introduced in the Senate by Senator John McCain on July 11, 2005, at which point it was passed on to the Committee on Commerce, Science, and Transportation. As of April 2006, the bill remains under review by the committee (U.S. Congress Senate 2005).

Several factors contribute to the complexity of rail security. First, rail cars operate by maintaining a rigid schedule on a fixed track. Once a car begins to slide off schedule, little can be done to fix it. Another factor is the public's willingness to undergo intense screening. Whereas flying is yet to become a routine activity in society, boarding a rail car is part of the daily routine of millions. Submitting to the same searches day after day is unacceptable to rail passengers.

It is also necessary to understand the expected results of a terrorist attack on rail systems. Where a successful attack on an aircraft usually results in a 100 percent fatality of all on board, and additional loss of life should the plane be used as a missile, an attack on rail systems have a low recorded fatality rate. According to a Congressional Research Service study on rail security, between 1998 and 2003, terrorists conducted 181 attacks on rail systems worldwide. Of these 181 attacks, only 431 deaths resulted, with one accounting for 252 deaths. Unfortunately, the Madrid and London attacks deviate from this trend, with 191 and 52 deaths occurring, respectively (Peterman 2005).

Another debate concerning funding is whether localities and transit agencies or the federal government should be primarily responsible for funding. On one hand, local transit authorities claim that federal funding is required because rail systems operate at deficit and the continued strain on local and state budgets limits further spending. Additionally, the proposed security measures are designed to protect the nation against foreign terrorists, making it a federal concern. On the other hand, federal taxes should not go toward issues in such isolated areas, and the security measures will help reduce local crime, making it a local matter (4).

In the midst of funding debates, the TSA has conducted several efforts to begin improvements on rail security. A major concern of passenger rail systems is that they rely heavily on routine and efficiency. It is expected that each day, the same number of people will ride the same cars to the same stops and at the same time. It is extremely predictable, making it an ideal target. All this creates a distinct challenge for the DHS. Nevertheless, the Transit and Rail Inspection Pilot (TRIP) was implemented through a multiphased system at several rail stations to test the feasibility of screening passengers and luggage. Each phase was conducted simultaneously at three different locations to test various concerns. The first testing took place at the Washington, D.C., Metro stop in New Carlton, Md. There, screening technologies were tested during rush hour boarding times: 8835 passengers and 9875 pieces of baggage were passed through an EDPP. TRIP Phase II examined 3,817 checked bags, 3,997 temporarily stored personal items, 527 unclaimed bags, and 253 items of drop-off cargo traveling on Amtrak trains at Union Station in Washington, D.C. The final phase of TRIP was conducted on a Shoreline East commuter train. Instead of screening passengers and luggage during the boarding process, this phase evaluated the efficiency of technologies screening for explosives while the car is in transit. The final phase successfully screened 5,817 passengers and 6,297 carry-on items (Transportation Security Administration 2006).

Results for testing were positive. On average, over 90 percent of passenger evaluation cards stated that the screening processes were satisfactory and had public support. In addition to the passenger support of the testing, it marked the first major security initiative for the passenger rail system. Future screening systems will not be as intrusive as airport screenings, which can be attributed to the overwhelming public and Congressional support. Despite the encouraging findings, implementation on a full-scale produces serious concerns. Every metropolitan city with a passenger rail system has dozens of stations, many of which are not designed to include efficient screening systems. Also, the cost of equipment and installation at every station is not feasible with current funding (Transportation Security Administration 2006).

Even with recent efforts to improve rail security, it is not likely to gain the same prominence as other modes of transportation. Proposed bills that significantly increase spending get stalled in Congress among review committees, and the public's eye is still focused on aviation and border security. On the other hand, despite its high vulnerability, attacks on subway systems generally result in low mortality rates. In addition, many experts believe the sheer number of subway stations make it impossible to conduct the same security overhaul that has been seen with aviation. Hence, funding should be directed at more intangible efforts such as intelligence gathering and improving national defense. Either way, it will be interesting to see how rail security is viewed in the coming years.

Conclusion

The face of transportation security is drastically different from the one prior to 9/11. It is no longer an issue of losing funding from Congress due to budget concerns, nor is it just a fear of overly paranoid commuters. Whereas decades of foreign terrorist attacks faintly echoed across the U.S. borders, the attacks of 9/11 awoke the nation to the possibilities of terrorists' capability to exploit the transportation system. The question everyone asked was, "how do we stop it from happening again?" Even with several years having passed since the attacks, much remains to be done to answer this question. However, polices and technologies created have significantly improved transportation security. Over $5 billion is spent annually on aviation security. With TSA established, baggage screening and onboard safety are no longer the overall responsibility of the airline industry. Federal mandates stating EDSs are placed in all major airports to help restore people's faith in flying.

Transportation and border security is indeed a perplexing issue that travelers encounter daily in innumerable ways. The possibility of future attacks will always remain. However, appropriately funding research for technologies such as UAVs and creating policies and systems capable of evolving with the times will reduce that threat. It is important to be responsive when initiatives become outdated. Before 9/11, airline experts knew CAPPS was antiquated, but nothing was done. Also, the government cannot wait until another domestic event occurs. The Madrid subway attacks in 2004 and the London bombings in 2005 make it clear that passenger rail systems are ideal targets for terrorists; however, rail security is still the most underfunded mode of transportation. Unfortunately, despite all the efforts by the DHS, many experts raise lingering concerns.

On December 5, 2005, the 9/11 Commission issued a report card for the government regarding their follow-up on the recommendations made in the commission's report; the grades were dismal.

Transportation Security

- National Strategy for Transportation Security: **C**
- Improve airline passenger prescreening: **F**
- Improve airline screening checkpoints to detect explosives: **C**
- Checked bag and cargo screening: **D**

Border Security

- Better terrorist travel strategy: **Incomplete**
- Comprehensive screening system: **C**
- Biometric entry–exit screening system: **B**
- International collaboration on borders and document security: **D**
- Standardize secure identifications: **B** (Eggen 2005)

This report card illustrates the difficulty in implementing such widespread improvement in a short period of time. Although the government has continually worked to develop programs to improve security, it is another challenge to seamlessly integrate them with the established system. Some issues lie with communication problems, others with Congress. Many issues trigger priority conflicts over funding and relevance. Whatever the problems may be, the Commission urged Congress to take the appropriate actions to secure the nation from another attack. During the release of the report, former chairman of the 9/11 Commission Thomas Kean stated, "We shouldn't need another wake-up call. We believe that the terrorists will strike again, so does every responsible expert that we have talked to. And if they do, and these reforms that might have prevented such an attack have not been implemented, what will our excuse be?" Only time will show how Congress acts with regard to this progress report.

Technology is progressing at an exponential rate. Determining how to implement it in the nation's security in a balanced manner will be an ongoing debate, but a much needed one to not only ensure safety but also liberty. Unfortunately, so much remains.

Case Study: Privacy Implications of CAPPS II and Secure Flight

Throughout history, governments have struggled with the conflict between civil liberties and security. This struggle is more evident since the 9/11 attacks. This case study will focus on TSA's reform of CAPPS, which led to the failed programs CAPPS II and Secure Flight, and the implications it has for the Privacy Act and other privacy legislation.

Following the conception of CAPPS II, privacy advocates were apprehensive of its obtrusive and secretive nature. Initially, TSA requested seven exemptions from the 1974 Privacy Act, an act specifically designed to prohibit the government from maintaining a confidential system of records on a group of persons.

The TSA argued that passenger records used with CAPPS II needed confidentiality in order to successfully monitor those warranting suspicion. Millions of citizen's background was to be inspected to attain a risk assessment, none of whom would have access to their file. If implemented, it would have been the largest confidential background checks in U.S. history (Sobel 2004).

In February 2004, the U.S. GAO issued its report on the legitimacy of the system. The fifty-three-page document is a scathing report on a range of problems with the system. Table 7.1 illustrates the unresolved issues of CAPPS II.

Table 7.1   Eight Key Issues Identified by Public Law 108–90 and the Status of Efforts to Address Them, as of January 1, 2004

Issues	Fully addressed	
	Yes	No
Developmental and operational issues		
1. Establish internal oversight board	√	
2. Assess accuracy of databases		√
3. Stress test system and demonstrate efficacy and accuracy		√
4. Install operational safeguards to protect system from abuse		√
5. Install security measures to protect system from unauthorized access		√
6. Establish effective oversight of system use and operation		√
Public acceptance issues		
7. Address all privacy concerns		√
8. Create redress process for passengers to correct erroneous information		√

Source: General Accounting Office 2004.

Upon receiving this report, public unrest grew and TSA's own review of the program revealed that a new plan was needed. As a result, in July 2004, former secretary of the DHS Tom Ridge announced the agency's abandonment of CAPPS II to pursue Secure Flight.

Though TSA guarantees Secure Flight will alleviate the privacy concerns surrounding CAPPS II, privacy advocates still are hesitant with the system. The initial testing phase of Secure Flight again requested Privacy Act exemptions and commercial data regarding passengers. Because of these privacy concerns, testing was postponed until September 2005.

In September 2005, a nine-member panel of privacy and security experts, known as the Secure Flight Working Group, assembled to review the progress of the Secure Flight. In its concluding report, the board submitted that Secure Flight still had yet to identify the basic goals of the program.

> TSA has not articulated what the specific goals of Secure Flight are. Based on the limited test results presented to us, we cannot assess whether even the general goal of evaluating passengers for the risk they represent to aviation security is a realistic or feasible one or how TSA proposes to achieve it. We do not know how much or what kind of personal information the system will collect or how data from various sources will flow through the system. (Secure Flight Working Group 2005, 5)

The February 2006 announcement that the current framework for Secure Flight was implausible and a "re-baselining" would have to be conducted in order to have a functional system only further complicates matters for TSA. The ongoing debate between TSA, Congress, and privacy advocates demonstrates the difficulty of balancing security and privacy in an era masked by fear of further attacks. But what can be assessed is that despite the presence of terrorist attacks, the American people still fervently cling to their fundamental civil liberties.

Discussion Questions

1. Is such an invasive screening process necessary for the aviation industry?
2. Should screening processes be a responsibility for TSA or individual airline agencies?
3. If they promise to discard all records, should TSA be allowed to use commercial data regarding passengers for testing phases? Why or why not?
4. How will more records help guarantee success for the program?

Key Terms and Definitions

Automated Commercial Environment (ACE). An automated data collecting system that would revolutionize the port industry by simplifying the processing system for incoming trade.

Aviation and Transportation Security Act (ATSA). An inclusive bill signed into law by President George W. Bush in 2001 that mandated sweeping changes with regard to aviation security, most notably, the formation of the TSA.

Computer-Assisted Passenger Prescreening System (CAPPS II). A prescreening system designed after 9/11, which assessed a passenger's potential risk by cross-referencing personal information with itinerary plans and federal watch lists. After receiving significant criticism, the program was abandoned in 2003.

Explosive Detection Systems. Machines similar to metal detectors that are designed to pick up trace elements of explosives.

Man Portable Air Defense Systems (MANPADS). Shoulder-armed missiles, widely popularized by terrorists for their powerful nature and prolific number on the black market.

Maritime Transportation Security Act of 2002. Much like the ATSA, an act signed in law to allow for sweeping changes to be made for maritime and port security by setting new standards for the industry.

National Targeting Center (NTC). A federal agency created to analyze information on people and events looking for information about potential terrorists.

Secure Border Initiative. The DHS's multiyear campaign to secure the nation's borders through an array of staffing, policy, and technological changes.

Secure Flight. The successor of CAPPS II offering a less intrusive, but still secure method screening passengers. However, similar to CAPPS II, Secure Flight has yet to be released due to operational problems.

Terrorist Screening Center (TSC). An organization created to consolidate the various enforcement agencies' watchlists, to supply a comprehensive list to better serve the nation's security efforts.

Transit and Rail Inspection Pilot (TRIP). A multiphased system implemented to test the feasibility of screening passengers and luggage at two rail stations and aboard one commuter train.

Transportation Security Administration (TSA). An agency created under the Aviation and Transportation Security Act to decide and implement appropriate actions needed to ensure security.

References

Airport Security Report. 2006. TSA puts breaks on "Secure Flight." March 1.
Chertoff, Michael. 2005. Remarks by Homeland Security Secretary Michael Chertoff at the Houston Forum. Houston Forum, Houston, Tex. November 2.
CNN. 2005. Man killed after bomb claim at airport. December 7. <http://www.cnn.com/2005/US/12/07/airplane.gunshot/index.html>.
———. 2006. Timeline of controversial ports deal. March 9. <http://www.cnn.com/2006/US/02/23/ports.timeline/index.html>.
Department of Homeland Security. 2003. Secretary Ridge announces significant steps in enhancing maritime security. October 23.
———. 2004. *Fiscal Year 2005: Homeland Security Grant Program* Office of State and Local Government Coordination and Preparedness Office for Domestic Preparedness. Government Printing Office, Washington, D.C.
———. 2005a. DHS organization: History. <http://www.dhs.gov/dhspublic/interapp/editorial/editorial_0133.xml>.

Department of Homeland Security. 2005b. Fact sheet: Secure Border Initiative. Press Release. November 2. <http://www.dhs.gov/dhspublic/interapp/press_release/press_release_0794.xml>.

————. 2005c. DHS Receives $2.4 Billion Increase for 2006 Appropriations. Press Release. October 18. <http://www.dhs.gov/dhspublic/display?content=4894>.

Department of Justice. 2003. British arms dealer Lakhani indicted for attempting to aid terrorists. Press Release. December 18. <http://www.usdoj.gov/usao/nj/publicaffairs/NJ_Press/files/lakh1218_r.htm>.

Eggen, Dan. 2005. U.S. is given failing grade by 9/11 panel. *The Washington Post*. December 6: A01.

Federal Aviation Administration. 2002. Fact sheets: Aircraft security accomplishments since September 11. <http://www.faa.gov/news/fact_sheets/factsheets/2002/factsheets_020905.htm>.

General Accounting Office. 2001. *Aviation security: Terrorist acts illustrate severe weaknesses in aviation security*. GAO, Washington D.C. September 1.

————. 2003. *Customs service modernization: Automated commercial environment progressing, but further acquisition management improvements needed*. GAO, Washington D.C. February 9.

————. 2004. *Aviation security: Computer-assisted passenger prescreening faces significant implementation challenges*. GAO, Washington D.C. February 7.

————. 2005a. *Information on certain illegal aliens arrested in the United States*. GAO, Washington, D.C. May.

————. 2005b. *Immigration enforcement: Weaknesses hinder employment verification and worksite enforcement efforts*. GAO, Washington D.C. August.

Gooley, Toby. 2004. C-TPAT: Separating hype from reality. *Logistics Management*. August 1. <http://www.logisticsmgmt.com/article/CA445765.html>.

Helm, Bert. 2005. Terrorist watch list tangles. *BusinessWeek Online*. May 11.

Hendricks, Tyche. 2006. Border security or boondoggle?. *The San Francisco Chronicle*. February 26: A1.

Hollings, Ernest F. 2001. Statement of Chairman Ernest F. Hollings to the Senate Commerce Committee Hearing on Seaport Security. July 24.

International Maritime Organization. 2002. IMO adopts comprehensive maritime security measures. Press Release. December 13. <http://www.imo.org/Newsroom/mainframe.asp?topic_id=583&doc_id=2689>.

Mefford, Larry A. 2003. Testimony before the Subcommittee on Cybersecurity, Science, and Research and Development, and the Subcommittee on Infrastructure and Border Security of the Select Committee on Homeland Security. 108th Cong., 1d sess. September 4.

Office of Inspector General. 2005. Review of the Terrorist screening Screening Center's efforts to support the Secure Flight program. OIG, Washington D.C. August.

Pike, John. 2005. Infrared countermeasures systems. GlobalSecurity.Org. <http://www.globalsecurity.org/military/systems/aircraft/systems/ircm.htm>.

Peterman, David Randall. 2005. *Passenger rail security: Overview of issues*. Congressional Research Service. Government Printing Office, Washington, D.C.

Savino, David. 2003. CDI Terrorism Project Factsheet: The Sky Marshal Program. Press release. <http://www.cdi.org/friendlyversion/printversion.cfm?documentID=845>.

Secure Flight Working Group. 2005. *Report of the Secure Flight Working Group*. Government Printing Office, Washington, D.C. 5.

Sandia National Laboratories. 2005. Explosives detection. Sandia National Laboratories. <http://www.sandia.gov/programs/homeland-security/explosives.html>.

Sobel, David. 2004. Testimony before the House Committee on Transportation and Infrastructure Aviation Subcommittee on "The status of the computer-assisted passenger prescreening system (CAPPS II)." 108th Cong., 2d sess. March 17.

Swarns, Rachel. Bill to broaden immigration law gains in senate. *The New York Times*. March 28.

Trade Facilitation Alliance. 2006. CBP plans on growing, evolving programs in 2006. February 20.

Transportation Security Administration. 2003. Secretary Ridge announces the awarding of $28 millions for Operation Safe Commerce. Press Release. July 24. <http://www.tsa.gov/public/display?theme=44&content=090005198003f277>.

———. 2005a. About TSA: <http://www.tsa.gov/public/display?theme=7>.

———. 2005c. Canine and explosives program. <http://www.tsa.gov/public/display?theme=32&content=0900051980034663>.

———. 2006. *Transit & Passenger Rail Security*. January 27. <http://www.unece.org/trans/doc/2006/itc/itcrt_sec/pres5.ppt>.

U.S. Congress. 2002. *Public Law 107–295: Maritime Transportation Security Act of 2002*. 107th Cong., 2d sess. Government Printing Office, Washington, D.C.

———. House. 2003a. Committee on Aviation. *Hearing on The Transportation Security Administration's Perspective on Aviation Security*. 108th Cong., 1st sess. October 13.

———. 2003b. Committee on Coast Guard and Maritime Transportation. *Hearing on Port Security*. 108th Cong., 1st sess.

———. 2005a. *H.R. 4437*. 109th Cong., 1d sess. Government Printing Office, Washington, D.C.

———. 2005b. *H.R. 4439*. 109th Cong., 1d sess. Government Printing Office, Washington D.C.

U.S. Congress Senate. 2005. *The Rail Security Act of 2005. S. 1379*. 109th Cong., 1d sess. Government Printing Office, Washington, D.C.

U.S. Customs and Border Patrol. 2005a. CBP adopts new tool for land border security: US-VISIT and CBP meet 2004 goals at the land border. *CBP Today*. March. <http://www.cbp.gov/xp/CustomsToday/2005/March/us_visit.xml>.

———. 2005b. National Targeting Center keeps terrorism at bay. *CBP Today*. March. <http://www.cbp.gov/xp/CustomsToday/2005/March/ntc.xml>.

———. 2005c. C-TPAT: Frequently asked questions. <http://www.cbp.gov/xp/cgov/import/commercial_enforcement/ctpat/ctpat_faq.xml>.

———. 2006. Fact sheet: Container security initiative. Press Release. March. <http://www.cbp.gov/xp/cgov/border_security/international_activities/csi>.

The White House. 2003. Homeland Security Presidential Directive. Press Release. September 13. <http://www.whitehouse.gov/news/releases/2003/09/20030916 5.html>.

———. 2004. Fact sheet: Fair and secure immigration reform. Press Release. January 7. <http://www.whitehouse.gov/news/releases/2004/01/20040107-1.html>.

———. 2005. Fact sheet: Securing America through immigration reform. Press Release. November 28. <http://www.whitehouse.gov/news/releases/2005/11/20051128-3.html>.

CHAPTER EIGHT

FUTURE IMPLICATIONS: IMAGINATION, INTEGRATION, AND IMPROVISATION

Table Top: Acting as an Oracle

As National Security Advisor to the president of the United States, it is your duty to analyze the national threat landscape, synthesize intelligence, and provide operational guidance to the Executive branch. In recent years, primarily marked by the spread of terrorism, your tasks have become increasingly difficult. Whereas the development of the DHS and the strengthening of the Intelligence Community has made important strides in combating the War on Terror, a myriad of critical security tasks have gone unfulfilled. Public support of the use of novel surveillance techniques has drastically waned, government tests have exposed weaknesses in the inspection procedures at the borders and ports, natural disasters have raised questions regarding the capabilities of emergency responders, and lackluster practices in information sharing have spread. After a long day full of nonstop dilemmas, the president calls you to the Oval Office for an informal meeting. After pouring you a stiff drink, he asks a blunt question, "What will the future of homeland security look like?" Initially caught off-guard by the query, you begin to ponder. What threats have we faced in the past and will they resurface? Will terror once again strike within our borders? How effective will the DHS be? How will legislation effect security efforts? What role will the Intelligence Community play? Are critical infrastructures likely to be targeted? How will risk communication and disaster preparedness be handled? Will our nation's modes of transportation and borders be secure? To adequately respond to the president's question, you must address these and other probing issues.

Introduction

This book has investigated the history and nature of the current threats facing the United States and the response of the government in combating these threats. It has also examined public policy implications and the state of information and intelligence analysis. Issues relating to Critical Infrastructure Protection and Information or Cyber Security have been explored. The text has also evaluated risk communication practices and the capabilities for emergency response. A detailed analysis was presented on the dynamics of border and transportation security. This final chapter will investigate future implications and integrate important themes and concepts for practitioners and policy analysts.

Trust and Fear

A constant theme of this text is the intricate personal and political relationship between security and privacy. Citizens of the United States have long cherished civil liberties, personal freedom, and privacy reaching back to the founding of the country. Ironically, security is often seen as too much until it is not enough. The privacy and security relationship has ebbed and flowed cyclically with events as the country grew and developed. Abraham Lincoln's suspension of the Writ of Habeas Corpus during the Civil War is often cited as an effective suspension of personal rights during wartime; however, some critics to this day judge Lincoln in a harsher light for these actions. One of the major concerns the American Colonist had was relating to the involuntary quartering of British soldiers. Moreover, the internment of Japanese Americans during World War II is another vivid example of the sacrifice of privacy and humans rights during a national crisis. The constant pendulum of government action checked by public outcry continued throughout the Vietnam War. However, after the 9/11 attacks, the debate reached a new level of intensity with the passage of the USA PATRIOT ACT. The current debate has been punctuated by the 2006 NSA spying controversy, where it was learned that President Bush authorized warrantless spying on American citizens (see the case study). There appears little question that privacy and security are intricate and precious personal issues and thus grounds for a spirited if not passionate political debate.

A Delicate Balance

Closely related to the debate between privacy and security is the issue of public trust and confidence. The primary reason the government would sacrifice the privacy and civil liberties of its citizens is to instill and assure public trust and confidence. Indeed, many of the actions of the government, such as requiring persons boarding airplanes to take their shoes off for examination, would appear to be as much aimed at instilling a sense of confidence as to thwart another attempted "Shoe Bomber." Moreover, the creation of the DHS, the largest reorganization of the U.S. government since World War II, could be interpreted as both a functional and symbolic attempt to promote public confidence and trust.

Vulnerability, Threat, and Cost

Clearly, the issue of public trust and confidence is a complex one and must be examined in the context of the interaction of vulnerability, threat, and costs as demonstrated in figure 8.1 (Amin 2006).

In this diagram, the shaded intersection of the three circles indicates achievable and sustainable action can be taken to address existing vulnerabilities, threats, and costs. One vivid example of the interplay of these factors is the jet airliner cockpit door example (9/11 Commission 2004, 84–85). It has been cited publicly that prior

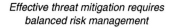

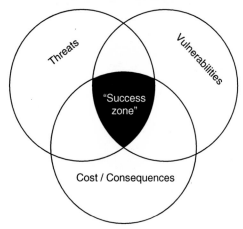

Figure 8.1 Quantifying Public Trust.
Source: Dr. Massoud Amin, University of Minnesota, Minn.

to the events of September 11, 2001, the U.S. government received reports that cockpit doors on large airliners should be strengthened along with accompanying pilot access procedures. However, the analysis of the threat to the flying public and the vulnerability of the pilot did not justify the considerable cost of strengthening the doors and government intervention required to change airline policies. In retrospect, along with many other issues that are painfully clear now, strengthening the cockpit doors and accompanying procedures seem like a prudent investment and fall in the shaded part of diagram one. Unfortunately, the challenge of the matter is that the government has to make hundreds of such decisions that could affect the safety of thousands of persons each day.

In order to extend the cost, threat, vulnerability interaction further, it is useful to look at the issues in an expanded framework, as represented in figure 8.2, referred to as the restructuring trilemma (Amin 1998).

In the diagram, director of the Center for the Development of Technological Leadership at the University of Minnesota in Twin Cities, Massoud Amin, captures the unique interplay of economics, politics, and technology. The trilemma reveals it is this interaction of economic, political, and technological considerations that permeates all public debates, government actions, and investments (Amin 1998).

Director of the Center for Risk Management of Engineering Systems at the University of Virginia, Yacov Haimes, suggests that planners should prioritize potential events based on probability and impact. Options tradeoffs and the effects of current decisions drive the future. Haimes proposes three Rs: redundancy, robustness, and resiliency. Redundancy calls for decentralizing targets and alternatives in an entrepreneurial manner. Robustness relates to reducing interdependencies and allowing systems to resist failure and withstand shocks. Resiliency describes the ability to

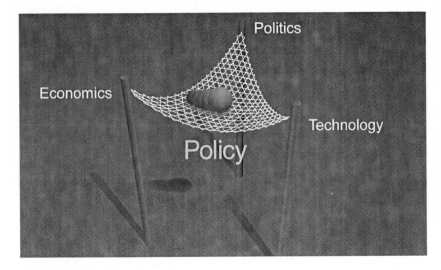

Figure 8.2   Public Policy Trilemma.
Source: Amin 1998.

recover and avoid irreversible consequences by overcoming failures and shortcomings (Haimes 2005).

Public Trust and Government Response

Not unlike security and privacy, public trust and the response of the government are closely interconnected. Federal, state, and local governments seek and need public confidence in order to continue in power. In a democratic form of government, politicians and governments can be replaced when the public loses confidence. There is nothing more sacred or vital to public trust than public safety and security. Once this is lost, any government can be quickly destabilized and ultimately replaced, albeit in a democracy through peaceful elections and transitions of power. The threat of terror or natural disasters opens existing fault lines in our society, and the government must carefully manage these vulnerabilities.

Normal Accidents

Public safety can be threatened by any number of catastrophes. Charles Perrow, sociologist and historian at Yale University, analyzed the social side of technological innovation and related risks by writing about the concept of "Normal Accidents." He concluded that the infrastructure of the nation is so extensive, complex, and sophisticated that a certain amount of failure is inevitable and *the cascading effects of interaction of variables is practically impossible to predict with certainty.* He contends that conventional approaches have failed because systems complexities make it impossible to engineer safety into the multitude of sophisticated systems touching our lives everyday and attempting to do so can often makes things worse. Perrow maintains that *the more "tightly coupled" or less slack in the system the more prone to cascading failure and catastrophic consequence* (Perrow 1999). This concept can be elaborated and categorized into three types of catastrophe: natural, accidental, and deliberate. It is argued that traditional organizations are not up to the challenge of prohibiting catastrophes, but can provide significant safeguards by reducing the concentration of power, size of targets, and concentration of hazardous materials by dispersing these targets. In addition, emphasis should be placed on natural incidents such as wind, water, and fire accidents that should be prepared for along with terrorist attacks. Perrow underlines that catastrophes are usually exacerbated by human and organizational failures as is evidenced by both the 9/11 attack and recent natural disasters (Perrow 2005).

A Major American City Is Lost: Hurricane Katrina

Perhaps there is no more vivid recent example of a natural incident aggravated by human and organizational cascading failures than the comprehensive response of the country to Hurricane Katrina in August and September 2005. It could be speculated that in the post-9/11 environment, the federal government was overly focused on protecting our borders from human threats from non-state actors such as al-Qaeda when Hurricane Katrina, the third strongest hurricane ever recorded in the Atlantic basin, came charging across the Gulf of Mexico into the Gulf Coast of Louisiana and Mississippi. Although such a grim scenario had been well documented, the Category 5 hurricane and the accompanying flooding of New Orleans devastated the gulf coast and seemed to leave all levels of government officials severely ill-prepared and uncoordinated in their response.

In what is emerging as one of the most destructive and clearly most costly disasters in the history of the nation, Hurricane Katrina's death toll exceeds 1,800 persons and property damage is estimated to reach seventy-five billion dollars. Tragically, in excess of one million persons were displaced and over two thousand are currently listed as missing. This level of human suffering, with so many persons being displaced by a combination of events, has not been witnessed in the United States since the Dust Bowl of the Great Depression in the 1930s, or perhaps the end of the American Civil War over 140 years prior. In a scenario that most would conceive as unthinkable, a major city, New Orleans, was decimated beyond recognition, and the entire Louisiana and Mississippi coasts were changed forever.

As the country recovers, rebuilds, and most importantly learns from the cascading tragedy of Hurricane Katrina, many questions can be asked about the long-term impact of this unprecedented disaster. Perhaps the most basic and important is, "Are the various infrastructures of this country robust enough to absorb such loss and what are the long term effects on the region and its citizens?" Government officials will continue the process of unraveling the planning, response, and recovery efforts for many years. One of the first of these after-action reports was released by the White House in February 2006, titled, *The Federal Response to Hurricane Katrina: Lessons Learned*. It cited clear failures by the DHS and other agencies in planning, communications, and leadership. The report proposed a broad restructuring of how the government should respond to the next catastrophe (Associated Press 2006). Chapter seven emphasized changes in eleven key areas that need to be implemented before the 2006 hurricane season, especially better disaster relief among federal agencies. The DHS in particular was cited for lacking effective and swift communications with emergency responders and the public, and for an inefficient system of supply management. In *The Federal Response to Hurricane Katrina: Lessons Learned*, the White House calls for an enhanced role for the Pentagon in planning, and a streamlined process for determining when the military should take over relief efforts in extraordinary situations. Finally, the government found a necessary commitment for better arrangements in transportation, housing, and medical services than were delivered in the aftermath of Hurricane Katrina (The White House 2006).

Not withstanding what subsequent official reports conclude, it is clear that there was a catastrophic breakdown among local, state, and federal officials that resulted in undue human loss of life, property, and untold suffering. Congressional and executive branch investigations will undoubtedly find methods to improve the coordination and response of the government. The lessons regarding planning and evacuation; intergovernment coordination; transportation, health, and other critical infrastructure; emergency shelters; preventing looting, price gouging, and physical violence are immense and evolving. A few of them include simple things like allowing persons to bring their pets with them from their homes to persuade evacuation. Others are more complex like examining if a private industry member, such as Wal-Mart, is more effective in responding with food, water, and shelter than the combined forces of local, state, and federal governments. Clearly, in the wake of these tragedies, persistent, societal issues such as race, fear, trust, greed, environmental management practices, and the role of the media need to be closely examined.

Fighting the Last War

As evidenced by Hurricane Katrina, one of the major reasons organizations and executives fail is that there is arguably a human preoccupation with preparing for the last scenario. In the case of the military, it is often said that generals prefer to "fight the last war." The same phenomenon easily transfers to government and private sector officials. Prior to 9/11, and in the wake of the Y2K conversion, it can be argued that the United States was extremely concerned, if not fascinated, with preparing for cyber attacks. Yet instead of a cyber attack, shutting down our critical infrastructures, the United States experienced a decidedly low-tech assault of suicide bombers turning their jet airliners into flying bombs. This was an unexpected and lethal combination of suicide bombing techniques perfected in the 1980s and 1990s, and the hijacking tactics popularized in the 1970s by Palestinian terrorists. Although evidence was later found about these preparations, it appears that the government could not assimilate the threat and take actions such as strengthening the pilot's cabin door. Although it now seems simple in hindsight, at the time government could not imagine such a dastardly scenario since there was no precedent. It was a failure of intelligence analysis, information sharing, communication, and imagination.

In the post 9/11 era and after the anthrax attacks in the fall of 2001, considerable attention was paid to the potential of nuclear attacks in the form of a dirty bomb or biological/chemical agents. Instead of a radiological, biological, or chemical attack in the fall of 2005, the country seemed ill-prepared to handle the punishing onslaught of natural disaster: Hurricane Katrina. As the debate about how the United States can better prepare for natural disasters, such as hurricanes, unfolds, the country must brace for the threat of a worldwide avian flu pandemic, which is speculated to have the potential to kill hundreds of thousands of people in the worst case scenario. The new war is about winning hearts and minds, not economic goals and territory. The key weapon is computer tools, especially instant electronic mechanism such as instant Internet sites complete with shocking video. It is easy to see that there are no clear choices for government leaders, planners, and responders. That is why imagination, integration, and improvisation are so crucial to the future safety of the nation.

Federal Government Organizational Response: The Creation of the Department of Homeland Security

The DHS was created in 2002, in response to the 9/11 attacks. It has been suggested that this was the largest bureaucratic reorganization in the history of the world involving 180,000 persons (United States Department of Homeland Security 2003). It has also been speculated that DHS is also now the world's largest bureaucracy with its accompanying turf battles and partisan politics. Charles Perrow predicts that the inherent inefficiencies of organizations will require ten years for the DHS to become fully functional, and that during this time the costs will greatly exceed the benefits (Perrow 2005).

After the creation of DHS, the concept of "national intelligence" was codified by the Intelligence Reform and Terrorism Prevention Act of 2004. President Bush signed the law that asserts, "our vast intelligence enterprise will become more unified, coordinated and effective" (The White House 2004). The Act calls for the integration of the domestic and foreign dimensions of U.S. intelligence to eliminate gaps in understanding national security threats. In addition, the White House recommends more depth and accuracy in intelligence analysis and ensuring that intelligence resources generate future capabilities. *The National Intelligence Strategy of the United States of America* highlights the challenge:

> U.S. national intelligence must be tailored to the threats of the twenty-first century, which seldom conform to the traditional profiles of hostile states and alliances. Adversarial states have learned to mask their intentions and capabilities, while terrorists and other non-state actors use commonplace technologies to boost their striking power and enhance their elusiveness. (Office of the Director of National Intelligence 2005, 1)

The strategy calls for achieving these goals through an unprecedented level of reform of government policies and procedures through integration, collaboration, and innovation. Interdependent teamwork and technological innovation are the guideposts of the strategy, which focuses on two strategic objectives: mission and enterprise. The mission objectives relate to the tactical ability to predict, penetrate, and preempt threats. The enterprise objectives relate to maintaining competitive strategic advantages and call for an intelligence transformation that is results focused, collaborative, bold, future oriented, self-evaluating, and innovative. This strategy will have to be quickly and effectively implemented as the officials predict, prepare, and respond to an ever-changing array of threats such as biological and chemical attacks, dirty bombs, coal mines, avian flu, and basic threats to the fragile health infrastructure of the nation such as various new forms of influenza. These weaknesses were vividly illustrated in the wake of Hurricane Katrina.

Education, Research / Technology, and Innovation as a Critical Infrastructure

Many observers believe that education holds the key to future economic and security sustainability of the United States. Since the 1980s there has been much attention on reforming basic (K-12) American education especially in mathematics and sciences with limited or mixed results. Today, urgency and importance is being paid to this area in large part because of security and economic competitiveness concerns. Much like the Sputnik incident of 1959, when the Soviets beat the United States in the race to put a satellite into space, the terrorist attacks of 9/11 have awakened the need for the nation to achieve higher levels in basic and higher education, once again, with an eye toward math and science in order to combat security threats with technological capacity and innovation.

The Ultimate Call for Education Reform

Higher education in the United States is also facing pressures to reform in order to meet the new challenges of society in the post-9/11 environment. Responding to a new world of changing boundaries, global competition, rising expectations, finite resources, exploding technologies, changing societal norms, national security concerns, and a changing economy are the impetus for higher education to advance their capabilities (Dotolo and Noftsinger, 2002, 19). According to associate vice president, executive director of the Institute for Infrastructure and Information Assurance at James Madison University, John Noftsinger, "It is driven by a technological revolution and national security challenge on a scale never experienced before" (20). He concludes, "The challenge of workforce development in an economy fueled by human talent as its major raw material underlines the opportunity" (20).

One of the clear responses to the post-9/11 environment has been the creation of a number of academic programs to educate persons seeking to work in the homeland security and defense area. Theses range from noncredit programs tailored to increase the skills of first responders such as fire fighters and emergency medical technicians to undergraduate and graduate programs in intelligence analysis and critical infrastructure protection. Some of the programs are titled as degrees in homeland security.

Schools such as University of Richmond, Rice University, Virginia Commonwealth University, and Cooper Union are currently offering specific courses relating to terrorism and homeland security. Other schools are taking a more pioneering approach. Texas A&M and University of Minnesota have been named Homeland Security Centers for Excellence. The DHS has commissioned these institutions to conduct research on various subjects of security. Most notable of all though, is the Homeland

Security University (HSU). The goal of HSU is to have facilities throughout the world that will educate security practitioners in the nation's efforts to combat terrorism. HSU has yet to conduct classes, but the institute does offers seminars regarding security issues, and as of April 2006, HSU has procured twelve facilities to achieve its mission (Homeland Security University 2005).

Prior to 9/11, Richard G. Little, director of the Keston Institute for Infrastructure at the University of Southern California called for the creation of an infrastructure professional program. Little found available undergraduate and graduate degree programs to be inadequate to educate the professionals required to plan, deploy, and maintain the extensive and complex infrastructure of the United States. Only through a new program that emphasizes integrated and cross-disciplinary dimensions will emerging professionals meet the challenges of the nation's complex infrastructure (Little 1999).

In response to calls such as these, James Madison University has created a degree program in intelligence analysis that has a distinct focus on critical infrastructure dependencies and how they can fail, and developing the critical thinking skills of students. Building on integrated and multidisciplinary tenets of the College of Integrated Science and Technology, this program seeks to produce graduates in three tracks: government sectors intelligence analysts, competitive business analysts, and emergency response planners. The Information Analyst Program at James Madison University prepares students to apply the principles of information analysis, synthesis, and data mining to problems in national, international, or business intelligence settings. Students are educated to be critical problem-solvers, using the latest technology coupled with sound problem-solving strategies, as well as lifelong learners. The program's faculty is committed to providing real-world applications in the classroom and students will participate in internship with intelligence industry partners. This program as well as others includes innovative methods such as war gaming and table-top exercises with a particular focus on data fusion and critical thinking skills.

Some institutions have created new administrative structures. George Washington University has named an associate vice president of Homeland Security. George Mason University has initiated the Critical Infrastructure Protection Project with James Madison University. James Madison University has created the Institute for Infrastructure and Information Assurance to support the CIP project and related research and public service activities. Carnegie Mellon has created the CERT-CC® (Computer Emergency Response Team-Coordination Center). Dartmouth Universities hosts the Institute for Information Infrastructure Protection (I3P). Purdue University supports the Center for Education and Research in Information Assurance and Security (CERIAS) research center. A comprehensive list of research institutes and programs is provided in chapter six.

The research in various higher education–based institutes spans the universe of biological, chemical, radiological defense, sensor integration, cyber defense and security, critical infrastructure protection, modeling and visualization, materials sciences including nanotechnology to research and develop new generations of security, and defense-oriented technology. The goals of these programs are to accelerate and integrate emerging basic research into developed technologies for the government and private marketplace.

National Laboratories and Federal Research
and Development Centers

The national laboratories of the nation along with the nation's federally funded research and development centers (FFRDC) are also researching these key areas. The key areas of homeland security research in the government, university, and business communities fall into the following categories: risk modeling, simulation and visualization, sensors development and integration, and nonproliferation of dangerous materials. Areas of interest include:

- Systems Evaluations
- Technology Assessments
- Operational Assessments
- Resource and Support Analysis
- Chemical and Biological Research
- Border and Transportation Security
- Radiological and Nuclear Countermeasures
- Explosives Countermeasures
- Cyber Security
- Critical Infrastructure Protection
- Control Systems

Sandia National Laboratory in conjunction with Los Alamos National Laboratory has created the National Infrastructure Simulation and Analysis Center to provide modeling, simulation, and analysis to address the threat of disruptions to the infrastructure of the nation. Sandia seeks to combat terrorism by applying a systems approach to developing real-world solutions based on thorough assessment of risk and innovative science and technology. Sandia also hosts the Program for Response Options & Technology Enhancements for Chemical/Biological Terrorism (PROTECT), which is a collaboration with the Argonne National Laboratory that addresses the vulnerability of citizens to bio-chem threats.

Project Starlight is a visual information system that uses advanced modeling to enable the user to search through volumes of data by employing graphical representations. Developed under the management of Batelle at the Pacific Northwest National Laboratory, Starlight visualizes relationships between people, places, activities, movements, and so on, which has led to the characterization of the program as an important tool for homeland security.

The DHS has funded Anser, FFRDC, to create the Homeland Security Institute (HSI). The HSI delivers independent and objective analyses and advises in core areas important to its sponsor in support of policy development, decision making, analysis of alternative approaches, and evaluation of new ideas on issues of significance. The primary mission of the HSI is to assist the DHS and its Operating Elements in addressing important homeland security issues, particularly those requiring scientific, technical, and analytical expertise. The DHS undersecretary for Science and Technology is responsible for managing the HSI and other FFRDC matters for the Department (Homeland Security Institute 2006).

The DHS and the DOD are aggressively seeking technological solutions to enhancing security in the United States through a number of programs such as the HSARPA, the Office of Research and Development, and the Office of Systems Engineering and Development to accelerate innovative concepts from the drawing board to deployment. There are a number of such programs in the DoD such as the Defense Advanced Research Program Administration (DARPA) and the Advanced Concept Technology Demonstration (ACTD), which have accelerated the deployment of research and technology to protect the nation.

Innovation as a National Imperative

Recently a number of major organization and national leaders have sounded alarms about the future economic and physical security of the nation. These organizations and leaders are calling for a nationally coordinated effort to accelerate the historical competitive advantage the United States has possessed in the area of innovation.

In early 2005, the Council on Competitiveness (COC) issued a report entitled, *Innovate America: Thriving in a World of Challenge and Change*. The report's theme asserts, "Innovation will be the single most important factor in determining America's success through the twenty-first century" (Council on Competitiveness 7). The report summarized the current challenge and issued an "Innovation Agenda" that focuses on talent, investment, and infrastructure. Recommendations under talent relate to building a national innovation educational strategy, catalyzing the next generation of innovators and empowering workers to succeed in a global economy. Recommendations for investment include revitalizing frontier and multidiscipline research, energizing the entrepreneurial economy, and reinforcing risk taking and long-term investment. The infrastructure requirements and interdependencies are creating a national consensus for innovation growth strategies, restructuring intellectual property regime, strengthening the nation's manufacturing capability, and using the health care infrastructure as a test bed for innovation.

In October 2005, the National Academies issued a report entitled, *Rising above the Gathering Storm: Energizing and Employing America for a Brighter Economic Future*. The commission that produced the report was chaired by former Lockheed Martin chief executive officer, Norman Augustine, and is commonly referred to as the "Augustine Report." The report synthesizes many concerns articulated in *Innovate America* but calls for discrete reforms. These reforms include: increasing the talent pool by vastly improving K-12 math and science education; sustaining and strengthening basic research; making the United States the best climate for attracting and retaining the best scientists in the world; and enhancing the overall climate for innovation including patent law and intellectual property practices (National Academies 2005).

At the end of October 2005, a group of concerned individuals from business, federal government, and academia, many of whom had been involved in the aforementioned initiatives, convened at the National Academies in Washington, D.C., to create an action plan for the nation based on the various reports. The Accelerating Innovation Foundation (AIF) emerged from this meeting. The goal of the AIF is to catalyze the recommendations of the various reports and support pilot projects based on these recommendations, which will be featured at an annual conference seeking to accelerate innovation across the nation at a grassroots level from community to community.

Historically, the United States has benefited significantly from the scientific and technological skills of foreigners who come to the United States for higher education or immigration for political or related reasons. Many observers make a strong argument that foreign talent has fueled much of the technological progress in research and development over the last twenty years. Ironically, in the post-9/11 environment, the ability of foreign students and workers to contribute to solving security challenges and economic productivity and competitiveness has been significantly reduced through a reduction in the number of persons being allowed to enter the country. At the same time, more and more functions are being outsourced to countries outside the United States. Outsourcing began in commodities such as textiles and furniture; however, today it includes more technical processes including software development. A number of concerned persons have expressed fears that weaknesses could be programmed into vital software by an unfriendly or unwitting country. These issues will continue to play out as economic pressures and the transitioning American economy continue to make outsourcing an attractive, if not politically popular, option.

A New Market Place: The Business of Homeland Security

A New Marketplace Is Born

In addition to their concerns about keeping the nation more competitive through innovation, the American business and industrial community has not surprisingly responded to the millions of federal, state, and local dollars that are being spent on homeland security in a search for solutions to make the nation safer and expand corporate profits. In what many observers see as the greatest government expansion since World War II, many large, medium, and small businesses have developed security-related products, business units, and even companies. There are for-profit companies whose sole business function is to conduct seminars and sell publications to guide aspiring companies to the perceived pot of gold in a fashion that is reminiscent of earlier gold rushes in the history of the country; except instead of selling shovels and spades they sell information and access. In some cases, companies have trotted out tired concepts or recast failed products under the ostensibly patriotic guise of homeland security. Traditional, large government contactors and systems integrators as well as small niche companies have all benefited from these massive expenditures. Some critics question whether these massive investments and the way the funds have been spent are actually making the country safe, or if government officials at all levels have squandered millions of dollars in an uncoordinated fashion in the name of security.

Ethical Considerations

The current business climate also raises ethical questions about companies and individuals who may try to take advantage of the vulnerable condition of the United States in order to profit financially. One of the keys to the future will be narrowing the gap between actual need, government response, and private sector entrepreneurship. Moreover, the ultimate goal will be to constantly increase technical efficiency while decreasing vulnerability within a cost structure that the nation can sustain.

Perhaps more important questions are: who makes these decisions: politicians, business persons, or scientists, and where are they best made—local, state, or federal level?

Imagination, Integration, and Improvisation

As this book and especially this closing chapter have made clear; predicting the future with assuredness has never been possible. Human and organizational limitations and constraints often conspire to make bad situations even worse. However, one of the most worrisome trends is the birth of a new hybrid organization that blends the vast financial resources, efficiency, and brutality of organized crime with the anonymous violence and fervor of extremist terrorist organizations. Their attacks focus on financial and symbolic targets and maximizing civilian casualties. Established organized criminals such as Ibrahim Dawood in south Asia are lending smuggling routes to al-Qaeda and supporting jihadists in Pakistan and elsewhere (Kaplan 2005, 42). Terrorist groups are clearly relying on the tactics and financial resources of organized crime to finance their global activities, "Both crime syndicates and terrorists groups thrive in the same subterranean world of black markets and laundered money, relying on shifting networks and secret cells to accomplish their objectives. Both groups have similar needs: weapons, false documentation, and safe houses" (Kaplan 2005, 42).

The "Is" of the Future

Many observers contend that the world is at a tipping point. Malcolm Gladwell discusses the concept of such instances in his book, *The Tipping Point*. Gladwell analyzes "a new way of understanding why change so often happens as quickly and as unexpectedly as it does." He further contends that social epidemics all have their own individual tipping points where exponential change begins to occur, and that this phenomenon can be applied to arenas such as social policy and business (Gladwell 2000). Fresh ideas similar to this are necessary to compete in today's world. It is clear that the challenges facing the democratic world and the United States as the only remaining superpower are complex, daunting, and constantly changing. The resolve to combat threats through constant vigilance and innovation will be a key component of future success. Along with resolve, another key defining characteristic of success will be resiliency: the ability to adjust easily and quickly to prevent, protect, respond, and recover from security threats. As evidenced by events since 2001, the American public and spirit is perhaps considerably more resilient than government policy. In order for resolve and resiliency to matter, there needs to be an unprecedented effort to break down communication and operational barriers for intra- and intergovernmental cooperation. The role of the media, which has taken serious criticism in the aftermath of the 2005 gulf disasters, also needs to be closely examined.

In this complex and ever changing environment of organized, global terrorism, humans are the most robust yet most fragile element in the system. As discussed in chapter five, humans are the infrastructure that connect and manage all of the critical infrastructure of the nation. The human element is both frightening and inspiring. Humans have great improvisational skills to flourish in the most difficult circumstances, as well as to make simple yet often cascading and catastrophic decisions. The improvisational skills of individual citizens of the United States have been displayed from the founding of the nation to the present, challenge after challenge.

The ability to innovate and improvise can be observed in many forms from the manufacturing plants to the battlefield to even cultural matters. Perhaps a lesson from American culture is a useful metaphor to inform future generations. America is renowned across the world as the birthplace of Jazz music. Barry Horowitz, professor of Systems and Information Engineering at the University of Virginia (Horowitz 2005), identifies Jazz as an appropriate metaphor for future planning and response in the homeland security arena. Jazz music is "a kind of music that, originally improvised but now also arranged, characterized by syncopation, rubato, and heavily accented rhythms, dissonances, individualized melodic variations and unusual tonal effects on the saxophone, clarinet, trumpet, trombone, etc." originated by Creole and African Americans in New Orleans (*New World Dictionary of the American Language* 1980, 755). As the definition of Jazz suggests, perhaps it is possible to develop a framework for improvisation that is planned yet accommodates reasonable and appropriate spontaneity and independent decision making. As in Jazz music, rhythm provides the framework, but the melody varies within each particular situation or gig, in musical terms (Horowitz 2005).

The human infrastructure can be encouraged and taught to improvise through imagination balanced with competence. Responders require both confidence in the framework they have been taught and their own innate skills to improvise within that system. Naturalistic decision making processes that accommodate intuition, simulation, gaming theory, and group decision-making processes are critical to future efforts. The current and inherent skill level of individuals can be further enhanced through innovative training techniques utilizing state of the art war-gaming theory and young America's penchant and unsurpassed skill in using video-gaming technology. These games are essentially modeling, visualization, and simulation technology turned into entertainment, which can now be used as a training methodology for war fighters of the future. The innovative capacity of youth armed with the latest technological, improvisational, and integrative skills holds the best hope for the future economic and physical security of democratic countries in the dangerous and complex climate of the world today.

Case Study: The NSA Domestic Surveillance Wiretapping Program

Authorized by President George W. Bush, the NSA wiretapping surveillance program has garnered much debate since a December 16, 2005, *New York Times* article revealed its existence. The story that disclosed the NSA wiretapping program stated that a presidential order, signed by George W. Bush in 2002, led to the monitoring of international telephone conversations and e-mails of hundreds, if not thousands, of people in the United States without the use of a court-issued warrant. *The New York Times* learned the basis for the surveillance was to track "dirty numbers" from within the United States to al-Qaeda operatives abroad. The surveillance has not been limited to those in direct contact to suspected terrorists abroad, as anyone linked to the domestic source could find their conversations wiretapped, as well. Supporters of the program believe the president should have the ability to conduct warrantless surveillance because of the speed with which the War on Terror needs to be fought. However, critics wonder why President Bush ignored the opportunity to ask Congress to include provisions for the NSA program in the USA PATRIOT Act authorizing the surveillance (Risen and Lichtblau 2005).

President Bush and Attorney General Gonzales Defend the Surveillance

President Bush immediately responded by addressing the Nation two days after the publication of the story. In order to head off any conspiracy theories of abuses of power, President Bush explained that the government had to confirm a link between the wiretapped person to a suspected terrorist before the surveillance could be authorized. In addition, the administration noted that the activities are reviewed every forty-five days by himself, the attorney general, and the White House legal staff. President Bush cited U.S. law and the Constitution as the basis for his authorization of NSA wiretaps (President's Radio Address 2005).

On behalf of the president, Attorney General Alberto Gonzales presented an argument to Congress on February 6, 2006. During this session, Gonzales asserted the Constitution requires the president to protect the safety of American citizens, and gives the president authority to see that the security is provided, thus providing Constitutional authority for the wiretaps (Gonzales 2006).

Gonzales identified the second authorization as derived from Congress when, under Gonzales's interpretation, both the House and the Senate gave the president authority to conduct the warrantless searches on September 18, 2001, through the "Authorization for Use of Military Force" (AUMF).

> In the AUMF, Congress did two important things. First, it expressly recognized the President's 'authority under the Constitution to take action to deter and prevent acts of international terrorism against the United States.' Second, it supplemented that authority by authorizing the President to 'use all necessary and appropriate force against those nations, organizations or persons he determines planned, authorized, committed, or aided the terrorist attacks' in order to prevent further attacks on the United States. (Gonzales 2006)

The prepared statement by Attorney General Alberto Gonzales specified that the surveillance program is only in effect when one person is located outside the United States, and there is "reasonable grounds to believe" that one of the communicators is linked to a terrorist organization. In addition, he informed Congress that leadership in both the House and the Senate had been made aware of the program. In Gonzales's opinion, "The program provides the United States with the early warning system we so desperately needed on September 10th" (Gonzales 2006).

Gonzales addressed Fourth Amendment concerns that could question the legality of the NSA wiretaps. He acknowledged that the surveillance may lead to false concern from those lobbying in the privacy arena. However, the need for this administration to do everything in its power to protect the American people is compelling, and therefore makes the intercepts reasonable (2006).

According to knowledgeable sources, *The Washington Post* has claimed the electronic surveillance yields very few suspects. The number given is less than ten citizens a year, who "have aroused enough suspicion during warrantless eavesdropping to justify interception of their domestic calls . . . That step still requires a warrant from a federal judge, for which the government must supply evidence of probably cause" (Gellman et al. 2006). The same article reports that supporters and those with inside knowledge of the program consider it to be a victory for the program if only a fraction of one percent of the flagged conversations gather meaningful evidence (Gellman et al. 2006).

Case History of Electronic Surveillance

Despite the reasoning put forth by President Bush and Attorney General Gonzales, many senior intelligence officials have declared the program illegal, as the NSA assumed the authority to wiretap communications of American citizens to persons abroad without a court order. An examination of the history of warrantless wiretapping and the passage of the FISA will provide a closer look at the legality of the program.

One of the first cases to challenge surveillance of the spoken word was *Katz v. United States*, 389 U.S. 347 (1967). Here the court ruled that the Fourth Amendment protected oral communications taking place in a wiretapped phone booth from electronic surveillance without a warrant. As a result, Congress passed Title III of the Omnibus Crime Control and Safe Streets Act of 1968, to, "provide for search warrants to authorize electronic surveillance for law enforcement purposes, but prohibiting such surveillance in other instances not authorized by law" (Bazan and Elsea 2006, 8). In addition, Title III specifically noted that nothing in the Omnibus Act could limit the president's derived powers from the Constitution to protect the United States from foreign attack, or to gather foreign intelligence to thwart such an attack.

A few years later, the Supreme Court weighed in on a specific domestic surveillance case in *United States v. United States District Court*, 407 U.S. 297 (1972), known as the Keith Case. The United States government requested a writ of mandamus to force a district judge to vacate an order that the federal government release electronically accessed conversations obtained without a warrant. The Supreme Court sided with the lower court that a warrant was necessary, given the argument presented by the government that the defendants were domestic security threats, and held, ". . . in the case of intelligence gathering involving domestic security surveillance, prior judicial approval was required to satisfy the Fourth Amendment" (Bazan and Elsea 2006, 9). In his Majority Opinion, Justice Lewis Powell wrote, "Fourth Amendment protections become the more necessary when the targets of official surveillance may be those suspected of unorthodoxy in their political beliefs. The danger to political dissent is acute where the Government attempts to act under so vague a concept as the power to protect 'domestic security.' Given the difficulty of defining the domestic security interest, the danger of abuse in acting to protect that interest becomes apparent" 407 U.S. 297 (United States Supreme Court, 1972).

The courts ruled in favor of warrantless wiretapping in *United States v. Brown*, 484 F.2d 418, 1974, which upheld a warrantless wiretap ordered by the attorney general for foreign intelligence purposes. In this case, information pertaining to Brown's arrest was not the target of the wiretap, but the information was ruled admissable (Bazan and Elsea 2006, 11).

The Creation of the FISA Court

As a result of the many cases reaching the upper levels of the judiciary system relating to intelligence gathering, and the highly publicized abuse of power by the Nixon administration, the Church Committee, chaired by Senator Frank Church, opened up an investigation into the history of wiretapping by the federal government. They found that every president since Franklin Delano Roosevelt used warrantless electronic surveillance in some capacity (12). However, it was the Watergate scandal that motivated Congress to pass FISA in 1978. The Act created the Foreign Intelligence Surveillance Court, referred to as the FISA Court, which oversees the provisions of FISA.

FISA outlines the ways in which the government can legally use electronic surveillance on a foreign power or agents of a foreign power. It actually alleviates the restrictions of Title III which, ". . . requires a showing of probable cause that a proposed target has committed, is committing, or is about to commit a crime, FISA requires a showing of probable cause to believe that the target is a foreign power or an agent of a foreign power" (18). This was the role of FISA until the 9/11 attacks, when certain provisions were amended by the USA PATRIOT Act. The certification that the electronic monitoring is for foreign intelligence was dropped and replaced with the understanding that a "significant purpose" of the surveillance be used for the gathering of foreign intelligence. On a day-to-day basis, the role of FISA is to grant warrants to the government to listen in on conversations overseas, where at least one party is either a suspected agent of a foreign power or a foreign power.

FISA does allow three exceptions that waive the requirement of a warrant: (1) if the surveillance targets communications between or among foreign powers, this includes technical intelligence deriving from a foreign controlled entity; (2) if there is a small chance the surveillance will include information from a U.S. citizen; (3) minimization requirements, as specified by the Act, must be met protecting American citizens from warrantless surveillance of their conversations (Legal Information Institute 2005).

The FISA Court versus Inherent and Statutory
Presidential Authority

In the current framework, one cannot have both the FISA legislation and the president's warrantless surveillance program. Either the president's power to obtain the communications must be derived from somewhere, or his actions are in violation of FISA. If the president does have legal authority, then FISA must be considered unconstitutional. The president has argued that he has inherent authority from the

Constitution to protect the American people, combined with statutory authority from the AUMF.

The administration cites *Hamdi v. Rumsfeld*, 124 S. Ct. 2633 (2004), as the relevant Supreme Court decision upholding presidential authority to conduct electronic surveillance. This specific decision affirmed presidential authority to, "detain a U.S. citizen as an 'enemy combatant' as part of the necessary force authorized by Congress in the AUMF, despite an earlier statute which provides that no U.S. citizen may be detained except pursuant to an act of Congress" (Bazan and Elsea 2006, 33). Despite the administration's claims of a necessary broad interpretation of the AUMF, the court declared a "state of war is not a blank check for the President when it comes to the rights of the Nation's citizens . . ." (33). In addition, the president argues that section 109 of FISA recognizes the NSA spying program as the surveillance is "authorized by statute" (37). The Act specifically states that, "A person is guilty of an offense if he intentionally—1) engages in electronic surveillance under color of law except as authorized by statute . . ." (Legal Information Institute 2005).

Many will agree that the president has historically been the chief officer dealing with foreign intelligence. However, it is a fallacy to assume that Congress should not have a role to play. No court has ruled on the authority of the Congress to regulate foreign intelligence (Bazan and Elsea 2006).

Opposition to the Program

Thus far, there has been notable, bipartisan objection to the program in Congress. Senator Patrick Leahy (D-VT), the ranking member on the Senate Judiciary Committee, prepared a resolution, "Expressing the sense of the Senate that Senate Joint Resolution 23 (107th Congress), as adopted by the Senate on September 14, 2001, and subsequently enacted as the Authorization for Use of Military Force does not authorize warrantless domestic surveillance of United States citizens" (Office of Senator Leahy 2006). A February 5, 2006, article printed by *The New York Times*, outlined the opinion of the chairman of the Senate Judiciary Committee, "The program 'is in flat violation of the Foreign Intelligence Surveillance Act,' said the chairman, Senator Arlen Specter of Pennsylvania" (Knowlton). In addition, Senators Dianne Feinstein (D-Calif.), Chuck Hagel (R-Neb), Carl Levin (D-Mich.), Olympia Snowe (R-Maine), and Ron Wyden (D-Ore.) wrote a letter to Senators Specter and Leahy asking for "inquiry and action" into the legality of the wiretap program (News from Senator Feinstein 2005). Many other members of Congress have asked their leadership to fully investigate the program.

On February 28, 2006, the Constitution Project and the Center for National Security Studies took legal action against the NSA spying program. These organizations filed a request to the FISA Court to investigate the legality of the program. It is the understanding of both these groups that the president is in violation of FISA, the Fourth Amendment, and as a result circumventing the American system of checks and balances (Constitution Project 2006).

Senate Hearing with Expert Testimony on the NSA Program

Also on February 28, 2006, Congress deliberated for a second time on the president's domestic spying program. Former intelligence officials and university law professors testified before the Senate Judiciary Committee about the legal justifications of the program.

Harold Hongju Koh, dean of the Yale Law School, sharply criticized any argument implying the president has the power to conduct such surveillance without oversight from Congress. Koh articulated his point, citing that the basis for a system of checks and balances is for the Executive Branch to get permission from another branch of the government before conducting a program that an Act of Congress (FISA) deems illegal. Not to mention the problems that may arise using evidence collected in a manner not yet recognized to be legal by the courts, "Under the ongoing program NSA analysts are increasingly caught between following orders and carrying out electronic surveillance that's facially illegal, and moreover evidence collected under the program will almost surely be challenged and it may prove inadmissible, making it far more difficult to prosecute terrorists" (Koh 2006).

On the other end of the spectrum, the Honorable James Woolsey, vice president of the Global Strategic Security Division at Booz, Allen, Hamilton defines the War on Terror as one different from the Cold War in every respect, and requiring new tools to combat the enemy. It is Woolsey's opinion that the inherent powers of the Constitution in Article II give the president the authority to conduct the NSA surveillance program. The speed with which the United States must act in the War on Terror is Woolsey's second legal justification for the program, "The one spy at a time surveillance systems of the Cold War, including FISA, through courts, are not designed to deal with fast moving battlefield electronic mapping in which an al-Qaeda or a Hezbollah computer might be captured which contains a large number of email addresses and phone numbers which would have to be checked out very [promptly]" (Woolsey 2006).

Timeline of Key Events

Here is a list of the major events that have occurred from December 16, 2005 to April 2006, concerning the NSA wiretapping controversy.

- December 16: After holding the story for more than a year, *The New York Times* unveiled the NSA wiretapping program, which began in 2002, sanctioning the NSA to perform domestic electronic surveillance without a court order (Risen and Lichtblau 2005).
- December 18: President Bush addressed the nation defending the surveillance program as legal and necessary in the War on Terror.
- December 19: U.S. Senators Dianne Feinstein, Chuck Hagel, Carl Levin, Olympia Snowe, and Ron Wyden wrote a letter to Senators Arlen Specter and Patrick Leahy requesting an investigation into the program by the Senate (News from Senator Feinstein 2005).
- January 1: The *New York Times* ran a story revealing objections to the spy program during John Ashcroft's time in office as attorney general (Risen and Lichtblau 2005).
- January 5: The Congressional Research Service released a report on the history of presidential authority to conduct warrantless surveillance.
- January 20: Senator Patrick Leahy introduced Senate Resolution No. 350 informing the president that the "Authorization for Use of Military Force" was not authorization for the NSA program (Leahy 2006).

- February 3: Senator Pat Roberts drafted a letter to Senators Arlen Specter and Patrick Leahy expressing his support for the NSA program, as a member of Congress who has been kept informed (Roberts 2006).
- February 5: Senator Arlen Specter told the media that he believed the president had broken the law, as the NSA program, "is in flat violation of [FISA]" (Knowlton 2006).
- February 6: Attorney General Alberto Gonzales appeared before Congress to defend the legality of the NSA program. Gonzales was not sworn in prior to the testimony.
- February 16: A party-line vote initiated by Senator Pat Roberts blocked an attempt by Senator Jay Rockefeller to vote on an investigation into the NSA program within the Senate Intelligence Committee (Office of Senator Rockefeller 2006).
- February 28: The Senate held their second meeting on the NSA program; this time with testimony from law experts in private practice and academia.
- March 7: Senate Republicans set in forth plans to introduce the Terrorist Surveillance Act of 2006, which would put an end to the program after five years unless renewed by Congress. The measure hit the Senate floor on March 16 (Morgan 2006).
- March 12: Senator Russ Feingold declared plans to call for a censure of President Bush. The following day he presented the resolution on the Senate floor (Office of Senator Feingold 2006).
- March 16: Senator Arlen Specter introduced the National Security Surveillance Act of 2006. The Act requires the attorney general to present evidence to Congress every forty-five days for renewal (Federation of American Scientists 2006).

Conclusions

As it stands, the Constitution does not delegate gathering foreign intelligence as a duty or responsibility of the Congress, nor is it a power expressed to the president. Since it would make little sense to assume the framers of the Constitution delegated foreign intelligence gathering to the states, one could argue that the president, with the oversight of Congress, has the power to conduct the collection of foreign intelligence (Bazan and Elsea 2006, 3). Historical examples have shown that foreign intelligence gathering has been conducted exclusively by the president with oversight from Congress (7). This delicate issue will take time and healthy debate, as a free, democratic society must decide where certain powers will lie within the government, and what will be the balance between security and privacy.

Discussion Questions

1. Do you believe that Congress should pass a resolution giving the Legislative Branch oversight of the program?
2. Based on Attorney General Gonzales's comments, does the president have the authority to conduct electronic surveillance on American citizens without a warrant?
3. Write a two-page response analyzing whether the characteristics of the nontraditional War on Terror grants the president authority to bypass the FISA Court in order to collect intelligence in a timely manner.

References

9/11 Commission. 2004. *The 9/11 commission report: Final report of the national commission on terrorist attacks upon the United States.* Authorized ed. Norton, New York: 84–85.

Amin, Massoud. 1998. Restructuring Trilemma. June.

———. 2006. Effective threat Mitigation Requires Balanced Risk Management. University of Minnesota, Minneapolis, MN.

Associated Press. 2006. White House unveils disaster plan revamp. *Daily News-Record.* February 23: 3.

Bazan, Elizabeth B. and Elsea, Jennifer K. 2006. *Presidential authority to conduct warrantless electronic surveillance to gather foreign intelligence information.* Congressional Research Service. Government Printing Office, Washington, D.C.

Constitution Project. 2006. Constitution Project and Center for National Security Studies file legal memorandum in foreign intelligence surveillance court. February 28. <http://www.constitutionproject.org/libertyandsecurity/article.cfm?messageID=145&categoryId=3>.

Council on Competitiveness. 2004. *Innovate America: Thriving in a world of challenge and change.* National Innovation Initiative Summit and Report. July 23.

Dotolo, Lawrence G. and Noftsinger, John B., Jr., eds. 2002. Leveraging resources through partnerships. *New Directions for Higher Education* 120. Wiley Periodicals, San Francisco: 19–20.

Federation of American Scientists. 2006. Dewine, Graham, Hagel and Snowe introduce the Terrorist Surveillance Act of 2006. Press Release. March 16.

Gellman, Barton, Linzer, Dafna, and Leonnig, Carol D. 2006. "Surveillance Net Yields Few Suspects." *The Washington Post.* February 5.

Gladwell, Malcolm. 2000. What is the tipping point? <http://www.gladwell.com/tippingpoint/index.html>.

Gonzales, Alberto R. 2006. Prepared statement of Hon. Alberto R. Gonzales, Attorney General of the United States. U.S. Department of Justice. February 6.

Haimes, Yacov. 2005. *Catastrophe: Coping through improvisation.* University of Virginia, Charlottesville, Va.: 17–18.

Homeland Security Institute. What is HSI? <http://www.homelandsecurity.org/about.asp>.

Homeland Security University. 2005. Homeland Security University and International College of Homeland Security Project. <http://www.homeland-security-college.org/ index.asp>.

Horowitz, Barry. 2005. *Catastrophe: Coping through improvisation.* University of Virginia, Charlottesville, Va., 17–18.

Kaplan, David E. 2005. Paying for terror. *U.S. News and World Report.* December 5: 42.

Knowlton, Brian. 2006. Specter says surveillance program violated the law. *The New York Times.* February 5.

Koh, Harold Hongju. 2006. "Statement on the wartime executive power and the NSA surveillance authority." United States Senate Committee on the Judiciary. February 28.

Leahy, Patrick. 2006. *S. Res. 350.* 109th Cong., 2d Sess. January 20.

Legal Information Institute. 2005. "U.S. Code: Title 50, 1802." Cornell Law School.

Little, Richard G. 1999. Educating the infrastructure professional: A new curriculum for a new discipline. *Public Works Management & Policy* 4, no. 2: 93–99.

Morgan, David. 2006. Senate panel rejects bid for NSA inquiry. *Reuters.* March 7.

National Academies. 2005. Executive summary. *Rising above the Gathering Storm: Energizing and Employing America for a Brighter Economic Future.*

News from Senator Feinstein. 2005. Feinstein, bipartisan group of Senators seek joint judiciary-intelligence inquiry into domestic spying. U.S. Senator Diane Feinstein. December 20.

*New World Dictionary of the American Language.*1980. Second College Edition. Simon and Schuster: 755.

Office of the Director of National Intelligence. 2005. *The National Intelligence strategy of the United States of America: Transformation through integration and innovation.*

Office of Senator Feingold. 2006. Remarks of Senator Russ Feingold introducing a resolution to censure President George W. Bush. March 13.

Office of Senator Leahy. 2006. Leahy on Friday introduces resolution underscoring that Congress did not authorize illegal spying on Americans. January 20.

Office of Senator Rockefeller. 2006. Vice Chairman Rockefeller's statement on the Senate Intelligence Committee's failure to vote on whether to authorize an investigation into the NSA surveillance program. February 16.

Perrow, Charles. 1999. *Normal accidents*. Princeton University Press, Princeton.

———. 2005. *Catastrophe: Coping through improvisation*. University of Virginia, Charlottesville, Va.: 17–18.

President's Radio Address. 2005. In focus: Homeland security. *The White House*. December 17.

Risen, James and Lichtblau, Eric. 2005. Bush lets U.S. spy on callers without courts. *The New York Times*. December 16.

Roberts, Pat. 2006. Letter to Senators Specter and Leahy. *United States Senate: Select Committee on Intelligence*. February 3. <http://www.fas.org/irp/congress/2006_cr/roberts020306.pdf>.

The White House. 2004. President signs Intelligence Reform and Terrorism Prevention Act. Washington, D.C. December 17.

———. 2006. *The Federal response to Hurricane Katrina: Lessons learned*. February.

United States Supreme Court. 1972. *United States v. United States District Court*. Case No. 407 U.S. 297.

United States Department of Homeland Security. 2003. Fact sheet: Leadership and management strategies for Homeland Security merger. Press Room. <http://www.dhs.gov/dhspublic/display?content=3155>.

Woolsey, James. 2006. Statement on the wartime executive power and the NSA surveillance authority. United States Senate Committee on the Judiciary. February 28.

INDEX

2003 Blackout, 113–16
  causes of, 114
  report on, 116
  timeline of events, 114–16

Abu Ali, Ahmed Omar, 74–75
Abu Ghraib scandal, 73
Achmetin, Mikel, 149
ACLU v. Ashcroft, 76
"all-hazards" approach, 30, 45, 50, 64, 140
all source analysis
  CIA and, 85
  defined, 95
  production and, 88–89
  TTIC and, 86
Al-Qaeda, 14, 41, 57, 179
  2003 Blackout and, 116
  Abu Ali and, 74–75
  Afghanistan and, 67, 70
  bounties offered for, 66
  innovative methods and, 16
  organized crime and, 187
  Padilla and, 71
  in Presidential Daily Briefing, August 6, 2001, 94
  random targeting and, 15
  surveillance of, 189
  terror cells and, 40
  War on Terror and, 189, 193
American Civil Liberties Union (ACLU), 61–62, 63–64, 76
American Library Association (ALA), 64
American Red Cross, 141
anthrax attacks, 138–39
anti-Western sentiment, 18
armed robbery, 15
Ashcroft, John, 61, 76, 193
assassination, 15

Assassins, 5, 12
attaché, 80, 81, 95
Attila the Hun, 6–7
Aum Shinrikyo, 12–13, 16
Automated Commercial Environment (ACE)
  automated data collection and, 164
  defined, 170
  funding, 163
aviation and airport security
  aviation defense technology, 154–56
  CAPPS II, 156–58
  Curb to the Cockpit initiative, 153–54
  overview, 152–53
Aviation and Transportation Security Act (ATSA)
  Curb to the Cockpit and, 153
  defined, 170
  TSA and, 150–51

Beslan School Hostage Crisis, 23
bioterrorism
  discussion questions, 140
  history of bio-defense, 125–28
  response to, 128–30
  shelter-in-place and evacuation, 130–35
bin Laden, Osama, 20
Black Hand, 15
Blue Team
  cyberspace and, 104
  defined, 116
Bolshevik Revolution, 13
Border and Transportation Security (BTS), 34
border security
  future of, 160–61
  overview, 158–59
  report card, 168–69

border security—*continued*
Secure Border Initiative, 159–60
technology and, 160
US-VISIT program, 160
Boyertown Area School District All
Hazards Plan, 137
Brown, Michael, 39–40
Brzezinksi, Matthew, 152
Bush, George H.W., 83
Bush, George W.
Abu Ali and, 74
ATSA and, 150–51, 170
bio-defense and, 125, 133
Century of Aviation Reauthorization
Act, 153
Department of Homeland Security and,
32–33, 45
enemy combatants and, 70–71
Executive Order 13228, 32, 50
Executive Order 13292, 90
Feingold and, 194
HSAS and, 111
HSPD-8, 45, 50
immigration reform, 29, 159–60
Intelligence Reform and Terrorism
Prevention Act, 83, 181
national security objectives and, 141
on poverty, 20
port security and, 165
Secure Border Initiative, 159–60
TSA and, 151, 153
TTIC and, 86
USA PATRIOT Act and, 57
warrantless domestic spying, 176,
188–90, 193

capitalism, 18, 149
CAPPS (Computer-Assisted Passenger
Prescreening System), 156
CAPPS II, 156–58
defined, 171
privacy implications of, 169–70
cascading failures
2003 Blackout and, 114
defined, 116
normal accidents and, 179
CBRNE weapons, 16, 46
Center for Risk Communication, 141–42

Center for Risk Perception and
Communication, 142
Centers for Disease Control (CDC), 130
Chechnya
kidnapping and, 15
Padilla and, 71
suicide terrorism and, 16, 21, 22–23
Chertoff, Michael, 33, 39, 159–60
civil liberties vs. security, 57
Clinton, Bill
bio-defense and, 125
FEMA and, 49
PDD-56, 83
PDD 63, 103
port security and, 161
Cold War
aftermath of, 67, 79–80
arms development and, 47
continuity and, 64
FEMA and, 49
NORAD and, 29
terrorism and, 18
translators and, 92
War on Terror compared to, 193
community shielding, defined, 145
Comprehensive Risk Analysis and
Management Network (CRN), 141
continuity of operations planning (COOP),
64–65, 76
Conyers, John, 60
counterintelligence, 80, 81–82, 95
Creasy, William, 126
crisis communication, defined, 144
Critical Incident Analysis Group, 142
critical infrastructure
2003 Blackout and, 113–16
defined, 100–1, 116
Department of Homeland Security and,
109
education as, 182–83
hazards and threats to, 105–9
history of, 101–5
Homeland Security Operations Center,
110–13
innovation as, 185–86
overview, 99–100
protection and response, 109–10
technology as, 184–85

Critical Infrastructure Protection Program (CIPP), 142
Critical Infrastructure Protection (CIP) Report, 144
Crusades, 7–8
Cuba, 13, 66, 70, 73
Curb to the Cockpit initiative, 153–54
cyber attacks
  CIPP and, 142
  critical infrastructure systems and, 105–9
  DHS and, 109, 112–13
  National Infrastructure Assurance Plan and, 103–4
  overview, 16
  PCCIP and, 102–3
  physical infrastructure and, 100
  preparation for, 180, 183
  risk assessment and, 125
  SHSGP and, 46
  vulnerability to, 105

Daniels, Mitch, 41
Dawood, Ibrahim, 187
DC sniper attacks, 119–20
dehumanization, 24
deindividuation
  other, 24
  self, 24
demonization, 24
Department of Defense (DoD)
  border security and, 160
  creation of, 28
  criminal investigations of U.S. Army, 73
  cyber terrorism and, 112
  DHS and, 42, 43, 48, 185
  DIA and, 87
  disaster recovery and, 31
  FEMA and, 49
  Hart-Rudman Commission and, 32
  Khamid and, 55
  National Guard and, 31
  Padilla and, 71
  TTIC and, 86
Department of Homeland Security (DHS), 33–37
  Advisory System, 38
  border and transportation security (BTS), 34

  Congress and, 42
  creation, 181–82
  Directive/HSPD-8, 50
  discussion questions, 50
  emergency preparedness/response, 34–35
  functions, 35–37
  funding, 43–44
  government-wide activities, 42–43
  higher education in, 46–47
  information analysis, 35
  infrastructure protection, 35
  key terms and definitions, 50
  mission, 34
  organizational deficiencies, 41–42
  organizational victories, 40–41
  private sector and, 48
  response to natural disasters, 38–40
  science and technology, 35
  state/local government and, 45–46
  strategic goals, 34
  strategic planning and public information, 37
  See also Federal Emergency Management Agency
depluralization, 19, 24
diplomacy, 66–68, 76
dirty bombs, 71–72, 180–81, 182
disaster planning, engaging the public in, 128–30
Disaster Relief Act of 1974, 29
distributed denial of service, 106, 117
domestic policy, 57–65
Dubai Ports World, 165

education reform, 182–83
electronic surveillance, 190–91
emergency guides
  Emergency Preparedness Guide, 141
  Introduction to NBC Terrorism, 140
  National Response Plan, 140–41
  National Strategy for the Physical Protection of Critical Infrastructure and Key Assets, 141
  Public Preparedness, 140
enemy combatants, 68–72
  defined, 76
  establishment of designation, 69
  Padilla and, 71–72

enemy combatants—*continued*
    questions about status, 70
    vs. prisoners of war, 69
    World War II and, 69–70
    See also Hamdi v. Rumsfeld; Padilla, Jose;
      Rasul v. Bush
Environmental Risk Analysis Program,
    143
espionage, defined, 95
evacuation
    defined, 145
    shadow-effect and, 134–35
    defined, 145
Executive Order 13228, 50
    See also Department of Homeland
      Security
Ex parte Milligan, 69
Ex parte Quirin, 69
Explosive Detection Systems, defined, 171

Federal Aviation Administration (FAA),
    152, 153, 156
Federal Emergency Management Agency
    (FEMA), 48–50, 141
federally funded research and development
    centers (FFRDC), 184–85
Feingold, Russell, 57, 138, 194
Feinstein, Dianne, 192, 193
Ferdinand, Franz, 15
"fighting the last war," 180–81
Foreign Intelligence Surveillance Act
    (FISA)
    creation of, 191
    electronic surveillance and, 190
    presidential authority vs., 191–92
foreign policy, 65–74
    alternatives: covert action, 66;
    diplomacy/constructive engagement,
      66; economic inducements, 66;
      economic sanctions, 66;
      extradition/law enforcement
      cooperation, 67; international
      conventions, 67; military force,
      67; rewards for information
      program, 66
    diplomacy/military action, 67–68
    enemy combatants, 68–72
    prisoners, ethical treatment of, 72–74

Foster, Donald, 139
Freedom of Information Act (FOIA), 130

General Accounting Office (GAO)
    report on ACE, 163
    report on CAPPS II, 169
    report on DHS effectiveness, 27, 41–42
    report on FAA, 152
    report on undocumented workers, 161
Geneva Conventions
    defined, 76
    diplomacy and, 67
    enemy combatants and, 71
    prisoners of war and, 72
    torture and, 73
    USA PATRIOT Act and, 56
geospatial intelligence, defined, 95
Gilmore Commission, 29
Gladwell, Malcolm, 187
Glass, Thomas A., 128, 129
Gonzales, Alberto R., 55, 189–90, 194
Graham, Bob, 161
Guantanamo Bay, 70–71, 73
Gupta, Rakesh, 4

Habeas Corpus
    Abu Ali and, 75
    defined, 76
    Ex parte Milligan, 69
    suspension of, 176
    violations of, 63
Hagel, Chuck, 192, 193
Hague Conventions, 67, 76
Hamas, 2, 15–16
Hamdi v. Rumsfeld, 70, 192
Harvard Center for Risk Analysis (HCRA),
    123, 143
Hatch-Rosenberg, Barbara, 139
Hatfill, Steven J., 139
Haupt, Hans, 69
Herod the Great, 6
Hezbollah, 2, 14, 15, 193
Hitler, Adolf, 12, 13
Hollings, Fritz, 161–62
homeland defense, 50
homeland security
    birth of, 31–33
    as business, 186–87

defined, 50
homeland defense compared to, 28–31
overview, 27–28
See also Department of Homeland
Security
Homeland Security Advisory System, 38,
111
Homeland Security Operations Center
(HSOC), 110–13
Homeland Security Policy Institute, 143
Humanitarian Law Project v. Ashcroft, 61, 76
Human intelligence (HUMINT), defined,
95
Hurricane Andrew, 49, 50
Hurricane Katrina, 179–82
"All-Hazards" approach and, 30
DHS and, 33, 50
FEMA and, 39–40, 49
IIMG and, 112
National Guard and, 29, 31
preparedness planning and, 64, 92–93,
101, 138
Hussein, Saddam, 12, 66

imagery intelligence (IMINT), defined, 80,
95
immigration
See border security
improvised explosive devices (IEDs), 16
Institute for Infrastructure and Information
Assurance, 143
intelligence
9/11 and, 93–95
all-source analysis and production, 88–89
analysis, 80–81
collection of data, 88
cycle, 87–92
defined, 96
discussion questions, 95
dissemination, 89–91
history of, 81–83
homeland security and, 91–92
introduction, 79–80
key terms and definitions, 95–96
levels of classification, 91
planning and direction, 87
processing, 88
U.S. intelligence community, 83–87

International Ship and Port Facility
Security (ISPS) codes, 163
Iran, 13, 66, 79

Jacobins, 10
John Doe, ACLU v. Ashcroft, 61
Johnson v. Eisentrager, 70
Journal of Homeland Security and
Emergency Management, 144

Katz v. United States, 190
key assets, 43, 44, 91
defined, 117
emergency guides and, 141
NIPP and, 100
threat advisories and, 111
Khamid, Amil, 55–56
Khamid v. Gates and Gonzales, 55
Khan, Genghis, 8–9
kidnapping, 15
Koh, Harold Hongju, 193
Kucinich, Dennis, 60

League of Nations, 3
Leahy, Patrick, 138, 139, 192, 193, 194
Levin, Carl, 192, 193
Libya, 13
London Train Bombings, 38, 92, 165–66,
168

Madrid Train Bombings, 15, 92, 166, 168
malicious software codes, 102, 112, 117
Malvo, Lee Boyd, 119–20
Man Portable Air Defense Systems
(MANPADS), 154, 171
maritime security
See port security
Maritime Transportation Security Act of
2002, 161–62, 171
See also port security
Marrero, Victor, 62, 76
McCain, John, 166
McKinley, William, 14
McVeigh, Timothy, 14
Measurement and Signature Intelligence
(MASINT), 80, 96
Meir, Golda, 11
Merari, Ariel, 21

Mitchell, Harold, 1
Mueller, Robert S., 139
Muhammad, John Allen, 119–20
Munich Massacre, 10–11

Nadler, Jerrold, 60
National Biodefense Analysis and
    Countermeasures Center (NBACC),
    126
National Guard
  emergency response and, 29, 30–31
  HSIN and, 111
  Hurricane Katrina and, 31, 39
  law enforcement and, 31
  Posse Comitatus and, 29
National Infrastructure Protection Plan
    (NIPP), 100, 104
National Intelligence Estimates (NIEs),
    defined, 96
National Security Letters (NSL), 61–62, 76
National Targeting Center (NTC)
  defined, 171
  establishment of, 151
normal accidents, 178–79
North American Air Defense Command
    (NORAD), 29
Northern Command, 31
North Korea, 13
NSA wiretapping surveillance program,
    188–94
  Bush administration's defense of, 189–90
  discussion questions, 194
  FISA court and, 191–92
  history of electronic surveillance, 190–91
  opposition to, 192
  Senate hearings on, 192–93
  timeline of events, 193–94

O'Connor, Sandra Day, 70–71
Office of Homeland Security (OHS), 30,
    32, 37, 50
Office of Management and Budget
    (OMB), 41
Office of State and Local Government
    Coordination and Preparedness
    (OSLGCP), 45, 51
Oklahoma City bombing, 4, 14, 31, 49,
    106, 127

Open-Source Intelligence (OSINT),
    80, 96
Operation Bojinka, 152
Operation Iraqi Freedom, 4
Operation Liberty Shield, 50–51
Oxley, Michael G., 57

Padilla, Jose, 71–72
panic
  avoiding, 125–30
  defined, 145
Perrow, Charles, 178–79, 181
Peter Sandman Risk Communication Web
    Site, 142
Pol Pot, 13
Pope Innocent IV, 9
Pope Urban II, 7
port security
  MTSA, 162–63
  new programs/technology, 163–65
  overview, 161–62
Posse Comitatus Act of 1878
  creation of, 28
  defined, 51
  exceptions to, 29
  immigration and, 29
Powell, Colin, 154
Powell, Lewis, 190
Presidential Daily Briefings (PDBs), 89
  August 6, 2001, 94
prisoners, ethical treatment of, 72–74
public policy
  ambiguity of, 55–56
  civil liberties vs. security, 57
  key terms and definitions, 75–76
  overview, 56
Putin, Vladimir, 23

rail security
  funding, 166
  overview, 165–66
  See also Transit and Rail Inspection
    Pilot
Rail Security Act, 166
random targeting, 15
Rasul v. Bush, 70
Raymond of Aguilers, 8
reconnaissance, 80, 82, 96

Red Team
  cyberspace and, 104
  defined, 117
Reign of Terror, 3, 10
risk analysis
  CRN and, 141
  defined, 145
  environmental, 143
  overview, 125
  publication on, 144
Risk Analysis (publication), 144
risk assessment
  CAPPS II and, 156, 169
  defined, 117
  ISPS and, 163
  modeling tool, 107
  overview, 125, 145
  rail security and, 166
risk communication
  agencies and organizations, 141–43
  defined, 144
  emergency guides, 140–41
  history of, 121–25
  publications, 144
  rules of, 122–23
  school safety and 135–37
  stages of, 121–22: explaining risk data
    better, 121; hazard and outrage,
    121–22; ignoring the public, 121;
    treating the public as full partner,
    122
  terminology, 123–25
  See also Seven Cardinal Rules of Risk
    Communication
Risk in Perspective, 144
risk management, defined, 125, 145
risk perception, defined, 145
Risk Sciences and Public Policy Institute,
  143
Roberts, John, 55
Roberts, Pat, 194
Robespierre, Maximillian, 3, 10, 12
Rumsfeld, Donald, 70, 71, 192
Rumsfeld v. Padilla, 71
Russia
  Bolshevik Revolution, 13
  Chechen rebels and, 16, 22–23
  FSB and, 81

RANSAC and, 142
  state-sponsored terrorism and, 13
  suicide terrorism and, 22–23
  translators and, 92
Russian American Nuclear Security
    Advisory Council (RANSAC), 142

Sageman, Marc, 18–19
Sanders, Bernie, 60
Sanhedrin, 6
Schoch-Spana, Monica, 128, 129
school safety
  Boyertown Area School Dist. All Hazards
    Plan, 137
  targeted school violence, 135–36
  threat assessment and, 136–37
Secure Border Initiative
  catch and return policy, 160
  defined, 171
  funding, 159–60
  overview, 159
Secure Flight
  controversy over, 156–58
  defined, 171
  privacy implications of, 169–70
Sensenbrenner, James F., 57
Seven Cardinal Rules of Risk Communication,
  122–23
Shane, Scott, 139
shelter-in-place
  call to, 131–32
  community sheeting, 133–34
  defined, 145
  duct tape and plastic sheeting, 132–33
  overview, 130–31
  types of, 132
Sicarii, 5, 11
Signals Intelligence (SIGINT), 80, 87, 96
Smith, Lamar, 160
Smith, Richard M., 139
Snowe, Olympia, 192, 193
social psychological conditioning, 19–20
Spanish Inquisition, 9, 10, 12, 14
Specter, Arlen, 192, 193, 194
Stafford Act, 29, 30
Stalin, Joseph, 12, 13
Stranislov, Alexsandr, 149
Sudan, 13

suicide terrorism, 16, 20–21
  background, 22
  discussion questions, 23–24
  overview, 22
  timeline of events, 22–23
Supreme Court, 29, 55–56, 190–91, 192
  enemy combatants and, 69, 71–72
  USA PATRIOT Act and, 57
Syria, 13, 55

table-top exercises
  defined, 145
  on border security, 149
  on critical infrastructure protection, 99
  on DC sniper attacks, 119–20
  on future threats, 175
  on Homeland Security, 27
  on information intelligence, 79
  on public policy, 55–56
  on source of terrorism, 1
Taliban, 12, 66, 67, 70
targeted violence
  defined, 145
  schools and, 135–36
Temujin, 8
terrorism
  causes, 16–18
  creation of terrorists, 18–20
  defined, 2–4, 24
  history of, 4–12
  key terms/definitions, 24
  religious, 14–15, 24
  revolutionary, 13–14, 24
  state-sponsored, 13, 24
  suicide, 16, 20–21
  tactics, 15–16
  types, 12–15
  See also suicide terrorism
Terrorist Screening Center (TSC), 149,
    150–51, 156
  defined, 171
threat assessment
  inquiries, 136, 145
  investigation, 137, 146
Torquemada, 9–10
torture
  Abu Ali and, 75
  defined, 76

Geneva Convention and, 72–74
  Khamid and, 56
  Torquemada and, 9
Training and Doctrine Command
    (TRADOC), 28
Transit and Rail Inspection Pilot (TRIP),
    167
  defined, 171
translators, 88, 92
transportation security, 150–51
  funding, 151–52
  key terms and definitions, 170–71
  report card, 168
  See also Transportation Security
    Administration
Transportation Security Administration (TSA)
  aviation security and, 167
  CAPPS II and, 156–58, 169–70
  Curb to the Cockpit and, 153
  defined, 171
  funding, 44, 153
  Operation Safe Commerce and, 164
  rail security and, 166
  responsibilities, 42, 150–51
  technology and, 155
Truman, Harry, 28, 82, 83
trust, public and
  government response and, 178–82
  privacy vs. security and, 176
  vulnerability, cost, threat, 176–78

United States v. Brown, 191
United States v. United States District Court,
    190
USA PATRIOT Act
  amendments to, 60
  creation of, 57–58
  defined, 76
  investigative capabilities, 59
  Judiciary and, 61–62
  monitoring of financial transactions, 59–60
  obtaining transactional records, 60
  opposition to, 63–64
  prominent provisions, 58–59
  reauthorization of, 60–61
  support for, 62–63
U.S. Commission on National Security in
    the 21st Century, 51

U.S.S. Cole, 4
US-VISIT program, 160

viruses, 106, 108
   defined, 117
   increased propagation of, 102
Visa Entry Reform Act of 2002, 150
vulnerability assessment, 110, 112
   cyberspace and, 104
   defined, 117

weaponization
   biological agents and, 126, 138
   defined, 146

weapons of mass destruction (WMDs),
   15–16
West Nile Virus, 129
wiretapping
   See NSA wiretapping surveillance
      program
Witt, James Lee, 49, 50
Woolsey, James, 193
worms
   defined, 117
   increased propagation of, 102
Wyden, Ron, 60, 192, 193

Zealots, 5, 12